P9-APR-743

LSD: PERSONALITY AND EXPERIENCE

WILEY SERIES ON PERSONALITY PROCESSES

IRVING B. WEINER, *Editor*
The University of Rochester Medical Center

INTERACTION IN FAMILIES
by Elliot G. Mishler and Nancy E. Waxler

SOCIAL STATUS AND PSYCHOLOGICAL DISORDER: A Causal Inquiry
by Bruce P. Dohrenwend and Barbara Dohrenwend

PSYCHOLOGICAL DISTURBANCE IN ADOLESCENCE
by Irving B. Weiner

ASSESSMENT OF BRAIN DAMAGE: A Neuropsychological Key Approach
by Elbert W. Russell, Charles Neuringer, and Gerald Goldstein

BLACK AND WHITE IDENTITY FORMATION
by Stuart Hauser

THE HUMANIZATION PROCESSES: A Social, Behavioral Analysis of Children's Problems
by Robert L. Hamblin, David Buckholdt, Daniel Ferritor, Martin Kozloff, and Lois Blackwell

ADOLESCENT SUICIDE
by Jerry Jacobs

TOWARD THE INTEGRATION OF PSYCHOTHERAPY
by John M. Reisman

MINIMAL BRAIN DYSFUNCTION IN CHILDREN
by Paul Wender

LSD: PERSONALITY AND EXPERIENCE
by Harriet Linton Barr, Robert J. Langs, and Robert R. Holt, Leo Goldberger, and George S. Klein

LSD: PERSONALITY AND EXPERIENCE

HARRIET LINTON BARR, Ph.D.
Eagleville Hospital and Rehabilitation Center,
Eagleville, Pennsylvania

ROBERT J. LANGS, M.D.
Division of Psychoanalytic Education, Downstate Medical Center,
Brooklyn, New York, and
Hillside Hospital,
Glen Oaks, New York

and

ROBERT R. HOLT, Ph.D.
LEO GOLDBERGER, Ph.D.
GEORGE S. KLEIN, Ph.D.
Research Center for Mental Health,
New York University, New York

Wiley-Interscience
A DIVISION OF JOHN WILEY & SONS, INC.
NEW YORK • LONDON • SYDNEY • TORONTO

Library of Congress Catalog Card Number: 72-37641

ISBN 0-471-05403-8

Printed in the United States of America.

10 9 8 7 6 5 4 3 2 1

To the memory of GEORGE S. KLEIN

Series Preface

This series of books is addressed to behavioral scientists interested in the nature of human personality. Its scope should prove pertinent to personality theorists and researchers as well as to clinicians concerned with applying an understanding of personality processes to the amelioration of emotional difficulties in living. To this end, the series provides a scholarly integration of theoretical formulations, empirical data, and practical recommendations.

Six major aspects of studying and learning about human personality can be designated: personality theory, personality structure and dynamics, personality development, personality assessment, personality change, and personality adjustment. In exploring these aspects of personality, the books in the series discuss a number of distinct but related subject areas: the nature and implications of various theories of personality; personality characteristics that account for consistencies and variations in human behavior; the emergence of personality processes in children and adolescents; the use of interviewing and testing procedures to evaluate individual differences in personality; efforts to modify personality styles through psychotherapy, counseling, behavior therapy, and other methods of influence; and patterns of abnormal personality functioning that impair individual competence.

IRVING B. WEINER

University of Rochester
Rochester, New York

Preface

This book describes a research study into the nature of altered states of consciousness, the personality factors related to the specific manifestations of such states as experienced by a given person, and the manner of functioning in these states. It dates back some years when members of the staff at the Research Center for Mental Health of New York University became interested in an experimental approach to the psychoanalytic theory of consciousness. These interests led to a search for a means of producing an altered state of consciousness in which it would be possible to enlist the cooperation of a subject in a range of psychological tests of his imagination, fantasies, and cognitive and other functioning. We inevitably came upon the early literature on the effects of mescaline and then the rather substantial literature describing the effects of a then unique drug, d-lysergic acid diethylamide (LSD-25). At that time the drug was something of a scientific curiosity and relatively unknown to the public. It was, however, a substance par excellence for our purposes and, after some preliminary testing with staff members, we undertook the controlled research study whose major findings are presented here.

The subsequent widespread use of this drug and the confused public and governmental response to it should not detract from its usefulness as a research tool that permits the scientific study of aspects of human behavior and functioning that are otherwise difficult to approach.

Our data had all been gathered long before 1967, when a rash of reports were published that raised the spectre of genetic damage from the use of LSD. A recent judicious survey and critical evaluation of all the evidence (Dishotsky et al., 1971) has come to the reassuring conclusion that "pure LSD ingested in moderate doses does not damage chromosomes in vivo, does not cause detectable genetic damage, and is not a teratogen or a carcinogen in man. Within these bounds, therefore, we suggest that, other than during pregnancy, there is no present contraindication to the continued controlled experimental use of pure LSD" (p. 439). We got in touch with as many of our subjects as possible during a period from 6 months to several years after the experiment, and in no case did we observe or learn about any untoward sequel that could in any way be attributed to the drug experience. Neither, we should add in fairness, did we observe any lasting benefit from what had been planned not as a therapeutic but as a purely investigative study, despite the claims of several subjects immediately after taking the drug that they had gained remarkable and personally useful insights.

We hope that this book will serve as firm evidence of the value of LSD as an investigative instrument, and that it may help lead to a reconsideration of the use of psychedelic drugs for scientific inquiry.

The work reported in this book was so completely a team endeavor, representing the major effort of the entire Research Center for Mental Health for several years, and that of the senior authors for a longer period, that it is not easy to specify the contributions of each member of our group; some of them, however, are clear.

The original impetus for this research came from George S. Klein's interest in the possibilities of using psychoactive drugs to study states of consciousness and their effects on thinking and attention. This interest dates back to the early 1950s, when he and Robert R. Holt carried out preliminary investigations of the effects of mescaline at the Menninger Foundation. He played a major part in the planning and conduct of the research, and in the analysis and interpretation of its findings. Our deepest regret is that he did not live to see the final product of his work.

An important stimulus for beginning this research was Robert R. Holt's interest in manifestations of primary-process modes of functioning and, in particular, in developing a thorough and objective system for scoring such manifestations in the Rorschach test. Under his supervision, Anthony F. Philip began a doctoral study, investigating the effects of LSD on Rorschach manifestations of the primary process, which was the starting point for the larger investigation.

The entire senior staff of the Research Center for Mental Health participated in planning the study, the experimental testing, and the personality assessment. Certain portions of the study were the special province of certain staff members, however: the Color-Word test and the Uloomoo-Takete experiment, George S. Klein; the Color-Form test, George S. Klein and Leo Goldberger; the Rorschach test and planning the Personality Assessment, Robert R. Holt; the development of the questionnaire, Harriet Barr and Robert J. Langs; the Human Figure Drawings and the development of the empirical questionnaire scales, Harriet Barr; earliest memories, Robert J. Langs; the cognitive test battery, Leo Goldberger and Robert R. Holt; the theme list task, Irving H. Paul and Robert J. Langs; medical histories and physical examinations, Robert J. Langs. Donald P. Spence,

Fred Pine, and Morris Eagle shared in the work of assessment and screening. Special credit is due to Walter S. Boernstein, whose Verbal Self-Portrait test contributed to our interpretation of the personality effects, and whose advice and experience were most helpful to us.

Of the many research assistants, now members of our profession, who did much of the day-by-day work of testing subjects and scoring the test protocols, Lester Alston, who supervised the testing schedules of the subjects and guided the complex sequence of testing, deserves special thanks. We wish to thank Sheldon Bach, Elena Barnet, Joanna Bressler, Phebe Cramer, Anne DeGersdorff, Carol Eagle, Harry Fiss, Arthur Goldweber, Bernice Hamerling, Helene Kafka, Harriette Weintraub Kaley, Anthony Philip, Norman Reiss, Reeva Safrin, Rita Simon, and Rebecca Strunsky.

Martha Gillmor showed us how to bring a complex mass of data and interpretation into what we trust is an intelligible form through her invaluable editorial advice. The administrative work of William Francis kept both the project and us from chaos over the years, and Melanie Chussid's zealous guardianship over our data files has countered the mysterious tendency of crucial data to vanish.

Finally, we wish to thank the National Institute of Mental Health for their support, over what is probably a longer haul than they originally anticipated, under the following grants: Research Grant MY-3670, Primary Process Thinking in the Effects of LSD-25; Program Grant MH-06733, Psychoanalytic Studies in Cognition; and Program Grant MH-17545, A Research Program in Cognitive-Affective Processes.

HARRIET LINTON BARR
ROBERT J. LANGS
ROBERT R. HOLT
LEO GOLDBERGER

September 1971
Eagleville, Pennsylvania
Glen Oaks, New York
New York, New York

Contents

Tables and Figures

LSD: PERSONALITY AND EXPERIENCE

CHAPTER 1

Introduction: A Research Strategy for Studying Personality and Differences in Drug Response

Throughout the ages man has experienced a variety of states of consciousness, and indeed from earliest known times has sought out consciousness-altering substances, most notably ethyl alcohol. Yet, as Auerbach (1953) persuasively argues on the basis of a keen analysis of literary texts, it is only in recent centuries that any but very exceptional persons have been self-conscious or aware of the quality of their awareness. Homer and his heroes, for example, were almost completely nonintrospective. In this historical perspective today's cult of consciousness, its "raising" and "expansion," and the vogue for mind-altering drugs of all kinds in particular seem to be the cresting of a long-gathering wave.

Typically, a scientist works on what excites him at the moment, which usually seems to be the unique outgrowth of a process of his work's inner development and not at all a reflection of a larger trend. Thus when two of us (RRH and GSK) began the first major program of the Research Center for Mental Health in 1953, it seemed to us a great and fortunate coincidence that our separate empirical and theoretical interests had converged on a desire to study disordered thought processes and simultaneously to work out in some detail Freud's theory of primary process as a way of conceptualizing them. Our first pilot studies with mescaline seemed to us only a logical extension of this program, one that could include a broader study of the states in which these two processes occur and also enable us to study other aspects of functioning in these states. We were already familiar with Huxley's (1954) *The Doors of Perception* and were vaguely aware that psychopharmacology was simultaneously becoming a highly active research field. In retrospect, we can see the evolution of our work as easily one way as the other: from the personal standpoint, as an organic process in the working out of a basically theoretical interest, and from a more sociological perspective, as a minor ripple on a large scientific swell.

Our theoretical interest, to be a little more concrete about it, began with a conviction that there was great potentiality for experimental psychology in what Freud wrote about the primary process—that apparently crude or primitive, but actually quite subtle, set of transformations that go into producing dreams, psychotic speech, neurotic symptoms, jokes, myths, and many other nonprosaic forms of human cognitive products. The primary process, we felt, just might turn out to be easier to translate into operational definitions and thus to work with in a controlled and quantitative way than many of the more familiar items in the Freudian theoretical stock. The general strategy was twofold; on the one hand, we made intensive study of the basic theoretical texts (particularly those bearing on the psychoanalytic theory of thinking) with the guidance of our friend and mentor, David Rapaport; and on the other hand, we started examining as many different kinds of disordered thinking as we could get our subjects to produce. Some of them we put to sleep, seeking in dreams the *via regia* to the unconscious that Freud had promised (see, for example, Fiss, Klein, and Bokert, 1966; Fiss et al., 1968). On the general hypothesis, growing out of *The Interpretation of Dreams* (Freud, 1900, Chapter 7), that the order and rationality of ordinary, secondary-process thought is maintained in considerable part by continued contact with the structure of reality, we tried various ways of impoverishing or blurring the input of environmental stimuli: by exposing subjects to stimuli that were too faint and brief to be clearly discriminated (Klein et al., 1958; Smith, Spence, and Klein, 1959; Klein and Holt, 1960; Klein, 1959b), getting them to respond to inherently vague and ill-formed inkblots (Holt, 1956; Holt and Havel, 1960; Holt, 1970), and by drastically limiting the variety and level of inputs in all stimulus modalities (Goldberger, 1961; Goldberger and Holt, 1958; Holt and Goldberger, 1960).

The pilot studies with mescaline convinced us that the so-called hallucinogenic drugs had many advantages as an independent variable in research of this kind. They seemed to put people into markedly altered states of consciousness—indeed, of the total organism—with notable effects on thinking and other functions (e.g., perceiving, remembering, defense against drives), while leaving them accessible to testing and self-observation. These effects were reputed to be profound, yet rather quickly reversible, so that some subjects could experience a virtually psychotic state of disorganization and shortly afterward be lucid enough to report on it extensively. Moreover, the chemical agents could be precisely measured, which promised to make replication easier than in the case of rather grossly describable manipulations such as sensory deprivation.

There was still another important element in the larger research program of which our work on drugs was a part. Our earlier work in cognitive styles and in diagnostic testing had taught us that an enormously important source of variance in any cognitive performance comes from the subjects themselves: the preexisting ways in which they are organized to deal with information. By such "ways" we refer to individual differences in a great variety of parameters, from abilities to cognitive control principles (Gardner et al., 1959), to all manner of personality traits and motives. Again and again we had seen the general point demonstrated that the fire that melts the butter hardens the egg; differently constituted subjects exposed to identical experimental manipulations reacted in diametrically (or orthogonally) different ways.

We had developed, therefore, a strategy of always including some assessment of individual differences in the experiments. For example, when we put subjects into our isolation room for 8 hours with vision, hearing, and touch effectively blocked or homogenized, we looked for individual differences in two ways. First, we measured a variety of reactions to the experimental situation and types of attempted adaptations ranging from simple verbal output, to the production of visual images, to sleep; then we interrelated these measures, finding *patterns* of adaptive and maladaptive response to the situation. Second, we gave the subjects a number of tests of personality and correlated the resulting measures with individual differences in reaction to the experiment, including the adaptive and maladaptive patterns just mentioned. The results (Holt and Goldberger, 1959) offered a good deal of insight into the kinds of people who reacted in distinctive ways to our experiment.

When we decided to study the effects of d-lysergic acid diethylamide (LSD-25) on cognitive-affective processes, with the general aim of learning more about primary-process thinking and other aspects of functioning, we followed the same strategy. First, we needed experimental tools with which to measure and observe an individual's functioning and experiencing in the altered states. We developed these through preliminary studies and in response to the specific areas of interest that soon came into focus. Second, we wanted to know as much as possible about the personal makeup of each subject in the study so that the experimental findings could be related to traits of personality. We therefore scheduled a series of psychological tests and interviews which became the raw material for a thorough personality assessment of each subject. The outcome was a two-year, double-blind research study; its results and their implications are unfolded in this book.

Our theoretical orientation is obviously psychoanalytic. By that we mean that, like the vast majority of other researchers on personality, we find many of Freud's concepts indispensable and the clinical orientation a great help in gathering and understanding data. Without such assumptions and concepts as unconscious motivation, the persistence of latent meaning throughout protean changes in manifest content, and the pervasive importance of sexuality, aggression, anxiety, and the modes of defense against such impulses and affects—without such basic tools of our trade—we would hardly know how to do more than scratch the surface of personality. We assume that the reader is generally familiar with these concepts and we use this Freudian framework of understanding our subjects and many of the phenomena they showed us, without further discussion. We intend to avoid metapsychology and other flights of theoretical imagination, believing that everyone's interests are better served if we stay closer to our observations. For those who wish to pursue the psychoanalytic theory of consciousness in some detail, it is reviewed in Appendix 1.

INDIVIDUAL DIFFERENCES IN DRUG RESPONSE

As we move at an accelerating pace toward ever greater usage of drugs, supervised and unsupervised, legal and illegal, differences among people in their response to these substances have come to the fore. Such differences, of the utmost importance both medically and socially, have been frequently noted but rarely accounted for or systematically investigated by any productive strategy. Psychopharmacologists are now gradually becoming aware of this gap in our information, but much remains to be done. The specific personality factors and other conditions that contribute to idiosyncratic, highly individualistic, and occasionally dangerous side effects of both a somatic and psychological nature in response to commonly prescribed medications are as yet imperfectly understood. Even more dangerous and less well studied, because of lack of proper supervision and controls, are the individual differences that occur in response to nonprescribed psychotropic and other abused drugs. It has become literally vital that we know as much as possible about the kinds of persons who are likely to have serious and tragic experiences, such as suicide attempts and acute and sometimes lasting episodes of psychosis, from ingesting these substances.

The total job is enormous. Ideally, we would like to be able to construct families of dose–response curves for each of the most widely used psychoactive drugs and to present statistical indications of the kinds of personality associated with each distinctive pattern of individual variation from the standard curves. Limited though our research is to a single dose of a single drug, and to a rather special sample of subjects, we believe that it has shown the power and effectiveness of our general research strategy as outlined above and detailed in the following discussion, and that its results will prove to be a lasting contribution.

A STRATEGY FOR STUDYING DIFFERENCES IN DRUG RESPONSE

Analyzing the Drug Response

The major outcome of our investigations has been to demonstrate important relationships between preexisting personality patterns and various states produced by LSD. To do this we began by mapping out the complex terrain of the drug reactions themselves. Using primarily the subject's reports of their experiences and, secondarily, observations of their behavior, we first clarified the manner in which separate components or symptoms of the drug reaction grouped themselves together (see Chapter 3). The first such grouping was constructed according to our own preconceptions as to whch of the drug's effects were related to one another, groupings that corresponded essentially to the usual clusters of psychological and somatic symptoms and functions. This organization proved less valuable, however, than the second grouping, which was based on a direct analysis of the data and revealed which reactions actually occurred together in the subjects.

We next used group data to examine the general effects of LSD on the performance of various tasks, and related individual differences in such performance to the drug reaction dimensions already found, thus expanding our understanding of both (see Chapter 4).

The most important and final step, however, was the identification of the *patterns* into which these dimensions or clusters of symptoms fell. By classifying the subjects into small groups, each characterized by a particular patterning of the component aspects of the LSD reaction, we were able to delineate the kinds of persons who reacted in these patterned ways (see Chapter 5).

What we have done has been to develop a typology of reactions to LSD. The level of analysis is the syndrome, rather than the symptom, and it was at this level that the strongest and clearest set of relationships between drug response and personality was found. Analysis at this level has proved most useful in the study of naturally occurring somatic and psychological pathology. Our work demonstrates that it is probably a very productive approach to understanding drug-induced alterations in functioning as well. We chose to concentrate on personality rather than cultural and ethnic background and attitudes, or physical characteristics, or medical and family history. We might also have studied the many variations in the possible conditions under which the drug can be taken, including the social and physical setting. This study says nothing about important factors such as these because such conditions were deliberately kept as constant as possible in order to maximize the effects of personality. It must therefore remain for further research to discover the effects of these other variables.

The Sampling Problem

The subjects we studied cannot be considered generally representative of any population, for they are an atypical group of young men (see Chapter 2). It was not our goal, however, to explore the frequency with which certain kinds of LSD effects occur in the general population, nor to define every possible effect of the drug in any population. Instead, we sought to delineate the patterns of altered states in one readily available group in order to define sharply and to study certain clusters of drug symptoms and to provide a research model for the study of any other possible clusters of response to this or any other drug.

The relationships we found between personality and drug response were highly consistent among the subjects within each of the reaction types. Thus, for each of these types, we have some confidence that other subjects with similar personalities would, under comparable conditions, react rather similarly to LSD. A different set of subjects would probably yield a different range of personality types and therefore a different proportion of each of our drug response groups. Another sample, with or without another level of dosage, might also show symptom clusters not seen in our subjects. Only further study will fill in these gaps.

A BRIEF LOOK AT PRIOR RESEARCH ON LSD AND INDIVIDUAL DIFFERENCES

The literature on LSD is far too extensive to be reviewed in any comprehensive way here. The reader who wants to delve into its fascinating historical development and gain a proper appreciation of the roles of many important contributors should consult any of several available surveys of this literature (e.g., Barber, 1970; Mogar, 1965; Tart, 1969b). The brief overview that follows is supplemented by the introductory comments to the various experimental substudies described later.

Hofmann's remarkable discovery of LSD in 1943 was followed by a series of papers (e.g., Rinkel et al., 1952; Savage, 1952; Salvatore and Hyde, 1956) describing many effects of the drug, ranging from subtle changes in experienced mood and perception to nausea to strictly physiological effects such as mydriasis (extremely dilated pupils). Clearly, the general effect must be called an *altered organismic state,* in the general sense of the word organism used by such writers as Angyal (1941) and Goldstein (1939). That is, the drug changes not just the state of consciousness, not just the physiological equilibrium, not just the relatedness of the person as a social unit to his sociocultural context, but all of these more or less simultaneously, so that simple chains of cause and effect can hardly be traced.

A group of systematic clinical and questionnaire studies (Rinkel et al., 1952; Savage, 1952; Salvatore and Hyde, 1956) clarified the emerging picture of the variously altered states produced by LSD, and the many functions affected by it. For example, Rinkel et al. (1952) reported that LSD disturbed thought, speech, affect, perception, behavior, and autonomic functions, describing drug-induced hallucinations and depersonalization. This study was one of many in a medical tradition that considers LSD a "psychotomimetic" (psychosis-mimicking) drug, since any intrusion of primary-process thinking can be viewed as an impairment and thus as pathological. In the view of some writers from a more recent school of thought, which takes a more romantic view of the primary process as intrinsically creative, the conclusions that LSD produces psychoticlike alterations of function "appear to be primarily a result of the use of the drug by white-coated psychiatrists in a sterile hospital setting" (Houston, 1967). Our approach to this issue (Langs and Barr, 1968) was to compare schizophrenics and LSD subjects directly on the same questionnaire instrument; we found that the majority of the drug reactions had little resemblance to the two schizophrenic syndromes studied, but that a few subjects did report experiences with striking similarities to those of certain paranoid schizophrenics.

It became evident quite early that LSD effects were actually a complex interactive function of the dosage, the subjects and their expectations, and the situation. Moreover, it began to be clear that there were several varieties of clinically observable reactions to the drug. The reports by Abramson and his co-workers (Abramson et al., 1955b; Levine et al., 1955a, b), describing a study in which subjects received a variety of doses of LSD and a placebo, explored subjective reactions with a 47-item questionnaire restricted largely to somatic and perceptual effects, and reported time curves of these effects. Salvatore and Hyde (1956) went a step further and grouped the symptoms their observers reported together into three clusters, each with a distinctive temporal pattern. The first cluster included gregariousness, anxiety, and hostility; the second neuromuscular and cutaneous reactions; and the third withdrawal, lethargy, depression, thought confusion, perceptual distortions, feelings of unreality, and inappropriate laughter and smiling.

A variety of tests have also been used to help quantify and to analyze more precisely the many effects of the drug. Levine et al. (1955a) studied responses to the Rorschach test, the Wechsler-Bellevue (1955b), and the Bender-Gestalt (Abramson et al., 1955c) under the influence of the drug, reporting a variety of impairments as compared to responses under normal conditions. They considered that their Rorschach results indicated a disruption of normal defenses with emergence of formerly submerged conflicts, overpersonalization of the subjects' reaction to the cards, a lessened capacity for intellectual surveillance and volitional control, regression, egocentricity, anxiety, an increase in socially directed defenses, distorted perceptions, paranoid tendencies, and more direct expressions of sexuality. Individual differences in these trends were noted, as were suggestions that these related to predrug personality, but they were not systematically explored. The Wechsler-Bellevue results indicated that LSD impaired several aspects of intellectual functioning, notably concentration and abstract and conceptual thinking, and created difficulty in shifting sets. Last, the Bender-Gestalt findings suggested shifts to psychoticlike performances, but the results were not definitive.

Bercel et al. (1956a, b) also studied Rorschach test performance in an effort to discover indicators in the predrug test that would predict psychoticlike Rorschach and clinical responses under LSD. Their post hoc analysis indicated that excessive productivity and pronounced sexual disturbances in response to the control Rorschach test were the best such indicators, and that most "psychotic" reactors could be identified. The control Rorschachs did not, however, permit them to anticipate the form of psychoticlike reactions that occurred. They noted, incidentally, that not all the subjects showed a general personality deterioration under the drug and that certain subjects who gave controlled, nonpsychotic responses to the Rorschach test were nonetheless, on clinical observation, "psychotic" and "paranoid" under the drug.

A less prominent thread in the fabric of LSD research has been the attempt to study its effects on a variety of experimental tasks. Perhaps the most extensive program of this kind has been reported by Klee and his associates (Klee, 1963; Aronson and Klee, 1960; Aronson, Silverstein, and Klee, 1959; Silverstein and Klee, 1960a, b; Weintraub, Silverstein, and Klee, 1959, 1960). They have shown that LSD has a minimal effect on paired-associate learning of neutral words but interferes with recall of such pairs if they are emotionally charged; it does not impair the retention of material learned under the drug; LSD disrupts the memory span for digits; it alters time perception; it impairs learning and performance of dual pursuit performance; it disrupts abstract thinking; it alters aspects of a subject's response to the word association test; and it produces paranoidlike reactions in certain predisposed subjects.

It is apparent that LSD has a profound effect on the total personality and on a wide range of specific functions which have been variously conceptualized. Savage (1952) has invoked Federn's concept of ego feeling to explain many of the drug experiences. Klee (1963), in one of the most systematic theoretical discussions to date, analyzed reactions to LSD in terms of altered ego functions of perception, thought, and motility, focusing primarily on the results of the researches by his group. In his paper, which appeared after we had formed our hypotheses and collected our data, he linked the perceptual changes under the drug (e.g., depersonalization, visual sensitivities and distortions, altered time sense) to changes in the body image and in the perception of the self, as well as to a breakdown in the stimulus barrier. He viewed the changes in thinking seen under LSD as shifts toward primary-process thinking, and in terms of a "dissolution of boundaries between the autonomous and conflictual areas of the ego" (Klee, 1963, p. 470). Defensive functions were altered under LSD, he thought, primarily in terms of a loss of "ability to employ defenses in the most adaptive manner" (Klee, 1963, p. 471).

Ludwig (1966) reviewed the phenomenology of altered states of consciousness, including states produced by LSD, considering the conditions necessary for their emergence, their characteristics, and the adaptive and maladaptive functions they may serve. The major characteristics of an LSD altered state, as Ludwig delineated them, are: alterations in thinking, disturbed time sense, loss of control, change in emotional expression and body image, perceptual distortions, changes in meaning or significance, sense of the ineffable, feelings of rejuvenation, and hypersuggestibility.

At the time our research began, there were no studies relevant to the question of personality factors in reactions to LSD. Subsequently, Klee and Weintraub (1959) found that paranoidlike reactions under the drug were most frequent in persons who are usually mistrustful, suspicious, and fearful, and who often use projection as a defense. Our analysis of data from the subjects in the present study confirmed and elaborated upon their findings (Langs and Barr, 1968). Rinkel and his associates (1961) have reported a preliminary study in which two constitutional types, athletic and asthenic, appeared to react differently to LSD.

More recently, McGlothlin et al. (1967), in a controlled study of some long-term effects of the ingestion of 200 μg of LSD, found that persons who emphasized "structure and control" responded minimally to the drug, while more intense reactions were seen in subjects characterized as preferring a more unstructured, spontaneous, inward-turning life. Such people also tended to score higher on tests of esthetic sensitivity and imaginativeness and tended to be less aggressive, less competitive, and less conforming than the underreactive subjects. Along other lines, Mogar and Savage (1964) have reported that response to LSD in brief psychotherapy could be related to personality variables: "subjects with a well-defined but flexible self-structure responded most favorably to the drug, while those with either under-developed or overly-rigid ego defenses responded less favorably" (Mogar, 1965, p. 388).

In sum, our project is not unique in examining a large number of LSD effects, in looking for patterns of symptom reports, in using psychological tests and experimental tasks as ways of studying the drug's impact, in conceptualizing findings psychoanalytically, or in seeking to relate the patterns of reaction to assessments of the subjects' personalities. Whether, as we believe, it is unique in combining all these attributes is less important than the fact that these constitute a rational strategy for exploring an extremely complicated psychobiological phenomenon.

CHAPTER 2

The Design of the Study and the Subjects

Since the goals of our research were multifaceted, a wide variety of experiments and other sources of observation were developed. The major focus was on the characteristics and varieties of the altered states of consciousness produced by, and the special properties of psychological functioning in, these states; beyond this, we hoped to relate our findings to the personalities of the subjects. To accomplish this, the personalities of the subjects were carefully assessed before they took the drug, and their experiences under LSD were monitored in great detail.

The drug states were followed in two ways. The first involved the use of a 74-item questionnaire developed through a review of the literature and from our own experiences as preexperimental subjects. This inquiry covers a wide range of potential alterations in perception, relationship with the environment, thought processes, emotions, experiencing of self, and bodily reactions, and was given 4 times during the experimental day. Second, each experimenter who worked with a subject systematically rated his behavior on 18 scales of observable effects; this was done from 6 to 12 times during the experimental day for each subject.

In addition, two types of control data were used to confirm that effects observed were indeed related to the drug. Wherever possible, pretesting in the waking state of consciousness was used as a baseline for each subject with which his performance under LSD could be compared. As an additional control, we obtained data from a group of subjects who underwent the same experimental procedure as the drug group, but did so after receiving a placebo. Through these comparisons, we learned much about the general or group effects of LSD and the altered states and altered functioning it produces.

To go beyond these broad generalizations, we utilized the personality data in interpreting a subject's performance on the tests administered to him under the drug. In addition, the pretest personality data were used to investigate broadly the individual differences in ways of reacting to the drug; that is, differences in the nature of the altered organismic state each subject developed. The latter, in all of its complexities, is the major focus of our research and of this book.

There were several possible approaches to understanding these individual differences in altered-state experience (see Appendix 2, Note 1). After considerable thought, we elected to deal with these in terms of people rather than test responses. The questionnaire responses regarding subjective experiencing and the behavioral observations were used together as the broadest means of sampling each subject's altered state, both as to content and over time. Measures based on these data were used to identify several groups of subjects through a person cluster technique, so that subjects who fell into the same group had similar altered-state experiences that differed from that of each of the other groups in at least some major areas. Once this was established, we ascertained whether subjects who showed similar experiences and behavior under the drug also resembled each other in their performance on the experimental tasks and, beyond this, whether or not they shared important predrug personality characteristics. Because they actually did so to a striking degree, we were then able to describe each group not only in terms of the kind of altered state that characterized it but also in terms of the type of person who tends to experience such an LSD state.

THE PLAN OF PRESENTATION

The complexity of the data means that there are drawbacks to any choice of presentation. The general group findings are presented first, however, because they convey an idea of the range of overall effects produced by LSD and also allow us to explore the implications of the specific drug-induced changes in performance in the various tasks. These are synthesized when the data are organized in terms of drug reaction-type groups, which provide the richest picture of the complex nature of our findings and allow us to consider the place of those findings in the broader context of personality research.

We therefore first describe in the balance of this chapter the personality assessment and selection procedures, the kinds of subjects who took part in the study, and the experimental setting and procedures, noting certain limitations that they imposed. Chapter 3 presents group results for the entire sample obtained through the questionnaire and the observations of behavior to give an overall picture of the drug's effects. Chapter 4 details group findings for each of the experimental procedures and tests, while Chapter 5 describes the six patterns of LSD reactions and the personality features associated with each. An individual case typifying each pattern is included. Chapter 6 discusses some theoretical and practical implications of our results.

SCREENING AND ASSESSMENT OF SUBJECTS

Several unusual constraints surrounded our choice of a group of subjects with whom to work. First, they had to be independent adults capable of assuming responsibility for themselves and stable enough not to have their adjustment seriously shaken by the powerful impact of LSD. These requirements immediately ruled out two favorite populations from which subjects are often drawn—college undergraduates and mental patients. Since the LSD study was part of a larger program of research on disordered thought, another requirement was that subjects have enough time available to work with us over a period of several months: the equivalent of a few days for the multiform personality assessment, and one period of 36 hours for the drug study proper (see below, p. 20f.). In addition, certain selected subjects were wanted for a study of the effects of a full day of perceptual isolation, for we wished to compare the alleged hallucinogenic effects of this kind of sensory deprivation with those of the psychedelic drug (Holt and Goldberger, 1960). Since a large investment of staff time was necessary to carry out the intensive assessment of personality on 50 men, we wished them to be accessible for other studies as well. Finally, subjects had to be intelligent and articulate enough to give introspective reports that would make possible a phenomenological analysis of alterations in their states of consciousness.

Where can such subjects be found? Employment agencies were ruled out because we had little to attract an unemployed person with the above qualifications since we could not offer steady employment and since the wage we could pay was not great. There is, however, one occupational group with the desired characteristics. In New York City, there are many aspiring actors who support themselves by temporary and parttime employment while waiting for theatrical work. By posting a notice at the office of Actors Equity, we obtained a steady flow of potential subjects who were looking for just the kind of intermittent work we could offer.

The subjects were thus professional actors, selected because of their availability, and limited to males in order to simplify the research design and its undertaking. They are, therefore, a group of young men, screened so as to eliminate grossly psychotic pathology, whose characteristics were then well delineated for this research. They are not representative of the general population, although they do offer a sampling of common character types.

Applicants were given the Minnesota Multiphasic Personality Inventory

(MMPI) as a first screening device. Those with scores outside of an acceptable range or with certain responses that were considered severe danger signs ("stop items") were eliminated at this stage. The 152 applicants who passed this step were called in for more intensive screening through a clinical interview and further testing, including the Rorschach test, the Thematic Apperception Test (TAT), and the Wechsler Adult Intelligence Scale (WAIS). Fifty subjects were finally accepted, 30 for the drug group and 20 for the placebo group.

The screening was intended primarily to eliminate those with psychotic or antisocial tendencies, paranoid features, and fragile or borderline adjustments. The cutoff points for the MMPI scales screened out those evaluated as severely depressed or clearly immature, those with an excessive number of somatic or functional complaints, and those who were notably paranoid, manic, bizarre in thinking or conduct, excessively obsessional, or extremely introverted (see Appendix 2, Note 2).

The clinical interview and Rorschach were used both for screening and, for those accepted, as part of the personality assessment for the study itself.[1] The clinical interview covered the subject's personal and psychiatric history, while the Rorschach was used to provide further diagnostic information, particularly about aspects of a subject's personality that are not available on a conscious level. The 50 subjects finally accepted for the study underwent additional personality assessment procedures, including Grygier's (1956, 1958) Dynamic Personality Inventory (DPI), Human Figure Drawing, and the writing of an autobiography; the WAIS and the TAT were also used in the personality assessment.

The WAIS was used primarily as a test of intellectual functioning, but the patterning of scores and idiosyncratic responses gave clues to psychopathology as well. The TAT was used to provide valuable information about personality dynamics, particularly a subject's self-concept, values, and motives, including those on a comparatively conscious level, as well as his characteristic ways of coping with his needs and his relationships with others.

The DPI is a comprehensive questionnaire including not only direct questions about the self, but questions concerning preferences and attitudes that serve as vehicles for the expression of more and less conscious elements of the personality. It yields scores for 33 scales, many based on psychoanalytic theory; well-established norms and validity data have been published. Human Figure Drawings were used in only a supplementary

[1] In addition to psychological screening, a physical examination was given. A blind diagnostic analysis of the assessment Rorschachs was made by Dr. I. H. Paul after the personality assessment ratings and independently of them.

way in the assessment, mainly to provide information about a subject's self-concept. The autobiography was written freely, but subjects were given a list of points to be covered: family background, early life history, current life situation, and plans for the future. Face sheet data were also obtained dealing with basic demographic data and educational, medical, personal, and family history.

The Personality Assessment

Although the assessment procedures yielded a wealth of clinical data for each subject, they did not do so in a form that lent itself readily to quantitative analysis. We decided, therefore, to study all of the clinical material on each subject and then to express the conclusions about his personality in ratings on a standard set of items. Using this material, staff members[2] independently rated each subject on 144 statements about personality, without knowledge of the subject's drug reactions, using 9-point scales to evaluate the extent to which each statement was true of him. These statements covered the areas of affects, thought processes, motives, defenses, inner states, identity, and interpersonal relationships.

The final ratings for all 50 subjects on the 144 personality variables were intercorrelated to determine whether their number could be reduced. Highly intercorrelated variables were combined when there was clear overlap in meaning. In this way the 144 items were reduced to 93 personality assessment variables; the complete list is presented in Appendix 2, Note 3.

DESCRIPTION OF SUBJECTS

Background

The average age of the 50 subjects was 28 years, ranging from 21 to 43; only 3 subjects were over 35. All but 7 had been to college and about

[2] Raters were members of the staff of the Research Center for Mental Health—faculty members, research scientists, and advanced graduate students in clinical psychology with training in personality assessment. Explicit definitions of the scale points for each item were first clarified in a series of staff meetings, so that ratings by different members would be comparable. Many of the raters had taken part in an earlier assessment program with fewer subjects (see Holt and Goldberger, 1959), each of whom had been independently evaluated by two raters; in that study the level of agreement was satisfactorily high. In the present study, to clarify specific points on which a particular subject's data provided insufficient or at times contradictory information, the subject was called back and interviewed again, after which the ratings were completed.

one-half (24) had graduated; three-fourths had taken professional courses in acting or music. As regards marital status, 7 were married, 3 divorced, and the remaining 40 were single.[3]

Their origins were quite varied. About two-fifths of the men were born in the Northeast, one-fifth each were from the South and Midwest; while the others came mostly from the West and Southwest. There was a wide spread of socioeconomic backgrounds, as indicated by their fathers' occupations, which were about equally divided among professionals or semi-professionals, white collar or small shopkeepers, and farmers or skilled or unskilled workmen. About half were reared as Protestants, and the remainder divided equally among Catholics and Jews; religious observance, however, was rare, and almost half the group identified themselves as agnostics.

The rate of family disruption from divorce or the death of a parent seems high. Thirteen of the men had lost a parent and the parents of nine others were divorced. In 10 of these 22 cases, the loss or separation occurred before the subject was 11 years old. About half of the subjects had experienced a gross trauma in childhood.

Personality Characteristics

Although these men vary widely in their abilities and personalities, they do, as a group, differ from a hypothetical average population in certain ways (see Appendix 2, Note 3). The assessment data indicate that they are, first, above average in intelligence, having a mean IQ of 126 and a range from 105 to 144. Their conceptual ability is excellent, they communicate ideas effectively, and their thinking is not likely to be stereotyped, inhibited, or concrete, although their concentration may be impaired by anxiety. They have a wide range of interests, particularly in artistic or other creative pursuits.

As a group, however, they do not have well-integrated personalities; two-thirds were rated as poorly integrated, over one-third very much so. Their predominant personality character structure was hysteric, characterized by pervasive use of the defense of repression and by emotional lability.[4] In addition, about one-half showed schizoid tendencies, indicating a defective capacity for deep emotional relationships and possible momentary impairments in reality testing.

They tend to be rather impulsive, exhibitionistic, and narcissistic, that is, egocentric and given to demanding, dependent relationships. They have a limited tolerance for anxiety, tending rather to avoid potentially anxiety-

[3] The high incidence of homosexuality is a factor in the low marriage rate.

[4] Four-fifths were diagnosed as having either a hysteric character structure or having marked hysteric features.

arousing situations. Under stress they tend to regress to a childish or passive role rather easily. They are not generous or sympathetic but, on the positive side, are rather spontaneous and emotionally expressive, well-poised and often charming in social situations, and relate easily (if perhaps often superficially) to other people.

Their overt expressions of hostility seem diminished, but there is much pent-up aggression that may emerge in fantasy or be projected onto others, sometimes to a paranoid degree. They tend to feel unloved, are highly sensitive to threat, and are likely to have an unconscious image of their bodies as damaged. Their anxiety level is quite high and the fear of a parental figure rejecting or abandoning them is a major source of anxiety. Masochistic and phobic tendencies are also common.

Their capacities for assuming adult responsibility are rather poor and in the face of obstacles they tend to abandon their goals rather than to persist. In their conscious values they reject conventional mores and authority in general, express tolerance for deviations in others, and assume a rather rebellious role, although in actual fact they are rather dependent and lacking in self-esteem.

They try to compensate by seeking acceptance and applause from others, by exhibitionism and, at times, by snobbishness. Denial of disturbing aspects of reality is a prominent defense, and isolation (dealing openly with disturbing material intellectually but repressing the appropriate emotional reactions) and reaction formation (controlling an unacceptable impulse by defensively emphasizing its opposite) are also used by them fairly frequently.

The most obvious pathological feature of this group is homosexuality. About two-thirds were evaluated as lacking an adequate masculine identification and about one-half had strong homosexual tendencies. Overt homosexuality was quite common and several were bisexual.

In summary, the subjects were intellectually bright and had poorly integrated, largely hysteric, and schizoid personalities. They were exhibitionistic and narcissistic, having much pent-up aggression. They were passive, vulnerable to stress, tended to be overtly anxious, and had impaired body images. Their major defenses were regression, projection, denial, isolation, and reaction formation. Last, homosexuality was a major area of pathology.

Comparison of Drug and Placebo Groups

The use of placebo subjects as a control group is valid only to the extent that the two groups are either well matched or differences are clearly defined and kept in mind when dealing with data that might be affected by them. Before comparing the drug and placebo groups on their pretest evaluations, we must briefly mention the problems that arose in the assignment of subjects to the two groups (see Appendix 2, Note 4).

We began to assign subjects by using the traditional method of random placement, only to discover through a preliminary analysis of certain aspects of the data that the first 19 drug and 10 placebo subjects were poorly matched, and that the differences could significantly affect drug-placebo comparisons in important areas. Random assignment was therefore abandoned and the remaining subjects were placed in a manner calculated to make the two groups more comparable. The end result was groupings of 30 drug and 20 placebo subjects which were not significantly disparate along any major dimension known to us at the time (see Appendix 2, Note 4). Since the matching could be explored only to a limited extent, the final groups did indeed differ in certain ways, although they proved to be comparable in most regards.

Background Data

Age, place of origin, religion, educational attainment, and marital status were well matched in the drug and placebo groups.

Among drug subjects their fathers' occupational levels were significantly lower; 11 drug subjects (37%) had lost a parent before reaching maturity but only 1 placebo subject had done so.

Intellectual Factors

The two groups were very well-matched intellectually in terms of total IQ (means of 125.5 and 126.1), WAIS subtests, pretest cognitive test performance, and the theme list task (see Chapter 4). The effects of LSD on intellectual functioning can therefore be evaluated without concern.

Personality Differences

In the personality assessment ratings, the greatest differences between drug and placebo subjects were in the areas of hostility and aggression. Placebo subjects were more openly hostile, more prone to anticipate being exploited, and more fearful of losing control over aggressive impulses. They were also judged to show more passive aggression and resistance. These ratings were complemented by the Rorschach summaries in which evidence of acted-upon aggressive impulses was seen in nine placebo subjects (45%) but in no drug group subject.[5] In contrast, all eight subjects with Rorschach evidence of overt depression were from the drug group.[6]

The difference in overt expressions of aggression is also confirmed

[5] Significant at .001 level.

[6] Significant at .02 level.

through the pretest earliest memories in which traumatic memories involving hostility or damage were described by significantly more placebo than drug subjects. Since there were more historical incidents of gross trauma in the drug group, this suggests that the differences are primarily the result of a strong tendency on the part of the drug subjects to inhibit their aggressive impulses. This is confirmed by an examination of the deviations from hypothetical norms in personality assessment ratings, in which the means of the placebo group for items dealing with expressions of hostility are within the normal range, whereas those for the drug subjects are notably low.

In other areas of personality, placebo subjects are more likely to experience their thoughts and impulses as ego-alien, to experience diffuse anxiety, and to feel guilt or anxiety over heterosexual impulses. They tend to act out, and their relationships are more tenuous and defensive. They may become disorganized under stress, and at times their defenses fail them. Their sexual identification is more feminine or homosexual and, last, on an overall scoring for ego strength (see Chapter 4), they score lower than the drug group.

Although the two groups differ in regard to these personality features, it should be remembered that they do not differ in most aspects of personality that were evaluated. They are similar in their general level of adequacy of functioning and in their use of a variety of defenses. They are also similar in the extent of their narcissism and exhibitionism and in their rather open expression of affect (other than hostility). They also do not differ in coping abilities and in their degree of independence, self-assertion, or self-esteem. Their attitudes toward convention and authority, and their goals and interests, are not different, and the adequacy and style of their thought processes are also quite similar.

We conclude, then, that the drug and placebo groups are adequately matched in many aspects of personality structure, ego functioning, and life style. As regards the special aspects of personality in which they do differ, most notably in the area of aggression, we must be alert to identify any of the experimental measures of LSD effects that might be affected by them.

THE RESEARCH PROCEDURE AND SETTING

The first contact our subjects had with the group of researchers was through the selection and personality assessment procedures already described. This consisted of several sessions of individual interviewing and testing by at least three different staff members. In the clinical interview, the potential subject was told that the study involved the taking of a drug (not identified), and that people differ markedly in their reactions to it. All were reassured regarding the safety of the drug and the experiment, and complete frankness was encouraged.

Throughout the entire study all subjects were seen individually, and only one subject took LSD or a placebo on any given day. On the day before he was to receive "the drug," each subject came in for about a half day of pretesting on the experimental tasks that required control data. The subjective questionnaire concerning drug effects was presented orally, and each experimenter who saw him filled out a behavioral observation sheet to provide base line data. The subject was then instructed to have a good night's sleep; to abstain from food, drink other than water (especially alcohol), and drugs from dinnertime on; and to report for the experiment without breakfast.

The entire experimental day was spent in the same laboratory, with the exception of brief periods for one or two of the experiments and visits to the bathroom. The room was painted a flat black, dimly illuminated, and hung with black draperies which deadened sounds; the general effect was rather eerie. Most of the time the subject sat in a comfortable easy chair. The room also contained a cot, on which some subjects lay down for brief periods when they wished, and there was apparatus for some of the tasks, including a tape recorder and microphone for recording much of the day's material.

At 8:50 A.M. the subject was given either 100 μg of LSD-25 (30 subjects) or a tap-water placebo (20 subjects) in a glass of lemon-flavored water, after which breakfast was brought to him.[7] At ½ hour after drug administration, which is the usual time of onset of reaction, the first questionnaire was presented, and from then until about 5:00 P.M., testing and interviewing were fairly continual with only a brief letup for lunch. Each subject was seen by from four to eight different experimenters, and he was not left alone at any time.

The subjects did not all take the same tests. Certain experiments were scheduled for only a portion of the subjects and, occasionally, a subject could not complete all of the scheduled tests. This was most likely to happen to those experiencing a maniclike reaction to the drug, which made testing difficult. The number of subjects who took each test is given in the reports of the experimental results.

Since the effect of the dosage of LSD used generally wears off in about 8 hours, official data-gathering was usually finished by 5:00 P.M. Thirty

[7] A double-blind procedure was used in the hope that none of the experimenters would know whether a particular subject had received the drug or the placebo. In practically all cases, however, it was soon obvious to the experimenters which subjects had actually received LSD.

of the subjects then spent the night in a dream research laboratory in connection with another study (Eagle, 1964). Of the others, placebo subjects were released after dinner, and drug subjects stayed with one of the experimenters until they were able to go home alone. All subjects came in the following morning for posttest interviews and control testing on some of the experimental procedures.

All subjects were seen in follow-up interviews several months later; some were interviewed again up to 2 years later. Two subjects had drug reactions that continued past the usual 8-hour period, and several were depressed or exhausted the following day (most common in subjects who had experienced maniclike reactions), but there were no persistent or recurring aftereffects. The longer-lasting reactions occurred in one panicky subject who spent the night with a staff member at his own request, and in another subject who experienced a very enjoyable, maniclike reaction which did not respond to Thorazine administered on the day following the LSD administration but which gradually disappeared over several days. The absence of harmful aftereffects may be attributed to the thorough screening procedure, aimed primarily at eliminating subjects whose emotional balance was precarious, and to the supervision which was continued as long as necessary in each case. During the follow-up period, none of the subjects took LSD again on his own, to the best of our knowledge; several said that the experience had been so unpleasant that no amount of money could induce them to take it again.

An important question that may be raised concerns the subjects' expectations before taking the drug. It should be remembered that the experimentation took place before the effects of LSD had become widely known. Later, a few guessed that they had taken mescaline, and a few, when told they had received LSD, said that they had heard something about its effects. The pretest questionnaire, by asking about a variety of bizarre reactions, may have established some expectations, although the instructions emphasized that "while all of these effects have been observed in some people who have taken this drug, different people react very differently, and you may have some effects but not others, or none of them at all." In any event, as elsewhere reported (Linton and Langs, 1962b), these expectations were obviously not sufficient to create the illusion of bizarre effects in the placebo subjects. The only spontaneous report of expectations came from several placebo subjects whose friends had previously been drug subjects; they expressed disappointment at not experiencing the interesting reactions about which they had heard.[8] Unfortunately, subjects were not systematically questioned about their expectations.

[8] Although subjects were asked not to discuss their experiences with each other, they did not all honor this request.

There is abundant evidence that reactions to LSD are affected by the setting in which it is taken (e.g., Hyde, 1960; Mogar, 1965; Pollard, Uhr, and Stern, 1965), and this undoubtedly applies to the present investigation. The setting was, insofar as possible, the same for all subjects, but the interpersonal aspects of the situation could not be completely controlled. One subject, for example, became more frightened, hostile, and suspicious when tested by an experimenter he disliked, but felt safe and relaxed with another experimenter who seemed to him "kind and like a father." The extent of such effects was not systematically studied. It can be assumed, however, that the bulk of the differences among subjects arose from pre-existing personality factors rather than from differences in the experimental situation.

It seems likely, however, that the laboratory setting placed certain constraints on reactions to the drug for most subjects. Extensive fantasy, marked regression and, in particular, hallucinatory effects, although they did occur, were not as common as has been reported in other studies using comparable dosage levels of LSD. Perhaps the constant barrage of testing did not allow such effects to develop as fully as they might have in other settings. By both filling the subjects' time and requiring them to relate to the experimenters and establish a task orientation, the situation implicitly demanded, for much of the time, reality-oriented, secondary-process functioning. While some drug subjects were often unable to maintain such a rational orientation, these pressures undoubtedly served to inhibit regressions in functioning.

The visually impoverished environment may not have been conducive to visual hallucinations, which were much less frequent than had been expected (body image distortions, in contrast, were quite common). Visual hallucinations, either drug-induced or naturally occurring, are likely to be triggered by real visual stimuli, beginning as distortions of actual percepts and then spreading (Bleuler, 1950). In our study the folds of the black draperies with which the room was hung were used in this way by some subjects, sometimes leading to the development of elaborate scenes.

The particular effects of 100 μg of LSD that we have observed must thus be understood to be the effects of the drug taken in the context of a particular experimental setting, aspects of which were not systematically defined in full. One could only speculate about the degree to which expectations of effects and other social factors affected the results described here; if the experiment were repeated under present-day conditions, both differences and similarities would undoubtedly occur. For our purposes, however, the naivete of our subjects was considered a great advantage.

As a final point, we should note that for all of the subjects this was their first experience with LSD. The novelty of the experience was thus an important determinant of the quality of their reactions, and it is likely that certain features, particularly anxiety, would be less prominent in subsequent LSD experiences.

With these considerations in mind, we now turn to the subjective questionnaire and, secondarily, to the behavioral observations that provided the basic tools with which we have defined and classified the LSD states of consciousness.

CHAPTER 3

General Drug Effects—Subjective Reactions and Observable Behavior

SUBJECTIVE REPORT: THE QUESTIONNAIRE

We used the subjective questionnaire for two major purposes: first, to monitor the states of consciousness throughout the experimental day, and, second, to provide an overview of the subjective aspects of these LSD states.

Although questionnaires have been used in previous studies, such as those of Abramson (1960; Abramson et al., 1955a, b), they have generally been limited primarily to somatic and perceptual experiences and have failed to take into account other important areas of functioning and experiencing characteristic of altered states.[1] The present questionnaire was designed not only to explore the subjective phenomena of the LSD reaction more thoroughly than had been done before but also to consider the drug reactions within the framework of psychoanalytic theory. By including items relevant to affect, cognition, and dimensions of self-experience such as body image, along with somatic effects, the questionnaire covers a broad range of subjective reactions. In order to develop meaningful and representative items, we reviewed the LSD literature and papers dealing with the psychoanalytic theory of consciousness (Klein, 1959a; Rapaport, 1957; Schur, 1955), with particular attention to the subjective correlates of altered states of consciousness. A preliminary version of the questionnaire was tested by several members of the research team who took LSD, and modifications were made. The final result of these efforts is presented in

[1] Perhaps the most useful previous questionnaire scale of drug effects is that derived from the Addiction Research Center Inventory (ARCI), a 550-item inventory developed by Hill, Haertzen, and their associates (Haertzen, 1965a, b; Haertzen, Hill, and Belleville, 1963; Hill et al., 1963a, b). Although the questionnaire devised for the present study was developed prior to the ARCI 172-item LSD scale, the two are similar in many areas. The present questionnaire, however, includes more items concerning psychoticlike effects than does the ARCI scale.

Table 3.1. The items are numbered 1 to 47, but the subparts of many of the questions bring the total number of actual items to 74.

Administration and Scoring

The questionnaire was given in interview fashion,[2] and for a number of items, qualitative information and clarification were specifically sought. In addition, all spontaneous comments were recorded.

There were seven administrations of the questionnaire in all:

1. Pretest day
2. One-half hour after drug administration
3. Two hours after drug administration
4. Five hours after drug administration
5. Eight hours after drug administration
6. Posttest day
7. Retrospective, given on the posttest day and asking for recall of all effects experienced at any time on the drug day.

Each separate questionnaire was scored for full and partial "yes" responses. These were summed for each questionnaire, yielding the *Total Questionnaire Score*; when the four experimental day questionnaires were totaled for positive responses, they yielded a comprehensive *Experimental Day Score* (See Appendix 3, Note 1).

Comparison of Drug and Placebo Subjects

We wanted to know first whether the questionnaire clearly distinguished the altered states from the waking state, differentiating the LSD from the placebo group. On the pretest questionnaire, administered the day before the experimental day with all subjects in the waking state, the groups did not differ (see Table A3.1). Under the experimental conditions, however, the questionnaire distinguished the drug and placebo groups at a high level of statistical significance, not only for the entire experimental day but for each of the four time periods sampled. In fact, the range of Total Questionnaire Scores in the two groups overlaps only slightly, indicating that there was virtually no similarity between the subjective reactions reported by LSD subjects and those reported by the placebo group.

[2] The experimenter gave the following instructions: "I'm going to ask you some questions about how you feel and what you have been experiencing. All of the things I'm going to ask you about have been observed in some people who have taken this drug but not in everybody. Don't worry about being consistent—just take each question as it comes. Answer each question on the basis of how you feel now or have been feeling in the last hour or so."

Table 3.1. Subjective Questionnaire: Percentage of LSD and Placebo Subjects Answering "Yes" to Each Item at Any Time during the Day

Pretest	Experimental day		
All Ss ($N = 50$)	LSD ($N = 30$)	Placebo ($N = 20$)	Question
2	60[a]	0	1. Have things felt unreal, as if you were in a dream?
0	43[a]	5	2. Have people looked different than they usually do?
0	40[a]	0	3. Have objects or the things about you looked different in any way?
10	57[c]	35	4. Do you find yourself talking about personal things you wouldn't usually talk about?
4	73[a]	15	5. Have you felt somehow as if you were melting or merging into your surroundings?
6	30[b]	5	6. Have you been thinking or talking a lot about your childhood (other than in response to our questions about it)?
6	83[a]	30	7. Have you felt occasionally that you have lost your sense of time?
2	73[a]	10	8a. Have you felt that you have lost control over yourself? *If not:*
4	50[a]	5	8b. Have you felt that you might?
6	60[a]	10	9a. Have you found it difficult to move?
10	32	15	9b. Easier than usual?
34	100[a]	50	10. Have you found it hard to concentrate on the tasks being given you?
14	63	45	11. Have you felt that certain things were especially clear to you or that you understood them better?
6	54[c]	30	12. Have you seen new connections between certain events or experiences that you hadn't seen before?
8	37	20	13. Have you felt depressed or sad?
6	93[a]	50	14. Has your body looked or felt strange in any way? [Any "yes"] *If so:*
2	73[a]	15	How? [Report of body image change]
4	80[a]	40	[Report of somatic symptom(s)]
14	50	35	15. Have you been especially happy?
10	77[b]	45	16a. Have you been feeling silly?

Table 3.1. (*continued*)

Pretest All Ss (N = 50)	Experimental day LSD (N = 30)	Experimental day Placebo (N = 20)	Question
4	63[a]	10	16b. Have you been acting silly?
12	47[b]	20	17. Have you been thinking about things you don't usually think about?
6	40[b]	10	18. Have you felt like a child?
4	50[b]	20	19. Have events or experiences seemed illogical or disconnected?
10	53[b]	23	20. Have you felt that under the drug you have acquired any new power or ability?
14	60[a]	20	21a. Has time been passing faster than usual?
8	70[a]	35	21b. Has it been passing slower than usual?
22	59[a]	20	22. Have some things seemed meaningless to you?
18	43[a]	10	23. Have you felt as if you were standing aside and watching yourself?
4	31[b]	10	24. Have you felt like an old person?
18	83[a]	20	25. Has any particular thing fascinated you—held your attention so that you found it hard to leave it?
0	50[a]	5	26. Has it felt as if some part of your body was disconnected or somehow didn't belong to the rest of your body?
6	60[a]	20	27. Have you been afraid or upset?
6	70[a]	10	28. Have you lost control of your thoughts? *If so:*
0	17[c]	0	28a. Have they taken possession of you?
0	13	0	28b. Does it feel as if someone else is controlling them?
10	60[a]	20	29a. Have you felt you would rather not talk?
8	60[a]	10	29b. Have you found it hard to talk?
18	60	50	29c. Have you been talking more than usual?
4	53[a]	5	30. Has it felt that time has come to a standstill or stopped now and then?
6	33[a]	0	31. Have certain objects or other things taken on meanings they never had before?
18	75[a]	35	32a. Have your thoughts been moving faster than usual at times?

Table 3.1. (*continued*)

Pretest	Experimental day		Question
All Ss (N = 50)	LSD (N = 30)	Placebo (N = 20)	
16	83[a]	30	32b. Slower than usual at times?
12	73[b]	50	33. Have you felt angry or annoyed? [Any "yes"]
4	41[a]	5	[Angry or annoyed at self]
8	59	45	[Anger or annoyance directed externally]
2	79[a]	15	34. Have you felt at times that you have lost control over your body or that you might?
			If so:
0	20[b]	0	34a. As if someone or something else has taken over?
14	100[a]	45	35. Do you think that your judgment and ability to evaluate have been different from usual? [Any "yes"]
			If so:
10	97[a]	10	How? [Report judgment impaired]
4	33	40	[Report judgment improved]
24	87[a]	30	36. Is it hard to hold onto thoughts, ideas, or images—do they seem to get away from you when you try to catch them?
4	53[a]	10	37. Have you felt like a different person at times?
2	67[a]	15	38. Have you felt that you were withdrawing from reality or losing your hold on the real world?
18	57[b]	30	39. Has your mind been a blank at times, so that you have had no thoughts at all?
0	40[a]	0	40. Have you been at all afraid that you might go crazy or lose your mind?
2	70[a]	0	41. Have you lost control over your emotions and feelings?
			If so:
0	30[a]	0	41a. Have they taken possession of you?
0	0	0	41b. Does it feel as if someone else is controlling them?
2	37[b]	15	42. Have you been seeing imaginary things?
2	50[a]	10	43. Have you felt as if some of what you have been doing is not really your doing at all?

Table 3.1. (*continued*)

Pretest All Ss ($N = 50$)	Experimental day LSD ($N = 30$)	Experimental day Placebo ($N = 20$)	Question
14	73[a]	10	44. Does one idea, thought, or image keep coming back again and again?
22	60[b]	30	45. Are you unsure of how others are responding or reacting to you?
			46. Have you had any of the following physical sensations?
20	90[a]	50	a. Dizziness or grogginess?
4	100[a]	35	b. Numbness or tingling?
6	73[a]	20	c. Chills or a cold feeling?
4	80[a]	10	d. Felt hot or sweating?
6	53[a]	20	e. Funny taste in your mouth?
0	33[c]	15	f. Unusual or heightened smells or odors?
0	73[a]	5	g. Felt nauseous?
2	53[a]	20	h. Blurred vision or trouble focusing your vision?
6	63[a]	25	i. Mouth dry or less saliva than usual?
4	34	20	j. Pressure or ringing in ears?
14	90[a]	40	k. Felt weak physically?
2	80[a]	35	l. Body felt lighter or like it was floating in space?
6	63[a]	25	m. Body felt heavier?
6	73[a]	15	47. Do you find that while you are answering a question you tend to forget what the question was?
4.32	38.95	11.15	Mean Total Questionnaire Score (Sum of all "yes" answers plus one-half sum of partial "yes" answers)
3.9	11.4	7.4	Sigma

[a] LSD > placebo at .01 level (one-tailed test).
[b] LSD > placebo at .05 level (one-tailed test).
[c] LSD > placebo at .10 level (one-tailed test).

The percentage of subjects in each group answering "yes" to each item on the experimental day is shown in Table 3.1; the groups are combined for the pretest percentages since their scores did not differ. As for the drug-placebo differences on individual questionnaire items, they were individually significant for 60 of the 74 items.[3] In most instances in which a significant

[3] Significance level was .05; 49 of these were at the .01 level.

difference was not reached, it was because the item was accepted infrequently by drug subjects; the placebo response was minimal in all areas. We can therefore conclude that the questionnaire was well suited to distinguishing the altered states of consciousness produced by LSD from the effects of a tap-water placebo. Furthermore, when their own pretest responses were used as a base line, the drug group showed a highly significant increase on the experimental day (see Table A3.1), whereas the total questionnaire scores of placebo subjects did not increase at all.

The two groups, as groups, were readily differentiated from each other by the questionnaire. As for the individual subjects, the total scores of 27 of the 30 drug subjects were higher than those of any placebo subject; 13 of the 20 placebo subjects had scores lower than any drug subject. The range of overlap of the distributions, therefore, included 10 subjects, 3 from the drug group and 7 from the placebo group.

Three methods were used to determine whether a more detailed analysis of the questionnaire could identify these 10 subjects correctly. These methods have been described fully elsewhere (Linton and Langs, 1962b); two involved modifications of the objective scoring, and one was qualitative. By using these methods, virtually every subject was correctly identified as belonging to the drug or placebo group on the basis of his subjective response.

The questionnaire, then, proved to be sensitive enough to classify the reactions of each subject as stemming from LSD or from the placebo. Placebo subjects in the present study did not experience reactions simulating the effects of the drug, although they had certain interesting features of their own which have been reported elsewhere (Linton and Langs, 1962b).[4]

As for the posttest questionnaire, given on the day following the experimental day, the mean number of items accepted by drug subjects (see Table A3.1) resembled the pretest mean; for the placebo subjects it was significantly lower than the pretest. The content of the items accepted on both days clarifies this finding. The items accepted most often on the pretest day by both groups reflect difficulty in coping with the experimental tasks and a certain degree of self-consciousness and apprehension. Two days later placebo subjects were more at ease and more familiar with the tasks. For drug subjects, however, the items accepted on the posttest day

[4] This finding contrasts with the report of Abramson et al. (1955c) that the reactions of their placebo subjects resembled LSD reactions. This may be partly the result of the content of their questionnaire, and partly because their placebo subjects were tested in groups together with drug subjects and, in many cases, had had previous experiences with the drug. Our subjects did not know what drug was being studied, had had no previous experience with LSD, and at no time observed the reactions of any other subject.

were different in content from the pretest. On the posttest day they too reported less difficulty with the tasks, but they also reported experiencing new meanings in objects and events, and a shift toward more depressive or less pleasurable affects. These were undoubtedly the aftermath of their drug experience (see Linton and Langs, 1962a).

Typical LSD Effects

What characterized the altered states our subjects experienced under LSD? This may be answered by looking at those items in Table 3.1 in which the experimental day percentages for the two groups differ by at least 50%.

Prominent among this group of items are indications of difficulty in thinking and in the control of the flow of thoughts. Subjects reported impairment of thought processes, judgment, and concentration, loss of control over their thoughts, and the feeling that their attention seemed to be captured involuntarily. Many of these reports (responses to items in Table 3.1) reflect a loss of control over the direction of attention, manifested in these subjects as trouble in keeping their attention on the task at hand and having attention drawn elsewhere without their volition.

All the items in the questionnaire that ask directly about loss of control also fell into the high-acceptance set of items. Included here were unspecified loss of control and loss of control over thoughts, the body, emotions, and behavior.

The subjectively experienced effects of the LSD states on the body were shown through somatic symptoms and body image disturbances. The former included numbness, feeling cold or hot, and nausea. Body image changes included changes in size, shape, weight, proportions, skin texture, or color. Feelings that the body had changed into that of a different person or the self at a different age were also reported, as was loss of the boundaries of the self. Subjects also felt weak physically and found it difficult to move.

Loss of contact between the self and the environment was reflected in feelings of unreality, loss of time sense, and loss of reality contact. Subjects also reported that they found it hard to talk; this may have reflected withdrawal as well as thinking difficulties and reduced motility.

These reactions may be considered the most typical features of the LSD states of consciousness in this group of subjects.

Although most of the other items were also accepted by more LSD than placebo subjects, particular attention is paid to only one set. These items, although accepted by less than a majority of LSD subjects, were accepted by no more than one placebo subject. They are thus effects that were highly specific to the drug states, although they appeared in only a limited number of subjects. This group of drug effects included distortions in the perception of people and objects, extreme feelings of loss of control, as represented by the feeling of being in the involuntary grip of thoughts or emotions, and the impression that an alien force had taken control of one's thoughts or body. Also included were fear of going crazy and fear of losing control. Possibly related to the issue of control was anger or annoyance at the self; spontaneous comments revealed that this often occurred when the subject was bothered by his inability to function in an adequate manner. The remaining two drug-specific items were thinking about childhood and seeing new meanings in objects or experiences.

To summarize the main characteristics of the LSD states in our subjects, these men experienced loss of control in a number of areas and many were frightened or angry with themselves as a result. As for their thought processes, loss of voluntary control over attention and generally impaired functioning were prominent. They felt that their bodies were affected physically and also reported difficulties in moving about and body image changes. Emotional control was impaired in such varied forms as fear, anger, or elation. Their feeling of contact with reality broke down, and some subjects experienced perceptual distortions.

Course of the LSD Reaction over Time

Over the 8-hour period studied, the overall strength of the subjective responses to LSD followed a characteristic course. The drug effect was well established by the ½-hour questionnaire, generally increased markedly by 2 hours, reached its peak at 5 hours, and then declined appreciably by 8 hours, although there was still a substantial effect at that time (see Table A3.1 and Fig. A3.1; for more details see Linton and Langs, 1962a). In the placebo group there was no characteristic time pattern. Fifty-seven per cent (17) of the LSD subjects were at the height of their drug reaction at the time of the 5-hour questionnaire; another 27% (8) reached their peak at 2 hours (1 subject peaked at ½ hour, and 4 at 8 hours). This distribution is significantly different from chance;[5] the peak times of placebo subjects were evenly distributed over the four questionnaire periods.

The LSD time curve just discussed is a group mean. The majority of subjects showed such a pattern, but a few did not. Some of the deviant patterns are considered in Chapter 5, in which the major varieties of LSD reactions found in this investigation are discussed.

Not only did different subjects exhibit different temporal patterns of responses to LSD but, for the group as a whole, different components of the drug reaction followed different courses. When the time curves of indi-

[5] .001 level, chi-square test.

vidual questionnaire items were examined, they were found to fall into five main types, each of which is shown in Fig. A3.1 (see also Linton and Langs, 1962a). These items are discussed briefly in Appendix 3, Note 2.

The Patterning of Subjective Reactions

The separate questionnaire items were grouped in two different ways. The first grouping included 16 scales, each made up of items whose content relates to the same area of functioning on an a priori basis.[6] The second grouping combined aspects of the drug reaction that actually occurred together in these subjects. These are the four empirical scales, and they represent the four major clusters of symptoms found in the drug group. [Their derivation has been described in detail elsewhere (Linton and Langs, 1964); their intercorrelations are given in Table A.3.2.]

Table 3.2 presents, for each of the 16 a priori scales, the items that comprise it and the empirical scale or scales that overlap with it. The titles of the scales are self-explanatory.

The four empirical scales are now briefly presented.[7]

Scale A

The items in Scale A can be grouped into three main areas: (1) loss of inhibitions, elation and a subjective experience that things are speeded up, (2) loss of control over attention and thinking, and (3) a subjective feeling of improved functioning, particularly the feeling of perceiving new meanings in experiences.

By 1/2 hour after taking LSD, each of these three kinds of effects began to appear. From the first area ease of movement and elation were evident. Loss of the ability to control attention first appeared as a kind of "fascination effect"—the subject's attention was involuntarily held by some re-

[6] These are the same scales previously reported (Linton and Langs, 1962a, 1964), with the difference that they have been renumbered in the order of their overlap with the empirical scales and one two-item scale has been dropped because of its unreliability. They have been retained because they provide a more detailed breakdown of the drug's effects than that given by the empirical scales; this is at times quite illuminating.

[7] The item content of the four empirical scales is listed in Table 3.3, along with the 14 items that did not fall into any scale, either because they correlated equally with more than one scale or did not correlate sufficiently with any (see Table A3.2 for the reliabilities of the four scales and their intercorrelations). The odd-even reliabilities are quite high; the intercorrelations, even though some are statistically significant, in no case approach the magnitudes of the reliabilities. We can thus be confident that the empirical scales represent major dimensions of the LSD experience that are internally consistent and, although related, distinct from each other.

Table 3.2. A Priori Questionnaire Scales

A Priori Scales	Questionnaire Items in Scale[a]	Number of Items	Related Empirical Scales[b]
I. Elation	15, 16a, 16b	3	A
II. New Meanings	11, 12, 31	3	A
III. Feeling of Improved Functioning	20, 35 (improved)	2	A
IV. Feeling Less Inhibited, Opened Up	4, 6, 9b, 17, 21a, 29c, 32a, 46l	8	A
V. Disturbed Time Sense	7, 21a, 21b, 30	4	A, (B)
VI. Difficulty in Thinking	10, 28, 28a, 32a, 32b, 35 (impaired), 36, 39, 47	9	A
VII. Feeling of Loss of Control	8a, 8b, 16b, 28, 28a, 34, 36, 40, 41, 41a, 44	11	(A), (B)
VIII. Visual Distortions	2, 3, 42	3	(A), B
IX. Loss of Contact	1, 7, 38, 45	4	(A), B
X. Ego Change, Alienation	18, 23, 24, 28b, 34a, 37, 41b, 43	8	(A), (B), (C)
XI. Loss of Meaning	19, 22	2	B
XII. Suspiciousness	28b, 29a, 33 (external), 34a, 41b, 45	6	B
XIII. Feeling Inhibited, Slowed Down	9a, 21b, 29b, 32b, 39, 46m	6	C
XIV. Body Image Change	5, 14 (body image), 26, 46l, 46m, (plus 18, 24 if body image effect reported)	7	C
XV. Somatic Symptoms	46a–k	11	(C), D
XVI. Unpleasant Affect	13, 24 (depressive), 27, 33, 40	5	D

[a] For some items only certain responses are scored; they are given in parentheses.

[b] Where only one empirical scale is given, it accounts for over twice as much variance of the a priori scale as does any other empirical scale. Scales in parentheses account for a substantial but smaller portion. Scales VII and X do not fall clearly into any one empirical scale.

Table 3.3. The Four Empirical Scales

Empirical Scale	Questionnaire Items in Scale[a]	Number of Items	Mean Drug Day Acceptance (%)[b]
Scale A	2, 4, 7, 9b, 11, 12, 13, 15, 16a, 16b, 17, 18 (in sense of carefree, spontaneous), 20, 21a (yes, don't know), 25, 28, 29c, 31, 32a, 35 (improved), 36, 37, 39, 41 (if elation), 41a (if elation), 44	26	51
Scale B	1, 3, 8a, 18 (if body felt small), 19, 22, 28a, 28b, 30, 34a, 41 (if fear), 41a (if fear), 42, 43, 45	15	35
Scale C	5, 6, 9a, 14 (body image), 18 (in sense of incapacity, helplessness), 24, 26, 29b, 32b, 34, 46a, 46b (in legs or feet), 46d, 46e (unpleasant), 46k, 46l, 46m	17	58
Scale D	8b, 27, 33 (at self), 40, 46f (unpleasant), 46g, 46h, 46j	8	42
Not in any scale	10, 21b, 23, 29a, 33 (external), 35 (impaired), 38, 41b, 46b (in face or head), 46b (in hands or arms), 46b (in body or trunk), 46c, 46i, 47	14	60

[a] For some items only certain responses are scored; they are given in parentheses.

[b] "Mean drug day acceptance" is the percentage of items accepted at least once at some time during the drug day by the average LSD subject; it is the same as the average acceptance per item.

current thought, idea, or image. The later reports of new insights and heightened powers of understanding were preceded at this time by the subject's feeling that he himself was different; inquiry disclosed that this did not mean feeling like someone else, but rather "fresher," "more mature," "more *me*."

By 2 hours the disinhibition expanded to include feeling and acting silly, the sense that time was passing quickly, feeling carefree like a child, and a sense of losing control over the elated affect. Loss of control over thinking became more explicit, including difficulty in holding onto thoughts or images and a loss of the sense of time (the two most frequently reported effects in this scale). The fascination effect appeared further in that objects or trivial events gripped the attention. Improved powers of judgment were reported and subjects stated that they were thinking about things they did not usually think about (most often related to self-understanding and the meaning of childhood experiences). The earlier perception of change in the self expanded to include an altered perception of others, not in the sense of physical distortion but rather in a sense that others were experienced "clearly, more vividly," or as a sense of "seeing people in terms of their essence."

The effects that emerged for the first time at the peak of 5 hours reflected primarily feelings of new understanding and further disinhibition. The latter included thoughts moving faster than usual and talking more than usual, sometimes about personal things one would not usually talk about. Thinking difficulties reached a point where the mind sometimes became a blank. The items that reflect more explicitly subjective reports of changes in the meaning of experiences, better understanding, seeing new connections between experiences, and the development of new powers emerged strongly only at 5 hours, with a marked decline after that time, suggesting that they represent the culmination of this set of reactions. Descriptively, subjects felt more astute and more perceptive. One said, for example, "Connections between things in my life and things in the tests, childhood recollections are clear to me now." In some subjects the heightening of perception was specifically sensory; colors and sounds became more vivid, and they saw new and personal meanings in the objects around them and in test stimuli. The personal meaning, however, did not have a paranoid quality (a crucial difference between Scales A and B). There was also some sadness described as a reaction to the newly acquired insights. This had a mellow, rather than a despondent quality; for example, "after philosophizing I would feel depressed, the bittersweet qualities of life."

The only effects remaining to any extent by 8 hours were elation, loss of the sense of time, recurrent thoughts, and some feeling of improved judgment.

In summary, Scale A effects included alterations in both the self-experience and the experience of the outside world. There were reduced controls over affect, particularly elation, impairment of attention deployment, and expansiveness, which are in some ways reminiscent of a maniclike reaction.

Scale B

The items in Scale B have the lowest incidence of those in any scale. Thus they include effects that are not common in our subjects but that we conclude are highly specific to the LSD states because they are almost nonexistent in the placebo group. Their content is the most psychoticlike of any scale and includes feelings of unreality and of experiences of losing meaning, perceptual distortions, the experience of losing control over a number of functions, and the feeling of being controlled by outside forces.

Although the items vary somewhat in their patterns, Scale B as a whole had the sharpest time curve of any scale, with a peak at 5 hours. The first manifestations, at ½ hour, were feelings of losing control (feeling that one's actions were "not my doing at all" and that one's body was controlled by outside forces) and, in a few cases, feeling physically small, like a child. By 2 hours these effects were joined by feelings of unreality and things seeming meaningless, visual distortions (both altered appearances of real objects and imagined percepts), feelings of being possessed by thoughts or having them controlled by someone else, and of having generally lost control.

These effects increased by 5 hours and were joined by clearer evidence of dissociation, as experiences became illogical or disconnected, time seemed to stop, and subjects became unsure of the reactions of others. In a few cases there was uncontrolled fear or anxiety. The only effects persisting to any extent by 8 hours were those of things seeming meaningless and the feeling that one's actions were not his own doing.

The subjects' explanatory comments shed further light on the meaning of Scale B. The most frequent reactions, as cited above, represent an overwhelming loss of the sense of self, so that the subject's own thoughts and feelings seemed foreign to him and he felt that he had lost control over his own functioning. There was also reduction in the hold on external reality, which itself became drained of meaning and assumed a dreamlike quality. The observing self became dissociated from the experiencing self: "It's as if someone else is chewing my food"; and experiencing became fragmented: "A pause between sentences, filled with time, seemed unending." One subject felt split into three identities: "the grinning imp" who could enjoy physical pleasures, "the one who denied" them, and "the rational me." Some subjects reported that they felt a physical regression to an infantile state; two felt curled up, "womblike"; others reported feeling small or talking baby talk.

These derangements in the experience of the self and of the environment were associated with paranoidlike phenomena. The same subject would first report that "things are meaningless" and later state "everything has meaning." Implicit meanings were read into a variety of situations that had become puzzling. Subjects wondered about "things the experimenters do, closing the door, shuffling papers, arranging the tape machine." There were fantasies about the experimenters' malevolent motives. The experience of having lost control over thoughts, emotions, or one's body led to ideas with delusional qualities. "Oh, yes, somebody must have control of them, I'm sure." These reactions were among those most often consciously suppressed while they were occurring under the drug and subsequently reported for the first time in recalling the drug experience the next day.

The visual distortions included some apparent hallucinations, but "imaginary interpretations of real things" were more common, such as images seen in the folds of the curtains. Some of the experiences were frightening, whereas others were pleasant; a few were extensive dramatic scenes.

Because Scales A and B implicate many of the same areas of functioning and they are correlated (see Table A.3.2),[8] it is helpful to compare them. The loss of control in Scale A pertains primarily to affect, attention, and ideation; in Scale B there is a more general and pervasive loss of control that seems to involve the whole self. In Scale B only, this experience is extended to the idea that someone or something else is controlling these functions. The change in relationship with the environment in Scale A is that of seeing new meaning in it; in Scale B the change in relationship results in loss of meaning and loss of contact with the environment. The self-experience in Scale A is one of increased competence accompanied by elation and an inner sense of acceleration that pertains to thoughts, actions, and the passage of time itself; in Scale B it is one of inadequacy, uncertainty, fragmentation, and impairment, accompanied by fear and a sense that time was stopping. Primary-process thinking is much more evident in Scale B than in Scale A.

Scale C

The items in Scale C deal primarily with alterations in the body image, somatic effects, and a generalized inhibition, both physical and mental. These reactions, particularly the bodily effects, have the highest experimental day frequencies and the earliest onset of any group of items, so that they dominate the initial stages of the total LSD reaction; they also persist for the longest time.

By ½ hour loss of control over the body was felt, as well as dizziness, weakness, and a feeling of lightness. Less frequent, but also manifest early, were the feeling that some parts of the body did not belong or were disconnected, heaviness, numbness in the legs, and feeling hot or sweating. By 2 hours, difficulty in moving was reported, as well as the sensation of merging into the environment and other body image changes, and unpleasant (for example, metallic or dusty) tastes. By 2 hours there were some effects not directly implicating the body; thinking was slower and in some cases thoughts of childhood came to the fore.

By 5 hours, the feelings of loss of control over the body and the sense that the body was disconnected lessened, but it became harder to talk, and feeling old or experiencing the helplessness of a child appeared. In a sense, both of these feelings express the total effect of the items in Scale C as

[8] It may be that Scale B represents an extreme extension of Scale A effects (see Linton and Langs, 1964, where this point is discussed).

verbalized by one subject: ". . . old and feeble, or like a baby, because I couldn't move." It may be on this basis that thoughts about childhood occurred. At 8 hours thinking was still slow and most of the somatic symptoms remained strong, but the more striking body image changes were mostly gone.

Some examples of the body image changes reported are: "a feeling of heaviness and lightness at the same time, as if there were two of me, one pressing against the other"; "the whole bottom part doesn't belong to the top part." These alterations were usually *not* accompanied by reports of anxiety, an interesting aspect of this scale.

Scale D

The items in Scale D include explicit reports of anxiety, fear of losing self-control or going crazy, and a group of related physical symptoms. Although the reactions in this scale were less frequent than those in Scale C, they also had a comparatively early onset. At ½ hour nausea and blurred vision were common, along with the feeling that control *might* be lost. By 2 hours pressure or ringing in the ears developed, as well as anger with one's self. By 5 hours, the feeling that control might be lost dropped off and was replaced by overt fear, in some cases specifically the fear of going crazy. Unpleasant odors (for example, sulfur) were also reported by a few subjects. At 8 hours the chief components still present were the somatic symptoms of nausea, blurred vision, and ringing in the ears.

A prominent feature of Scale D is the feeling of being *on the verge* of losing control. As one subject put it, ". . . on the threshhold of loss of control of the body and possibly also of the mind." The few subjects who actually vomited after taking the drug had significantly higher scores than other subjects on Scale D but not on the other scales. The subjective anxiety and the physical symptoms may be either concomitant reactions on different levels or causally related; we have no way of evaluating this issue.

OBSERVATIONS OF BEHAVIOR

As noted in Chapter 2, the *objective* measure of the state of our subjects was obtained by having the experimenters rate each subject on 18 scales characterizing their behavior, mood, manner, and spontaneous verbalizations. Whenever feasible, each experimenter made these ratings immediately after testing or interviewing a subject.[9]

The 18 variables were rated on 4- or 5-point scales, with each scale

[9] Each subject was actually rated from 6 to 12 times on the experimental day, by from four to eight different experimenters. On the pretest day, from 2 to 4 ratings were made of each subject.

point defined on the rating form by a verbal description, and clarified by discussion among the raters. In analyzing the data, however, we combined some variables and dropped one, which yielded a final list of 11 variables, of which 4 were combinations made on the basis of high intercorrelations, closeness in meaning, and similarity of patterns of correlation with the other variables. The following combinations emerged (the other 7 measures were retained in their original form).

I. *Regression*—combining four scales: Thought Confusion, Loss of Reality Contact, Regressive Behavior, and Open Uncontrolled Verbalizations (the average intercorrelation among these was .82).

IV. *Silliness*—combining Silly Behavior and the rating of affect as Labile (correlation = .73).

V. *Depression-Elation*—a bipolar scale formed by averaging Depression vs. Elation and Verbal Inhibition vs. Pressure of Speech, and rating of Affect as flat (average intercorrelation = .86).

X. *Hostility-Negativism*—formed by averaging Hostility and Negativism (correlation = .79).

On most of the scales, the higher the score, the greater the deviation from normal behavior. Two scales, Affect (Depression-Elation) and Motility (Slow and Fast), were bipolar, so that both extremes represent abnormal behavior.[10]

For each measure all pretest and all experimental day ratings were averaged, providing two scores for each subject on each measure (Table 3.4). The groups were well matched on the pretest day, both showing deviations in affect and some anxiety. Placebo subjects, however, were more likely to be suspicious, a difference that could well result from chance, although it is consistent with the personality differences between the two groups (see Chapter 2).

On the experimental day the two groups were completely different from each other, so that their Total Behavioral Scores scarcely overlap. In the placebo group 14 subjects showed less behavioral deviation than on the pretest; 6 increased. In the drug group, however, 28 of the 30 subjects

[10] On Scale V (Affect) a subject whose average for the drug day was at the midpoint of the scale could have shown normal affect at all times or he could have been manic half the time and depressed the other half. On Scale VI (Motility), the extremes represent hypermotility and motor retardation. Therefore these scales are presented in two ways. For Scale V the first score ranges from depressed to elated; the second (V-A) measures how totally deviant the affect was. For Scale VI, the first score ranges from slowness of movement to hyperactivity; the second (VI-A) measures the degree of total deviation from a normal activity level, whether higher or lower.

Table 3.4. Behavioral Observations of LSD and Placebo Subjects[a]

		Mean Scores[b]							
		Pretest Day			Experimental Day			Significance (two-tailed) of Pretest to Experimental Day Shift	
	Behavioral Scale	LSD	Placebo	Significance of Difference	LSD	Placebo	Significance of Difference	LSD	Placebo
I.	Regression	−.01	.01	—	.39	−.01	.001	.001	—
II.	Visual Distortion	.00	.00	—	.41	.01	.001	.001	—
III.	Inappropriate Affect	.03	.04	—	.56	.06	.001	.001	—
IV.	Silliness	.09	.06	—	.43	.04	.001	.001	—
V.	Depression (+) vs. Elation (−)	.06	.10	—	.09	.19	—	—	—
V-A.	Affect, absolute deviation	.27	.30	—	.62	.30	.001	.001	—
VI.	Motility: Slow (+) vs. Fast (−)	−.02	.06	—	.10	.05	—	—	—
VI-A.	Motility, absolute deviation	.19	.11	—	.48	.21	.001	.01	—
VII.	Withdrawal	.06	.18	—	.20	.16	—	—	—
VIII.	Anxiety	.66	.66	—	.99	.30	.001	.05	(−).001
IX.	Bodily Preoccupation	.07	.08	—	.83	.05	.001	.001	—
X.	Hostility-Negativism	.10	.04	—	.28	.12	.05	.01	—
XI.	Suspiciousness	.06	.19	.05	.27	.02	.001	.05	(−).05
	Total Behavioral Deviation	2.89	2.56	—	7.82	2.22	.001	.001	—

[a] All significance levels are based on two-tailed tests. For pretest to experimental day shifts, the *t* test for correlated means was used; minus signs in the last column indicate significant decreases in the placebo group.

[b] Each variable was rated on a 4- or 5-point scale, with scores adjusted so that a score of zero represents "normal behavior," that is, no discernible effect.

increased; the 2 who decreased were also the 2 LSD subjects with the lowest Total Questionnaire Scores.

The difference between groups can best be seen by comparing the changes from the pretest to the experimental day for each group (last two columns of Table 3.4). For every variable except Withdrawal (VII), the drug group showed a significant increase and also became significantly different from the placebo group; for both Affect and Motility, however, the increase is only in the total amount of deviation.

Further, the experimental day scores of placebo subjects were significantly correlated with their pretest scores, suggesting that both sets of ratings represent their characteristic behavior in a laboratory situation of the type used. Drug day scores of the LSD subjects, in contrast, were uncorrelated with their pretest scores, indicating that behavior under LSD was not each person's typical behavior but rather was specific to his LSD state.

Relationships among Behavioral Effects

Intercorrelations among the various behavioral ratings revealed which aspects of behavior went together; most were in keeping with expectations. The details of these relationships are presented in Appendix 3, Note 3, and in Table A3.3, while the following are the most important of these findings:

1. Inappropriate affect (III) was associated with all of the other affective deviations (IV, V, VII, X, and XI), motility deviations (VI-A), and regressive behavior (I).
2. Anxiety (VIII) and bodily preoccupation (IX) went together as they did in the subjective questionnaire (Scale D); both were associated with regression (I) and motility changes (VI-A), while anxiety was associated with hostility (X) and suspiciousness (XI), which formed a pair themselves.
3. Altered motility (VI-A) occurred along with some of the most pervasive behavioral changes in other areas.
4. Depression (V) occurred along with retardation and withdrawal, while elation was associated with pressure of speech and hyperactivity, as well as silliness.
5. Regression (I) constituted the most psychoticlike behavior and correlated with almost all of the other behavioral deviations.

SUBJECTIVE REPORTS VS. OBSERVATIONS OF BEHAVIOR

Each subject's own report of his experiences under LSD was compared with the experimenters' ratings of his behavior to the extent that the two overlap. This was done to check the accuracy and validity of the two sources of data and to detect possible areas of concealment or uncertainty. Toward this goal, several specific comparisons were made which are briefly summarized here (see Appendix 3, Note 4).[11]

First, we explored the behavioral correlates of the four empirical scales derived from the subjective questionnaire. This comparison revealed striking overlap (see Linton and Langs, 1964, for full details):

Scale A (maniclike expansiveness and difficulty with attention) correlates with behavioral scales: Regression (I), Visual Distortions (II), Inappropriate Affect (III), Silliness (IV), Elation (V), Total Affect Deviation (V-A).

Scale B (psychoticlike effects) correlates with: Regression (I), Visual Distortions (II), Inappropriate Affect (III), Silliness (IV), Elation (V), Anxiety (VIII), Bodily Effects (IX).

Scale C (body image changes) and Scale D (somatic effects and fear of losing control) correlate with: Anxiety (VIII) and Bodily Effects (IX).

The second method of comparing the self-report and observations was to correlate the more specific a priori scales with the scores derived from the experimenters' ratings. We predicted 49 such correlations and were correct to a significant degree. To these were added a few unpredicted correlations, yielding a picture in which the subjective report emerged as the more reliable and useful of the two measures (see Appendix 3, Note 4). This was seen most clearly when a third means of comparison was used, one in which the items most directly related to each other from the two sources were compared subject by subject. This revealed that, while the two sets of scores were consistent for most subjects, when they differed it was usually because the subject had reported an effect that the experimenter had failed to detect.

In terms of the behavioral scales, predictions related to Regression (I), Visual Distortions (II), Inappropriate Affect (III), and Silliness (IV) were confirmed in the subjective reports most strongly, while Anxiety (VIII), Bodily Effects (IX), Hostility (X), and Suspiciousness (XI) were also confirmed. Predictions failed, however, for Affective Shifts (V-A), Motility Shifts (VI-A), and Withdrawal (VII).

In three areas the discrepancy between the two sources of observation suggested concealment or denial. Suspiciousness was detected by our observers more often than it was reported by our subjects. Posttest inquiry revealed that some subjects feared to report it during their drug experience.

[11] Table A3.4 presents all the correlations between the behavioral measures and the four empirical scales, along with selected correlations between the former and the 16 a priori scales.

This was also true in the area of hostility, particularly because some subjects were afraid to report anger which experimenters detected. Last, some subjects minimized their feelings of anxiety because they feared being more overwhelmed if they admitted it. In every other area the self-report was more complete and revealing than our observations. Thus subjects were, on the whole, capable of observing and reporting their experiences under LSD accurately.

We may conclude, then, that the subjects' responses to the questionnaire may be taken as valid in most respects and as a more reliable and complete source of information about the altered organismic states produced by LSD than the observations made by the experimenters. The questionnaire was capable of detecting finer differentiations in subjective experience in areas in which the two sources covered the same content, and it also tapped many areas not available to direct observation. We therefore make greater use of the subjective reports in defining the various altered states observed under the drug and use the observations to supplement the subjects' own descriptions of their experiences.

CHAPTER 4

The Effects of the LSD States on Experimental Test Performance

In order to sample and test a wide range of functioning in the LSD states, a variety of procedures were administered. These ranged from standard cognitive and personality tests to experiments specifically designed for our research. Although we developed hypotheses for many of these studies, all were undertaken in a search for new observations and formulations.

For each of these procedures, the results were evaluated in the context of both the placebo control data and, whenever possible, test data obtained from drug subjects in the nondrug state. We first ascertained if and how functioning was altered by the LSD states, and then studied individual differences in such altered functioning. These individual differences were examined by relating the findings from each procedure both to other aspects of the drug response and to several dimensions of the pretest personality data. To a limited extent we also examined relationships between the findings from different experimental procedures.

Since the personality correlates of different kinds of LSD reactions are considered at length in Chapter 5, we limit ourselves in this chapter to correlations with two broad measures derived from the personality assessment. The first is a scale of ego adequacy; this scale is essentially a measure of ego strength, or autonomy and competence. This measure subsumes several major aspects of personality: coping ability; self-concept, including self-esteem and self-image; modulation of affect and level of anxiety; object relationships and ego interests; type of thinking and judgment; and maintenance, adequacy, and regressiveness of defenses. The second is a measure of paranoidlike tendencies, or tendencies that predispose a person to develop an altered state with paranoid features. It includes such features as hostility, depression, fear of exploitation, and an impaired sense of identity. The Ego Adequacy and Paranoid-Prone scales are described in Appendix 4, Note 1. In addition to these two measures of predrug functioning, a third, IQ, was also related to the experimental results when appropriate.

THE EXPERIMENTAL TASKS

The Cognitive Tests

The literature on attention and LSD states led us to predict that performance on standard tests of cognitive functioning would be impaired. We expected, however, that not all tests would be affected to the same degree. The ability to sustain attention is thought to be particularly impaired in altered states. It therefore seemed likely that tasks requiring only a brief period of effort or those on which subjects use a relatively overlearned, automatized set of responses (such as easy arithmetic problems which require no analysis) would be less seriously disrupted than those requiring longer, focused periods of attention. Similarly, since the drug states tend to impair active efforts at directing attention, it was postulated that tasks requiring primarily the use of passive attention or a receptive attitude would be less affected than those requiring active attending. The eight tasks selected for the evaluation of the effect of the LSD states on cognitive functioning were therefore chosen so as to vary in their degree of complexity and in the amount of active mental effort and attention they demanded.

Method

All subjects were tested twice, under control and experimental conditions, using alternate forms. Experimental day testing was done in the middle of the day, when the effect of the drug was at its peak in most subjects. The battery consisted of:

1. Digit Span test, from the Wechsler-Bellevue Intelligence Scale.
2. Short Passage Comprehension test, adapted from the Iowa Silent Reading Test.
3. Long Passage Comprehension test, adapted from the Iowa Silent Reading Test.
4. Word-naming test, in which the subject was asked to name, within a 3-minute period, as many words as possible having a given number of letters (three or four).
5. Serial Sevens test, in which the subject was asked to count backward by intervals of 7 from a given number (103 or 101).
6. Simple Rhyming test, in which the subject was asked to name, within a 3-minute period, as many words as possible that rhyme with a given word (fist or rise).

7. Robinson Rhymes test [devised by Mary Frances Robinson (1946)], which required the subject to keep several things in mind, while using overlearned material. For example: Name a color that rhymes with the word for writing fluid.

8. Robinson Numbers test, similar in structure to Robinson Rhymes, but dealing with numbers. For example: Name a number which when doubled and added to two gives six.

Results[1]

On the experimental day the cognitive performance of the placebo group was superior to that of the drug group on all eight tests. These differences were, however, significant for only four of the tests: Word-Naming, Serial Sevens (for both time and errors), Robinson Rhymes, and Robinson Numbers. As predicted, the tests that were most impaired appear to be those that demand more active mental effort and sustained attention, either because of a degree of complexity that requires the subject to carry out several processes at once, to juggle several sets and shift back and forth between them, or to overcome a highly overlearned process. Specifically, the Word-Naming task requires the subject to call up words from a potentially vast storehouse, scan them to check the number of letters, recall whether or not the word has already been given (since he was asked not to repeat himself), and carry on this entire process without hesitation since the goal is to produce as many correct words as possible in a limited time. The Serial Sevens test requires the subject not only to counteract the highly overlearned process of counting forward but also to count backward by units of seven, thus calling for the process of subtraction or, as was frequently the case, leading a subject to covertly count backward, which appreciably increased the time needed for the task. It was on this task that drug subjects most often strayed into other preoccupations, such as with fantasy, imagery, or their physical state, so that the experimenter had to prod them to continue. This may have happened because of this task's special demand for persistent effort in the absence of any element that could inherently engage or attract the subject's interest.

The two Robinson tests have in common the fact that several schemata or sets must be maintained at once, a rather complex process. In addition, the task requires both shifts in attention and maintenance of persistent attention. If the subject is searching for "a food that rhymes with the name of something we use when we sew" (bread-thread), he must first

[1] The data analysis is presented in Appendix 4, Note 2, and has been published elsewhere in more detail (Goldberger, 1966). The results for the eight subtests are presented in Table A4.3.

activate a food schema and maintain attention on it (for example, meat, milk, eggs, butter) while at the same time activating and attending to a sewing schema (for example, needle, thread, thimble, scissors); he must then check one against the other for rhyming, thereby alternating the focus of his attention. Subjects varied on this task in their style of matching schemata. Some were haphazard and disorganized, while others remained rigidly fixed on one idea and gave up or reached the time limit without shifting from it. Both of these strategies of attending occurred more frequently under the drug, while more flexible strategies predominated under the placebo.

Finally, the Robinson Numbers task requires that the subject maintain a focus of attention on an entire mathematical problem and also attend to the necessary backward steps required to solve it, doing each correctly while not losing track of the other. The drug subjects could not do this efficiently as shown by their almost significantly greater need to have the problem repeated.

By contrast, in tasks in which the groups did not differ significantly, subjects were not required to make active, persistent efforts to maintain and shift attention. The Digit Span task requires only a brief focusing of attention. In the Comprehension task, whether long or short, the subject listens to a paragraph and then picks out what he has heard from a multiple choice list. These tasks require only passive attention and a receptive set. They contrast with the Theme List task in which retention is tested by active recall without an offering of choices, and the recall of neutral material was highly impaired by the drug (see below).

The rhyming task raises a question because its degree of difficulty and attention requirement might appear to be similar to that of naming of words. The Word-Naming task, however, is a two-stage process (thinking of a word and checking out the number of letters) calling for some shift in attention and for decision making. Rhyming, however, is essentially a one-stage, sensory process; once a word comes to mind, its correctness as a rhyme is evident. It therefore entails only the passive process of recognition. Further, dealing with a word in terms of its sound is a relatively primitive kind of behavior, and it is in fact well known that clang associations are often increased in altered states of consciousness. Viewed in this light, it is not surprising that simple rhyming was less impaired under LSD than was word naming.

In cognitive tasks that are presumably neutral emotionally, then, the LSD states affect certain kinds of functions more than others. Tasks requiring active mental effort, either to counteract a highly overlearned process or to deal simultaneously with the several aspects of a complex task, are seriously impaired; in these tasks complex shifts of attention are required. There is no appreciable impairment, however, when the task requires only brief moments of focus and maintenance of attention and when the chief requirement in the task is that of passive rather than actively mobilized attention.

Individual Differences in Cognitive Impairment[2]

Although the LSD states clearly impaired the ability to perform on four cognitive tests, not all subjects were equally affected. In looking at these four tests separately, we found that about half of the subjects were seriously impaired in each test to a degree well beyond the deterioration shown by any placebo subject. An index of total cognitive impairment was formed,[3] and it indicated that the cognitive performance of eight (36%) subjects was seriously impaired, whereas nine subjects (41%) did at least as well as the average placebo subject; the remaining five (23%) showed some deterioration but did so within the range of impairment seen in the poorer-performing placebo subjects.

What accounts for these differences among subjects in the degree of cognitive impairment they experience under LSD? In order to understand them better, it must first be noted that among the four cognitive tests in question, impairment scores on Word Naming, Serial Sevens, and Robinson Numbers are highly intercorrelated,[4] whereas impairment in Robinson Rhymes has lower correlations.[5] We also find that the first three tests are very similar in their patterns of relationships to other variables, whereas Robinson Rhymes has its own pattern. The experimental findings are presented accordingly.

Pretest cognitive performance and impairment under LSD for both groups of tests were examined in relation to Verbal IQ,[6] Ego Adequacy, and degree of anxiety observed under LSD at a time close to the cognitive testing. When we considered the first three tests taken together—Word

[2] See Table A4.4 for a presentation of the major findings described here in their essence.

[3] This was done by subtracting from a subject's score on each of the tasks the score that would have been predicted from his pretest performance using placebo criteria, and then summing these for the four tests. Twenty-two drug subjects took the cognitive test battery.

[4] Intercorrelations are, respectively, .69, .83, and .68.

[5] The correlations of Robinson Rhymes with the other tests are .50 (Word Naming), .32 (Serial Sevens), and .55 (Robinson Numbers).

[6] The cognitive tests were correlated with three factors derived from the WAIS: the verbal, attention-concentration, and analytic factors (see Cohen, 1957; Witkin et al., 1962). They were highly correlated with the first two, but only modestly with the analytic factor. Since the verbal and attention-concentration factors are represented by the verbal tests, verbal IQ seemed to be the most relevant measure to use.

Naming, Serial Sevens, and Robinson Numbers—we found that pretest performance is primarily a function of Verbal IQ and Ego Adequacy, and that the contributions of these two variables to nondrug cognitive performance are independent of each other. The degree of impairment under LSD, however, is related primarily to the ongoing anxiety level, with subjects who are overtly anxious in the LSD state showing marked deterioration in their performance on these three tests.[7] The striking thing about this finding is not that anxiety impairs secondary-process, attention-demanding, cognitive performance, which is a well-known phenomenon, but the fact that this is so exclusively a function of the anxiety component of the LSD reaction. Impairment on these tests is unrelated to the blatant subjective and objective regressive effects of the drug states, such as psychoticlike experiences, body image alterations, a subject's own report of thinking difficulties, loss of reality contact, and regressive behavior.

The Robinson Rhymes task operated quite differently. First, pretest performance in this task was not significantly related to pretest performance on the other three impaired cognitive tasks, to Verbal IQ, or to ego strength. Under the drug the ability to cope with Robinson Rhymes was also unrelated to the extent of anxiety. The critical factor in maintaining adequate performance on this test under LSD was adequacy of ego functioning, despite the fact that pretest performance was unrelated to this factor.

The drug day Robinson Rhymes performance was, in addition, related to several aspects of the questionnaire reports of our subjects' altered states. These reflected a loss of reality constraints (but *not* distortions of reality) and a flighty kind of thinking. We speculate that this complex rhyming task differs from the other three cognitive tests in that achievement in this test may be helped by an unfocused flight of ideas and a playful orientation toward the task. A clue to the difference between the two sets of tasks is found if we examine the subjects who were not anxious. They all did better than anxious subjects on the three interrelated tasks, but on the rhyming problems the nonanxious subjects who stayed closely in touch with reality all did very badly. This is because every subject in that group was noted as being clearly depressed. As we shall see later, it was subjects of superior ego strength who were most likely to give themselves up to a pleasurable state of fantasy and drive expression under the drug, maintaining an open and playful attitude toward their experience.

In summary, then, the complex cognitive tasks requiring both active and sustained attention were most impaired in the LSD states. Of these tasks,

[7] Impaired performance under LSD is also related to low ego adequacy scores, but this is only because subjects with inadequate ego functioning were more likely to become anxious.

impairment in three (Word Naming, Serial Sevens, and Robinson Numbers) was determined almost entirely by the immediate level of anxiety. On the fourth task, Robinson Rhymes, impairment under LSD was related to the degree of predrug ego adequacy and to the extent to which subjects reported experiences of loss of reality constraints and flighty kinds of thinking under LSD.

The Color-Word Test

In the Color-Word test, the subject looks at a page of incongruent color-word combinations, such as the word "green" printed in blue ink, and is asked to name the colors, ignoring the words. Thus, two mutually incompatible response tendencies are aroused, and he is asked to suppress a strong, highly overlearned, relatively automatized response (reading words) in favor of an unfamiliar task demand (naming the contradictory colors). This can be done only by maintaining a high level of focused attention directed consistently, evenly, and flexibly, in order to suppress a ready response. The ability to resist the interference of the incongruent words in the naming of the colors is termed "flexible control," whereas "constricted control" refers to difficulty in resisting this interference (Klein and Smith, 1953; Klein, 1954; Gardner et al., 1959). Previous studies have shown that this cognitive control style is highly stable. We were therefore interested in learning whether LSD states would affect such an enduring characteristic of a person's cognitive style and, if so, in what way.

Method

The criterion task, which has been used in many previous studies of cognitive controls (cf. above and Hardison and Purcell, 1959; Loomis and Moskowitz, 1958; Wolitzky, 1967), is based on Thurstone's (1944) adaptation of the test devised by Stroop (1935), and is described more fully in Appendix 4, Note 3. After it has been determined that his reading speed is within normal range, the subject first names the colors of ink in which groups of asterisks are printed on a page (four colors are used), as quickly and accurately as possible. This colors-alone series serves as a baseline and is followed by the color-word series, which consists of the four color names printed in incongruous colors. The subject must name the colors aloud as quickly and accurately as possible, ignoring the words. The test was given on both pretest and experimental days, and three measures are obtained:

1. *Colors-Alone Time.* The number of seconds needed to read the colors-alone page. This measure reflects the subject's ability to concentrate and persist in an unfamiliar task. Even though the stimulus does not em-

body conflicting cues, the task is intrinsically more difficult than reading words, and an aphasiclike blocking often occurs.

2. *Interference.* The time taken to read the color-word series (adjusted statistically so as to eliminate the effect of each subject's colors-alone time). This represents the additional delay in color naming produced by the tendency to read the words and the need to suppress this tendency.

3. *Variability* in the times taken to "read" the five separate two-line segments of the color-word series. This represents the degree of erratic or variable performance.

Results[8]

The colors-alone reading was very strongly and significantly slowed down in the LSD states. Thus, while the placebo group improved on the experimental day, a practice effect found in previous studies, the drug group became significantly worse than they had been on the pretest day. In spite of this strong drug effect, each subject was affected to a similar degree so that their levels of performance relative to each other were unchanged. We see, then, that subjects under LSD maintained their characteristic style of color naming, even though they were all slowed down.

Interference, in contrast, was not consistently increased or decreased under LSD; the adjusted experimental day mean interference scores on the Color-Word Series were virtually identical for the drug and placebo groups. A drug effect is suggested, however, by the fact that drug day interference scores of individual drug subjects were not predictable from their pretest performance but were related to certain other drug effects described below.

Variability in Color-Word reading was increased significantly under LSD; 54% of the drug subjects showed a substantial increase in this score while only 21% of the placebo subjects did so. The placebo group as a whole did not become more variable.

Summarizing the general effects of the LSD states on the Color-Word test, it was found that color naming became much slower, while the relative ability of different subjects to perform this task was maintained. On the Color-Word page, performance became much more erratic. Interference proneness, a usually stable cognitive style, was greatly altered, but not in a consistent direction.

Relationships with Other Variables[9]

The drug's effect on colors-alone reading time was unrelated to either the cognitive test battery results or the empirical subjective reaction ques-

[8] The detailed findings are presented in Table A4.5.

[9] The correlations of each of the measures of drug effects on the color-word task with the cognitive test battery and the empirical scales from the questionnaire are presented in Table A4.6.

tionnaire scales. This is in keeping with the fact that the LSD subjects maintained their pretest cognitive styles of color naming under the drug, and supports our previous interpretation that the general slowing in colors-alone time is a nonspecific effect of the LSD states.

Changes in interference proneness, however, were associated with other LSD effects. An increase in interference proneness was associated with a strong Scale B subjective experience, which includes the most psychoticlike LSD effects, among them loss of reality contact, perceptual distortions, and alterations in perceived meanings. Resistance to interference in the Color-Word series requires persistent maintenance of attention and controls in order to separate consistently the two incompatible meanings encoded in the same stimulus. The Scale B effects represent the most striking losses of controls under the drug. In addition, increased interference was associated with difficulty in learning new, neutral verbal material in the Theme List task (see next section). The evidence suggests that the key factor here is an impairment in comprehension related to a grossly disturbed LSD state.

The variability of Color-Word reading time, however, is quite a different matter. Highly variable drug day performance (a reflection of a constant struggle to establish controls in the face of great difficulty) was associated with high scores on questionnaire Scale D, which reflects experienced anxiety and fear of losing control. It was also related to impairment in the three cognitive tests whose disruption was, as we have seen, primarily a function of anxiety. It was unrelated, however, to impairment in the Robinson Rhymes test or to the Questionnaire Scale B effects, which reflect the actual loss of controls rather than the fear of losing control. Since variability is a direct measure of fluctuations in attention, this pattern of findings provides direct support for our previous interpretation that the anxiety component of the altered LSD states impaired performance on the three cognitive tests through its effect on attention. We may conclude, then, that anxiety disrupted the active, even, consistent dispensation of attention to tasks that required sustained attending. As a result, the performance of subjects who became anxious under LSD became highly erratic on a variety of tasks.

To summarize, we have found that impairments of different aspects of performance in the Color-Word test have different implications. Impairment in color naming per se was great under LSD, but unrelated to personality factors or to other aspects of the drug reaction. Increased interference proneness under LSD was associated with drug-induced ego breakdown, particularly loss of control, alterations in perceived meanings, and difficulties in comprehension. Increased variability within the Color-Word series directly reflects the alternate disruption and reinstatement of the ability to use focused attention that is associated with anxiety. Impairment of active coping resources appears to be the crucial factor in interference proneness, whereas the struggle to maintain or to reinstate control lies behind a highly variable performance.[10]

Theme Lists: The Retention of Drive-Related and Neutral Material

Controlled studies that have compared the learning and recall of drive-related (sexual or aggressive) material with that of neutral material (Kott, 1955; Riggs, 1956; Smith, 1954) have found that they do not differ in the ease with which they are retained. It has been found, rather, that learning and recall depend most on the formal properties of the stimuli and that content plays a role only in terms of its degree of familiarity and the interest and attitudes of the subject toward it. This appears to contradict psychoanalytic theory, which suggests that the drive properties of a stimulus play an important part in the ease with which it is learned and retained. These studies have, however, typically used subjects who were fully alert and attentive, and it seems likely that this is an important factor in the failure to find a drive effect. As Rapaport (1942, 1958), Klein (1959a), and many others have pointed out, psychoanalytic theory postulates that adults have relatively autonomous capacities, relatively free of the influence of drive and emotion, which enable them to perceive and learn in accordance with reality. These relatively autonomous cognitive functions depend, however, on the maintenance of a fully waking state of consciousness for effective functioning, relatively free from the pressure of drives. It is our hypothesis, therefore, that in the altered states produced by LSD the autonomies of cognitive functions are not fully maintained. On this basis we predicted that drive content would prove a greater influence on learning, retention, and recall under LSD than in waking states.

Method[11]

The ability to learn and retain verbal material was assessed by the Theme List technique, a procedure devised by I. H. Paul (1958, 1959, 1964) for a series of experiments on memory styles. A theme list is a loosely connected set of passages forming the plot outline of a story. Four theme lists were constructed for the present study. Two had manifest drive-related content, one aggressive and the other sexual, and two were drive-neutral, serving as control lists and equated insofar as possible for all formal variables.

[10] Sample patterns of reading times associated with different kinds of LSD states are given at the end of Appendix 4, Note 3.

[11] See Appendix 4, Note 4, for details of the method and findings, including the two control theme lists. The scoring and procedure have been described in greater detail elsewhere (Paul, 1964).

The aggressive theme list was:

The Vampire

Theme 1: The bearded captain was a damn big man that hot night.
Theme 2: Men were guzzling burning rotgut.
Theme 3: They cut him down with cruel barbs.
Theme 4: A vicious stroke lacerated five.
Theme 5: She watched the bloody fight.
Theme 6: A butcher knife plunged deep.
Theme 7: There was a satisfied peace.

The sexual theme list was:

Forbidden Sin

Theme 1: He watched intently the blonde strip in the dark.
Theme 2: Wriggling she showed her belly.
Theme 3: Lights dimmed on gleaming skin.
Theme 4: She rubbed naked breasts.
Theme 5: He peeked through fingers covering his eyes.
Theme 6: Down on the bed she peeled off black panties.
Theme 7: "God, is that man or woman!"

Subjects were tested in the morning and again in the afternoon on both the pretest and experimental days, with a different list on each occasion, using a controlled sequence. Immediate recall of each list was sought after a 5-minute diversion. On the morning of the experimental day, before the new theme list was given, the subject was asked to recall the previous day's lists as precisely as possible. Although various aspects of the subject's reproduction of the material were scored, we are concerned here only with the accuracy of recall, measured by the number of information units correctly reproduced.

Results

For immediate recall (5 minutes after presentation), placebo subjects did equally well on the two days. They did tend to recall the sexual theme list better on either day, probably because that list was intrinsically easier, although an erotic drive effect cannot be entirely ruled out.[12] There was, however, no evidence of a general effect of drive content on retention under nondrug conditions.

The drug states, on the other hand, significantly impaired learning and immediate recall of the theme lists, and this effect was different for the drive and control lists. While both types of lists were significantly more

[12] This point is discussed in detail in Appendix 4, Note 4.

poorly retained under LSD, the impairment was significantly greater for the control list than for the drive list. Thus under LSD the aggressive list and the sexual list were *both* better retained than their respective controls. The main drug effects on the Theme List test are presented in Table A4.7.

As for the experimental day reproduction of the previous day's theme lists (24-hour retention), the drug and placebo groups differed in the expected direction but only at a borderline level of significance. This suggests that the impairment of "short-term retention" under the drug may not be primarily an inability to *retain* learned material, but rather a failure to learn adequately under LSD in the first place. The relationships with other aspects of the drug reaction support this interpretation.

Relationships with Other Drug Variables

Theme List accuracy scores are related to two kinds of variables:[13] measures of the subject's capacities in the normal state and measures of the drug's effects. The data show, first, that pretest accuracy[14] has substantial relationships with both IQ and Ego Adequacy; under the nondrug conditions it was the brighter and more autonomous subjects who learned both drive and neutral lists better. The learning of the drive lists under LSD, which was more resistant to impairment than the neutral lists, was significantly related only to the pretest accuracy score. Apparently, the drive content of these lists served as a means of maintaining focused attention and, thereby, as a bulwark against the inroads that LSD states usually make on cognitive functioning. As a result, learning and retention were relatively stable under the drug. This conclusion is supported by the fact that drug day drive list learning accuracy was unrelated to impairment on the other cognitive tests or to the questionnaire or behavioral manifestations of drug effects.

The two aspects of Theme List performance that were impaired under LSD were, as we have seen, the recall of the previous day's lists and the learning of the neutral list. These two kinds of impairment were significantly related to each other ($r = .57$) but not so highly as to be identical in their implications. Both measures were, first of all, significantly related to Ego

[13] Table A4.8 includes all correlations between IQ, Ego Adequacy, and four accuracy scores from the theme list task. Since the Ego Adequacy score and IQ were unrelated to each other, they represent measures of two independent aspects of adequate functioning.

[14] Under pretest conditions the accuracy scores for drive and neutral lists were highly correlated ($r = .69$) and had similar relationships with other measures, so they were combined into a single measure. The same holds true for drug day recall of the two pretest lists ($r = .68$), so a single measure was used for them as well. It is only in new learning under LSD that the drive and neutral lists have different implications.

Adequacy; subjects whose ego functioning is normally better were less impaired under LSD in both long-term and immediate recall. In their correlates with LSD state reactions, however, they differed.[15]

The relationships between these two scores and other measures of the effects of LSD reveal that poor recall of the pretest lists under LSD was strongly associated with impairment in the cognitive test battery. As with the other cognitive tests, this was associated with marked manifest anxiety, not, however, in terms of its momentary state, but rather in terms of the average level of anxiety observed throughout the drug day. This was because recall was tested about 1 hour after the drug was taken, when the LSD effects were just beginning to appear. Thus those subjects who recalled the previous day's lists poorly early in the drug day tended to be the ones who later became manifestly anxious and showed impairment in the cognitive tests. As for effects at the time of the Theme List recall testing, poor recall was related to the first signs of regressive behavior, such as confused thinking, and to loss of contact with reality. It seems probable that the subjects who showed those early effects, while still able to control the visible manifestations of their anxiety, were already experiencing impairments in attention and concentration leading to interference with memory functions.

The learning of new, relatively neutral material in the LSD-altered states, in contrast, was not related to any measure of anxiety, and its correlation with the nonrhyming cognitive tests was only of borderline significance. Rather, impairment of immediate recall under the drug was strongly related to the subject's own report of ongoing effects, primarily the psychoticlike Scale B effects, but also the expansive Scale A effects. Five of the more specific a priori scales were significantly associated with difficulty in learning the neutral lists: visual distortions, loss of meanings, loss of control, loss of reality contact, and thinking difficulties.

The only aspect of overt behavior that was related to impaired learning of neutral material was evidence of visual distortions, providing further evidence that these subjects were experiencing a change in the meaning of external stimuli. When the entire day's behavior is considered, it is also associated with regressive behavior.

This part of the Theme List task differs from the other cognitive tasks in that it requires the subject to learn meaningful material. The other cognitive tasks and the recall of previously learned theme list material suffer from the interference with attending produced by anxiety. In contrast, the learning of new, meaningful material under LSD suffers most if the person is in a regressive state in which objects and events lose their usual

[15] These relationships are presented in Table A4.9.

meanings. This is reflected in the remarks of some subjects that under the drug the theme lists seemed disorganized and the separate themes merged together. The data indicate that the actual cause of the learning difficulty was an inability to grasp readily the meaning of the themes. This is supported by its correlation with the interference score on the Color-Word test. Previous studies indicate that the meaning of the words in that test must be grasped before the interference produced by them can be overcome.

We may now summarize the Theme List findings and their implications. It is not surprising that the altered states of consciousness produced by LSD interfered with the ability to learn and retain connected meaningful material. What is noteworthy is that the impairment occurred primarily in the learning of neutral material. Such impairment was attributable only in small part to the difficulties in concentrating and attending so prevalent in LSD-altered states; it was primarily accentuated by difficulties in the ability to grasp and comprehend the meaning of the themes experienced by subjects who had a particularly regressed drug state. Drive content apparently facilitated learning through its power to attract and focus attention, which exceeded that of the more neutral control material. Thus the drive-related meanings were able to attract attention more readily than neutral material, thus assisting the subject in compensating for the interference in the function of attention experienced in the LSD states.

We also conclude that, in the usual state of consciousness, cognitive functioning is relatively autonomous within the limits tested by the theme lists. As a result, the functions of comprehending meaning and directing attention can operate relatively free of drives and affects. Thus there was no consistent difference in the learning of drive vs. control material on the pretest day. In the altered states produced by LSD, however, the autonomy of cognitive functioning was impaired, so that drives came to play an organizing and selecting role. Our findings show that there is indeed a relation between emotions and memory (Rapaport, 1942), but that this relationship is in part vitally mediated by the state of consciousness.

Our results also point up an essential difference between the learning of new material and the recall of previously learned material. Learning new material is facilitated when the content is drive related, a condition that aids its organization into a comprehensible and focused whole, but the recall of previously learned material is not affected by this factor. The latter is aided instead by concentrated effort and the consistent dispensing of attention in the required direction and, like several other cognitive tasks, it is disrupted by anxiety. Finally, both of these processes—the active feat of comprehension and the concentrated focusing of attention—are maintained best under LSD by those subjects whose ego functioning is most adequate in the nondrug state.

Responsiveness to the Expressive Connotations of Words as Both Peripheral and Focal Stimuli[16]

It has been shown by many researchers that words may be responded to not only in terms of their presumed objective meanings but also on the basis of their expressive or physiognomic qualities (Arnheim, 1949; Koffka, 1935; Werner, 1966; Scheerer and Lyons, 1957; Hochberg and Brooks, 1957). For example, certain words appear to people to be inherently ominous or joyful, regardless of their defined meaning, solely on the basis of their sound qualities. The present experiment was designed to evaluate the effects of LSD states on responsiveness to these latter qualities under two kinds of conditions: when the stimulus or word to which they belong is peripheral to the subject's primary field of attention, and when the word itself is the focus of attention.

It seemed likely to us that LSD states would produce a loss of boundaries between the diverse elements of a total stimulus situation, so that the schemata evoked by the stimulus would be less likely than usual to remain distinct from each other. In this experiment physiognomic qualities were activated incidentally as attributes of a peripheral stimulus element (a word) presented together with a focal stimulus (a drawing of a young man's face). The expectation was that under LSD the expressive attributes of the word would be more likely to intrude upon descriptions of the face. In addition, we sought to compare drug and placebo subjects in their responsiveness to these expressive qualities when the word in question was the focal or central stimulus.

Method

The words "Uloomoo" and "Takete" have been found, in other studies, to have highly contrasting connotations. In our experiment we told half of the subjects that the person pictured was a primitive man named Uloomoo, and the other half that he was named Takete. Each subject was asked to rate the face on two lists of bipolar adjective pairs. He was then asked to rate the words alone as words (one of which he had not seen before), using the same adjective pairs.

Ratings were made on two lists, each consisting of items rated on a 7-point scale, defined by opposing pairs of adjectives. List I consisted of 25 items previously found by Hochberg (1957) to differentiate between

[16] See Appendix 4, Note 5, for the details of the procedure and results.

Uloomoo and Takete; the adjective pairs in List I are essentially physiognomic, with metaphoric connotations (for example, low-high, smooth-rough). List II, which was developed for this experiment, consisted of 44 pairs of personality traits (for example, skeptical-dogmatic, compliant-independent). The nature of this experiment made it impossible to obtain pretest data, so we must rely on comparisons between the two groups on the experimental day.[17]

We were interested in exploring several issues with our data. First, we wanted to know whether the drug would reduce or enhance the differentiation that subjects normally make between the two stimulus words. Second, would the boundaries between the pictured person and the word used as his name be reduced under LSD? Finally, if there was a fusion between the attributes given the face and the name, we wished to specify its nature.

Results

Turning now to the results, we first explored whether the ratings did, indeed, distinguish among the various stimuli.[18] We found that for placebo subjects the conceptions of the face and of each of the words were quite independent of each other. This was not true of the drug group, however. The ratings of the face and the name given to it bore a highly significant resemblance to each other, and neither resembled the adjective descriptions of the word not paired with the face; this pattern held true for every drug subject. This effect was stronger for List II adjectives, which describe personality traits, although it also occurred for List I, which consists of more impersonal physiognomic qualities.

We then looked at the actual content of the ratings.[19] For List I, our subjects generally differentiated between the two words in the same way Hochberg's (1957) college students had in the normal state: Uloomoo was perceived as more low, rounded, soft, dull, passive, relaxed, and smooth; Takete was seen as more high, angular, loud, sharp, active, tense, and rough. These differences were extremely significant in the placebo group; for subjects under LSD they were, by and large, in the same direction, but

[17] This test was given to too few drug subjects for us to relate individual differences in the effects found to other aspects of the drug reaction.

[18] This was done by computing for each subject the average scale distance between each pair of sets of ratings over the total set of items; with these averages we could not only compare the drug and placebo groups, but could test either against the average discrepancies that would have occurred by chance. Smaller-than-chance discrepancies indicate some similarity between the two concepts being rated; a discrepancy at the chance level means that two concepts are no more similar than any pair of unrelated concepts. See Table A4.10.

[19] See Table A4.11.

not as marked. This is because drug subjects did not differentiate significantly between Uloomoo and Takete along conventional lines when the word was paired with the face. Thus, in the LSD-altered states, the usual connotations of the words were modified, presumably by taking on some of the face's qualities.

Drug subjects also differentiated between the two words on fewer items from List II than did the placebo subjects. More interesting, however, is the fact that on this list the two groups differentiated between the words on completely different sets of items. Thus the groups were in agreement on the physiognomic connotations of the two words but not on their personality implications.

List II consists of attributes that describe people and can be used to express a more personal secondary elaboration of the common core of physiognomic qualities described by List I. We find that the two groups of subjects elaborated that common core in different areas. Placebo subjects apparently valued the basic Takete qualities positively and extended them to include, from List II, qualities that created an image of an energetic, assured, brash, and attractive person. Uloomoo, by comparison, was for them more tame, inhibited, retiring, and weak.

Drug subjects, however, differentiated between the two words primarily along interpersonal lines. For them the connotations of the core qualities of Takete were quite unpleasant and threatening, while Uloomoo was seen as more agreeable, warm, and open.

The lack of pretest data makes it impossible for us to determine whether these differences are drug state effects or derive from predrug personality differences between the two groups. Our data suggest, however, that the drug state did influence the perception of the two words, coloring the LSD subjects' ratings.

The Word–Face Interaction

The greater-than-chance similarity between the drug subjects' ratings of the face and its name indicates that LSD did indeed weaken the boundaries between the two, since no such similarity was found in the placebo group. The fact that the usual distinctions between Uloomoo and Takete did not completely hold when the word named the face indicates that the core of physiognomic meaning suggested by either word was differently elaborated when it was evaluated alone and when it was evaluated as the name of a person, or that the attributes of the face modified the connotations of its name to some extent. We also examined the possibility that the influence works in the opposite direction as well.[20]

[20] This question was examined by means of two special measures: (1) the face

We found that both effects were found significantly in the drug subjects but not in the placebo subjects. The face, however, was a stronger stimulus than the words; the effect of the face on the name was about twice as large as the reverse effect.

In summary, then, the Uloomoo-Takete experiment produced two main findings: (1) under LSD there was a significant loss in boundaries between the face and the associated name, so that the two schemata, readily kept separate by placebo subjects, were measurably assimilated into each other under the drug, and (2) subjects under LSD nevertheless remained capable of responding to important connotations of the word and face stimuli in a manner not unlike that of alert placebo subjects. While the expressive or physiognomic attributes of the word did, as we predicted, modify the response to the face, the face seems to have affected the response to the words to a greater extent. Furthermore, what crossed the boundaries between the face concept and the name concept were not the primary physiognomic qualities of the two stimuli but rather the more inferential set of personality attributes.

We suggest two reasons why the influence of the face was the greater. The most obvious is that the face was rated first; once a face-name schema was formed, it persisted for subjects in the drug state, so that the name-alone schema was partially assimilated into it. The second factor is that the face is a much stronger stimulus, providing clearer clues for the kinds of ratings for which we asked, particularly on the personality attributes in List II. This not only limited the amount of peripheral influence the name could exert on the face but also generated a strong schema which could carry over to the words.

The Use of Color vs. Form in Perceptual Organization[21]

The Color-Form experiment is an investigation of the predicted shift to a more primitive level of functioning in LSD states. It is a study of perceptual organization in a task in which the subject's "choices" are spontaneous rather than consciously determined. It has been demonstrated in developmental studies that the organization of a percept through the use of color represents an earlier, less mature level of functioning than the organization of a percept on the basis of its form-qualities. Further, color organization has less reality-attuned utility than organization through form;

---

ratings were scored for the six items that best differentiated between the words Uloomoo and Takete, and (2) the ratings of both words were scored for a set of eight adjectives that were typically assigned to the drawing of the face. The results are presented in Table A4.12.

[21] For a summary of several studies bearing on this issue, see Meili-Dworetzki (1956). See Appendix 4, Note 6, for the details of the procedure and results.

the latter is best suited for a stable perception of the environment. If our assumptions about the regressive effects of LSD states are correct, we would expect that, in a task that requires the subject to respond either to the form *or* to the color of a stimulus, subjects under the drug would tend to organize their percepts more through color and less through form than subjects in the nondrug waking state.

Method

In most Color-Form tests the options are obvious, so that they lend themselves to a deliberate, conscious choice, rather than facilitating a spontaneous reaction. This drawback is overcome in the test devised by Schmidt (1936) and used by Thurstone (1944), in which two patterns of colored spots are projected alternately in such a manner that apparent movement can be seen in either a clockwise (right) or counterclockwise (left) direction. If a subject sees movement in one direction, he sees moving circles and stripes that change color; if in the opposite direction, he sees moving red and green spots of constant color but changing shape. The subject is not aware of the basis of his perception, however, and he is usually unaware that the rotation can be seen in more than one direction until he has stared at the screen for a while and, in most cases, experiences a spontaneous reversal of direction. In our study there were two trials of 1 minute each on the pretest and experimental days.

Two scores were obtained for each trial: % Color and Alternation. % Color is the percentage of the time during which movement was seen that was determined by color (all subjects saw movement during virtually all of the exposure time). A high score thus represents greater color-dominance, and a low score greater form-dominance. Alternation rate is the number of spontaneous reversals in the direction of movement that the subject experienced.[22]

Results—General Drug Effect

The pretest % Color scores of the two groups were well matched, movement being determined by form about three times as often as by color for both groups. On the experimental day, while both groups responded to color more than they had on the pretest, the increase was significantly greater under the drug condition, and virtually every LSD subject showed an increased use of color. Despite this, form remained the more influential determinant of apparent movement, color reaching 50% for only one

[22] This score was converted to logarithms, which give a more normal distribution of scores than the raw number of alternations. A subject whose perceived direction of movement did not change was therefore given a raw score of 1 and a logarithmic score of 0. In this report Trials I and II are combined for each day.

drug subject. Furthermore, placebo subjects maintained their ranking on % Color on the two days, but the drug group did not.[23] The use of color is therefore a highly stable characteristic of an individual subject under nondrug conditions, but the LSD states disrupt this aspect of cognitive style.

The analysis of the effect of the LSD states on alternation rate suffers from poor pretest matching of the groups (see Appendix 4, Note 6). The alternation rate of the drug group did not change significantly, whereas a very significant increase occurred in the placebo group; the placebo increase, however, occurred mainly in subjects who experienced few or no pretest alternations, and there were no such subjects in the LSD group. Furthermore, the correlation between pretest and experimental day alternation rates was extremely high and was identical in the two groups, indicating that the rate of alternation of the percept is a highly stable characteristic of the individual subject that was *not* altered by the LSD states.

The use of color and alternation rate were very highly correlated under nondrug conditions so that a high rate of alternation was associated with greater determination by color, whereas subjects whose perception of the wheel was organized primarily through the cues of form experienced little alternation. Under LSD, however, this relationship vanished completely.

To summarize the essential findings, the LSD states did not affect the subjects' characteristic alternation rates. The drug states did, however, strongly affect the influence of color on the perception of apparent movement, breaking the link between color and alternation rate, so that individual cognitive styles of color use were not carried over into the drug state and, further, for practically all subjects, the extent of color determination increased. In terms of this measure, then, LSD tended to make perception more primitive, less affected by form (a characteristic associated with control).

Relationships between the Color-Form Test and Other Measures

Pretest use of color and alternation rate were unrelated to any measure of the drug reaction. Since alternation rate showed no measureable drug effect, we focused on color determination in exploring individual differences in the LSD subjects.[24]

[23] The pretest vs. experimental day correlation for placebo subjects was .73.

[24] In evaluating these relationships, two controls were used. One was to use a special score which we called *C′*, as a purer measure of the drug effect than the % Color increase (see Appendix 4, Note 6). The other control was the use of questionnaire and behavioral measures obtained at a time as close as possible to the Color-Form testing. The relationships between *C′* and the questionnaire scales are shown in Table A4.14.

Greater reliance on color under LSD is associated with the expansiveness and psychoticlike effects of questionnaire Scales A and B, unrelated to Scale C, and somewhat *negatively* related to the fear of losing control of Scale D. The relationships between color usage and the more specific a priori scales clarify the picture. Within the Scale A effects, color preference is significantly related only to the expansive feeling of losing one's inhibitions. The highest correlations with the Scale B effects are with visual distortions, loss of contact, experiencing an unreal, dreamlike state, and loss of the sense of time. Color usage was not, however, related to the Scale A effects of elation or the feeling of having acquired new powers, or to the Scale B effects of thinking difficulty, meaning loss, or the feeling of having lost control. We may say, therefore, that LSD created an increased reliance on color as the basis for perceptual organization and did so most strongly in those subjects whose LSD state was characterized by a lifting of certain normal constraints, including those of reality-oriented perception.

In addition, extensive use of color was significantly associated with body image changes, while more direct somatic symptoms were significantly associated with greater reliance on form. The latter was also associated with a variety of unpleasant affects related to the fear of going crazy or losing control.

Only two behavioral scales related significantly to use of color: loss of reality contact and regressive behavior. This is in keeping with the subjective questionnaire results.

Changes in the use of color determinants in the Rorschach were examined on the notion that they should have specific relevance to the color-form test. A significant but unexpected relationship was found.

Subjects whose reliance on color increased in the Color-Form test were those whose use of color in the drug day Rorschach *decreased*. As we shall see when we analyze the Rorschach findings, this decrease was associated with an increased involvement with fantasy and inner life, which is in keeping with a reduced use of reality-attuned form in determining movement in the color-form test.

To discuss the implications of our results briefly, we typically identify objects by their shapes and are thus able to react appropriately to them. The perceptual constancy of form and general reliance on form are therefore more adaptive than comparable emphasis on color in creating a stable external world with which the perceiver can cope. The strong reliance on form in the usual perceptual organization of adults is thus inseparably tied up with a stable perception of reality and an active, rather than a passive, relation to it. In the Color-Form test, an increase in the use of color can occur only at the expense of giving up some measure of form constancy, which is normally more important for stable perception than color constancy.

Several strands of evidence in the present study support this interpretation. First, there is a strong relationship between pretest use of color and the placebo effect, which indicates that subjects who rely less on form are more passive and suggestible. The most striking evidence, however, is that of the correlates of high color usage in the LSD states. The greatest shift toward color (i.e., the greatest loss of form constancy) occurred in subjects whose drug experience emphasized loss of reality contact, regressive behavior, distortions of perception of the outside world and their own bodies, and increased involvement with their inner life.

While we have emphasized the importance of form constancy in coping adaptively with the demands of everyday life, this is not to say that it is entirely without a price, particularly if it is too rigidly maintained. In our experiment the subjects who "gave up" a measure of form constancy in favor of color were those who had a much richer LSD experience, while it was the most rigidly defended subjects, fearful of losing control, who maintained form constancy to the greatest extent.

The fact that the best questionnaire correlate of color usage was visual distortion is of special interest. On the simplest level both represent a loss of reality orientation in visual perception. In addition, the relationship suggests speculations about the mechanisms for the visual distortions and hallucinations that some people experience under LSD and, by extension, in psychotic states. Perhaps the perception of real objects can be so affected by inner needs as to constitute illusions or hallucinations only in people who do not maintain the perceptual constancy of visual forms. We also know that unstable perception is characteristic of certain psychotic states. Breakdowns in veridical perception provide a gap that may be filled by internally based "percepts." Furthermore, the increase in the role played by the colors of objects when form constancy breaks down, with the more emotional and drive-laden connotations of color, would also facilitate the emergence of internally based, psychodynamically determined material.

One final point: throughout this study form remained the preferred basis of perceptual organization. The one subject for whom, under the drug, this was not true was the one who experienced the strongest LSD effect, including marked loss of reality orientation. Thus while the LSD states did reduce the reliance on form, it was rare indeed that form failed to maintain at least some edge. This corresponds to our more general impression that our subjects usually maintained a considerable degree of reality orientation throughout the experimental day.

THE PROJECTIVE TESTS

The personality changes produced by the LSD states were explored through three projective techniques—the Earliest Memory, the Rorschach test, and the Human Figure Drawing Test—given before and during the drug experience. These tests are especially sensitive to changes in instinctual drives and ego structures, such as defenses, as well as to changes in the self-concept and the person's relationship to the environment.

Earliest Memories

The earliest memory a person is able to recall may be conceived of as reflecting both the residue of important past life experiences, current drives and conflicts, and his defensive operations and modes of adaptation. Recent studies have illuminated the relationships between earliest memories and total personality by demonstrating correlations with clinical diagnosis (Langs et al., 1960), clinical psychiatric assessment (Levy and Grigg, 1962), character structure (Langs, 1965b), and, predictively, with a variety of personality features (Langs, 1965a).

Very little systematic work has been done on the questions of the stability of earliest memories or their modification in altered states of consciousness, although some interesting leads have emerged from psychoanalytic case reports and discussions (Freud, 1899; Glover, 1929; Greenacre, 1969; Kris, 1956; Niederland, 1965; Reider, 1953; Saul et al., 1956). Nor has there been any experimental study of the effects of LSD on the recall of earliest memories, although in subjective reports many people who have taken the drug claim that they have recovered very early experiences, and our knowledge of the general effects of LSD on cognitive functions would lead us to expect "regressive" trends. In light of other data from our research, individual differences in such effects would be expected to be prominent. The present study specifically explored these issues.

Procedure and Results[25]

The basic data that we collected were subjects' responses to the request: "I want you to go back into your childhood as far back as you possibly can, and tell me your very first memory—the earliest thing you can remember in your life."

First memories were collected on both pretest and experimental days,

[25] See Appendix 4, Note 7, for the details of the procedure and results; see also Langs et al. (1960; Langs, 1967).

and each memory was scored for a wide range of specific categories. Although the many scoring categories provided interesting descriptive data, most were assigned to too few cases to yield significant results. Broader findings did emerge, however (see Table A4.15). It was found, first of all, that the drug and placebo groups did not differ appreciably in the proportions of subjects who produced new memories on the experimental day. Examination of the kinds of changes that were found, however, revealed that it was only in the drug group that the new memories reported were ones that the subject had never recalled before, were rambling or disconnected, or had content with regressive features.

As regards the expected individual differences, two dimensions of personality are associated with change in the earliest memory in both groups and, further, a major measure of the drug effect is related to change in memory for the LSD group (see Table A4.16 for details). The first dimension is the paranoid-proneness scoring of personality assessment items described at the beginning of this chapter. Six drug subjects and eight placebo subjects had scores indicative of substantial paranoidlike tendencies, and these subjects, with one exception, gave the same memory as that of the pretest day. This suggests that paranoid-prone subjects resorted to a defensive clinging to the memory reported previously, regardless of the state of consciousness.

The pretest diagnostic Rorschach summary provided the second dimension. In it a number of subjects were rated as "tending to regress to a passive childish position under stress." With one exception it was only such subjects from both groups who gave regressive memories, although not all subjects so described did so. Subjects who reported new, nonregressive memories, however, did not differ from those with stable first memories in this respect.

These two aspects of personality, which predispose both drug and placebo subjects to have stable or unstable earliest memories, are not in themselves sufficient to produce a regressive earliest memory, however. This was related primarily to LSD state factors. Within the LSD group those producing more regressive memories differed very significantly from nonchangers on questionnaire Scale C[26] which, it is remembered, represents body image changes, selected somatic effects, and a general slowing down of functioning under the drug.

When all three elements occurred together (Scale C drug effects, personalities with a tendency to regress, and an absence of paranoid feasures), 6 out of the 7 such subjects produced regressive earliest memories. In contrast, only 1 of the other 21 LSD subjects did so (he was not noted

[26] This difference is significant beyond the .001 level.

as tending to regress but was nonparanoid and showed a strong Scale C effect); this is an extremely significant finding. It is apparently the confluence of these three elements that contributes to the recall of regressive earliest recollections since, when each is considered alone, it also characterizes a certain number of subjects who do not produce such recalls.

The fact that the Scale C effects are most directly implicated in a shift to more regressive earliest memories under LSD is worthy of further consideration. It is the body image Scale C effects that differentiate the regressive changers most strongly, while the somatic and inhibitory effects do so to a lesser extent. These subjects also have much higher scores than other subjects on items related to changes in experienced identity. Thus the common characteristic of the a priori scales that are most strongly associated with regressive shifts in the earliest memory is that of an alteration in the experience of the *self,* which is apparently the matrix in which such memory alterations develop.

In fact, the one subject of this type who did not report a more regressive earliest memory under LSD reported another memory change that bore very much on his identity. Later in the day he felt that he was reliving, with great emotional intensity, a hitherto isolated adolescent experience that had been crucial in determining a neurotic (homosexual) course of personal development.

The role of paranoid trends in the personalities of some subjects with unchanged memories can now be clarified further. We suggest that repeating the same memory, whether under the drug or placebo, served a defensive function; this is supported by the fact that under LSD paranoid-prone subjects were likely to give a terse, constricted recall of the memory they had reported on the pretest day. The LSD state of the subjects with vulnerability to paranoid tendencies, whether their reaction was pervasive or minimal, was characterized by a special patterning of effects; alterations in the self were much less in evidence than alterations experienced outside of the self, such as visual distortions and changes in the meanings of events. Clinging to the same earliest memory, then, can be seen as part of the more general process typical of paranoid defenses which ward off any recognition or acceptance of changes within the self.

We can conclude, then, that the presence of paranoid tendencies is consonant with a rigid personality structure in which first memories are fixed and which blocks the kind of drug reaction that would have facilitated the emergence of new first memories.

In summary, this study of earliest memories under LSD has demonstrated that an altered-state reaction that abounds in changes of the experience of the self provided the setting in which the recall of first memories shifted to a regressively presented and often previously unrecalled experience.

Such a shift did not appear in the placebo group. Subjects with paranoid-prone personalities tended under both drug and placebo conditions to adhere defensively to the same first memory, whereas nonparanoid subjects often recalled a different memory, regressed or not. Subjects who, as judged from their pretest Rorschachs, were prone to regress under stress were the ones who tended to recall regressive new earliest memories in the LSD state. The results suggest that the first recollection is a relatively stable and personally characteristic structure within the ego. In persons with a particular type of loose ego organization, an altered state of consciousness abounding in changes in the self may modify this memory structure and permit the appearance of a repressed, more primitive recollection. This new recollection may also be more consonant with the prevailing modes of experiencing and level of functioning in the altered state.

Primary-Process Manifestations in the Rorschach Test[27]

The Rorschach test is the richest projective instrument we have for learning about personality. Through this test we can often explore in depth a person's inner life, including the extent and nature of his fantasies, the manner in which he handles his impulses and emotions, the adequacy and formal properties of his intellectual functioning, and his characteristic defenses and controls—whether adaptive or pathological and adequate or not.

Our interest in the Rorschach was twofold. First, it was used in the screening and assessment of our subjects. Second, it was readministered on the experimental day while our subjects were under the drug or the placebo, in order to evaluate the effect of the LSD states on manifestations of primary process or primitive modes of thought.[28] Two main dimensions were studied. The first is primary-process *content,* which refers to any response discernible as an instinctual drive derivative, either sexual or aggressive. The second is primary-process invasions of thought or perception, which are aberrations in thinking or perceiving reflected in the open use of the formal mechanisms of the primary processes (condensation, displacement, symbolism, and so on) and, more generally, in the appear-

[27] The authors are indebted to Dr. Anthony F. Philip who conceived and carried out the Rorschach study as his doctoral thesis (1960). Most of the findings presented here come from our reanalyses of his data. See Appendix 4, Note 8, for the details of the procedure.

[28] This was done by means of a special system for scoring primary-process manifestations developed by Holt (Holt, 1956, 1959, 1966, 1970; Holt and Havel, 1960; Holt et al., 1969). In this system each response made by the subject to one of the blots is scored for a number of different expressions of the operation of primary-process mechanisms (see text and Appendix 4, Note 8).

ance of idiosyncratic, bizarre, and grossly disturbed responses. For brevity, these are called the *formal features* of the primary process.

In addition, each primary-process response is studied for the subject's use of a variety of *controls and defenses* in dealing with the primary-process manifestation. Some of these are also evaluated in terms of how adequately or inadequately they are utilized, and some, by their very nature, represent pathological defenses.[29] There are two additional special indices, the *defense demand* of the response (DD), and its *defense effectiveness* (DE). Defense demand attempts to measure the shock value of, or tension created by, a given primary-process response and the amount of demand it poses for adequate defensive or controlling operations. Defense effectiveness measures the adequacy with which this demand for control and defense is met in terms of qualitative features of the response that contains primary-process expressions.

In addition to Holt's scoring, certain standard scores were used and are described below. We are concerned here primarily with the changes that the LSD states produced in the Rorschach test responses. The experimental day testing was done in the middle of the day when drug effects were typically at their height. In general we expected under LSD an increase in primary-process content and formal invasions, a greater defense demand and impaired defense effectiveness, along with the usual individual differences in such regressive trends.

Results—General Drug Effects

One of the most impressive findings is the high degree of correlation (or similarity of subjects' relative standing) between pretest and drug day scores, even where there is a substantial drug effect. For example, the total number of formal primary-process features of the most blatant sort (called *Level 1*) increased significantly under LSD; nevertheless, the correlation between the two days for this score was very high. This increase occurred only in high reactors, as measured by the subjective reports of the questionnaire. These high reactors had, however, more than twice as many such responses on the pretest day as did the low reactors; their increase was almost twofold under the drug. Low LSD reactors not only had fewer Level 1 formal features on pretest but did not increase in these responses under the drug, resembling the placebo subjects in this respect.

These trends hold true for many of the major Rorschach measures and they indicate that the LSD states did not produce their effects out of whole cloth, but brought out aspects of the personality that were already present,

[29] There are, in all, over 100 specific categories used to score content, formal invasions, controls, and defenses. They can also be combined into summary scores, such as the total number of primary-process responses.

although latent in most cases (this point is amply demonstrated in Chapter 5). It seems reasonable to expect that a projective instrument such as the Rorschach, with its ability to detect manifestations of the primary process not apparent in other encounters with the person, should be a sensitive and effective instrument for eliciting individual differences in response to the pressures toward regressed functioning created by LSD.

Major Summary Scores. The total number of responses given to the Rorschach test was not affected under LSD, but the total proportion of responses with primary-process manifestations did change in certain ways under the drug.

We studied first the two content scores that summarize libidinal and aggressive expressions. Level 1 consists of blatant, direct-drive material, such as seeing sexual organs or murder. Level 2 consists of more socialized expressions of instinctual drives, such as seeing a couple kissing or a military insignia. There was no net change in these scores under LSD. There were, however, some changes in the specific content categories within them, which are considered later.

As we have just seen, formal features of the primary process are likewise divided into two levels. Level 1, the more blatant level of disturbance, includes such features as fusions or fluid transformations of percepts, autistic logic and logical contradictions, verbal condensations, and loosening of memory. Level 2 includes such features as arbitrary or unlikely combinations, contradiction of realistic expectations (inappropriate activity), and verbal slips. It is in these formal properties of cognition that we find a strong and important drug effect, highly significant for Level 1, although only borderline for Level 2. All of the specific Level 1 categories scored showed an increase under the drug. The increase in total Level 2 formal features was less significant because, while some of these mechanisms were used more often under LSD, others were used less often (see below).

Turning next to defense demand, we find that the LSD states significantly increased this measure of the effort needed to maintain an adequate, well-defended Rorschach response. Further, the effectiveness of the controls and defenses used to deal with the pressures created by the primary-process material tended to be good under all conditions, as expected for a non-hospitalized group. Only one subject, while under LSD, actually had a negative mean defense effectiveness score (which, by definition, indicates a pathologically regressed state, such as psychosis). Nevertheless, overall, defense effectiveness deteriorated significantly under the drug.

One component of defense effectiveness, the weighted form level, which measures how well a subject's responses fit the actual configurations of the blots, is of special interest because (according to Mayman, 1960) it measures "reality adherence," the ability to attune cognition to reality. Rather surprisingly, a significant drug effect was not found for the LSD group as a whole (although the average form level of the drug group declined while that of the placebo subjects increased minimally). Form quality *was* affected by LSD, but individual differences were crucial. If drug subjects are again divided into high and low reactors, we find that there was a significant drop in form level for those with a strong or pervasive drug reaction. In contrast, weak reactors, like the placebo subjects, improved slightly. Taking three of the components of the form-level score separately, we find that subjects experiencing a strong LSD effect produced fewer superior forms and more vague ones, while weak reactors and placebo subjects did the reverse. A third component of the weighted form level, grossly poor forms (*F*—), also increased markedly in strong reactors.

Since many of the responses that subjects gave on the second or experimental day represented essentially the same images they had given on the pretest, the improvement in placebo subjects and weak LSD reactors probably represents mainly a clarification of what was previously seen. The deterioration associated with a strong drug effect, however, indicates that we must consider this impairment among the effects of the LSD states, keeping in mind that it appears largely among subjects with markedly altered states of consciousness.

The final general scores to be considered before proceeding to the specific primary-process scores are human movement response (*M*) and responsiveness to color (*Sum C*). They are of interest not only as separate dimensions but in their relationship to each other. The interpretation of *M* is quite complex; it is generally considered to be related to the degree of inner life experienced by a person. A large number of *M* responses therefore would indicate access to fantasy, imagination, and cues from within (which may be either adaptive or pathological), while few or none would suggest a constriction of inner fantasy life. The extent to which responses are determined by color, on the other hand, is an index of the person's responsiveness to stimuli from without, particularly to other people, and reflects both his capacity for relationships and his emotional responsiveness. While the quality of these relationships is reflected in various ways, perhaps the single most important feature is the relationship between color and form. Responses based on the form of the blot, with color used appropriately (*FC*), indicate that the responsiveness is modulated by rational considerations (adequately or poorly), while those in which color is the primary determinant, with the role of form minor (*CF*) or absent (*C*), reflect the absence of such controls. The balance between *M* and color is called the "experience type." If *M* is predominant, the person's orientation is internal; if color predominates, he is considered more externally oriented. If both *M* and color are abundant, both kinds of responsiveness are present; a paucity of both indicates a constriction of both inner life and the capacity to respond to the external environment.

The number of *M* changed under LSD for many subjects, but the change was not in any one direction. Responsiveness to color, however, decreased significantly so that under LSD more subjects produced protocols emphasizing *M,* without the balancing effect of color responsiveness. This inward shift is the Rorschach counterpart of the withdrawal from involvement with the surroundings seen in many of our subjects under LSD, a shift accompanied by considerable self-absorption.

The reduction in the use of color is not evenly distributed over the different kinds of color responses, however. *CF* and *C* responses were dropped more consistently than were *FC* and, within both categories, arbitrary or inappropriate color responses decreased significantly,[30] while appropriate color responses did not. This is surprising, since we might have expected LSD to lead to a less rational use of color. Instead, we found that color responses in which form plays a major role and in which the two elements are appropriately integrated were well maintained under LSD. Further, inappropriate and uncontrolled responsiveness to color stimulation decreased.

Overall, then, the awareness of stimulation from within represented by *M* was maintained under LSD and assumed more importance than on pretest through the reduced external responsivity indicated by the decrease in color responses; the balance within the color responses per se shifted to more appropriate control as subjects who could not combine form and color adaptively on pretest gave more appropriate combinations under the drug.

Specific Content Scores. The only clearly significant group effects in regard to primary-process content were in the Level 2 Aggression scores (Level 1 Aggression is rare under any conditions). The two major categories are aggressors (images of hostile or threatening persons, animals, or objects, like "a lion," "a sword," or "people fighting"), and results of aggression (images of destruction, death, or injury, like "a charred stump," "a headless woman," or "a peg leg"). The balance between these two measures shifted significantly for each group of subjects, but in opposite directions. The drug group saw more images of damaged creatures and objects and fewer images of aggressors under LSD, compared to pretest. It seems likely that this expresses the feelings of helplessness, impairment, and general passivity produced by the drug states. The placebo group, however, saw more aggressors and fewer results of aggression than previously. This,

[30] These are responses in which the color is either used inappropriately without adequate rationalization ("a green man"), or in an arbitrary or schematic manner (e.g., to delineate map areas).

Rorschach Correlates of Other Drug Effects

Two issues are of interest. The first is the prediction of drug effects through the pretest Rorschach, which is not examined in detail here (see Chapter 5). The second is our primary concern in this section: the relationships between the subjective effects of the LSD states and the changes in Rorschach test responses. The four empirical questionnaire scales provide the most comprehensive way of examining different aspects of the drug reaction, so we concentrate on a thorough analysis of the Rorschach change correlates of each scale.

Scale A. The subjective effects that typify this scale are loss of inhibitions, elation, and feelings of new insights. Subjects with strong Scale A effects showed, on the drug day Rorschach, a loosening or breakdown of their controls over the formal properties of cognition reflected in a greater defense demand in their percepts, poorer defense effectiveness in their handling of this tension (including poorer form level), and a higher percentage of Level 1 formal invasions. Except for some Level 1 formal features, none of these qualities was notably conspicuous in their pretest Rorschach records. They did, however, have more primary-process *content* in their pretest Rorschachs than other subjects, particularly in regard to Level 2 percepts, the more socially modulated ones. This kind of controlled openness to primary-process material in the waking state (as indicated by Level 2 content) is therefore associated with the expansive kind of drug effect represented by Scale A. Under the drug, however, these subjects relaxed their ego controls and felt less necessity to conform to logical reality. As a result, the formal properties of their responses were affected, while the amount of primary-process content was actually reduced, so that it was no longer greater than that of other subjects.

Among the specific formal features of their responses, verbal oddities were prominent: occasional incoherence, queer or peculiar verbalizations, and verbal condensations. Inappropriateness also appeared, both in activities inappropriate to the figures seen and in affective contradiction (i.e., emotional reactions inappropriate to the reported image).

A greater use of creativity is suggested by a marked increase in the use of both esthetic and humorous contexts for their responses, and more symbolic use of images. These subjects also shifted toward a more introversive experience balance, not so much through an increase in human movement as through a decrease in color responses, particularly *CF* (responses in which color is more important than form as a determinant). Such a shift suggests an increased involvement with imaginative processes at the expense of responsiveness to their surroundings.

The expansiveness of the Scale A subjective effects is, then, correlated in the Rorschach primarily with responses that reflect a loosening of normal ego controls, an introversive shift, and an outpouring of imaginative material often not in accord with the demands of reality. The use of humor, esthetic contexts, and symbolic imagery indicates that these distorted primary-process expressions were probably both pleasurable and highly acceptable to these subjects.

Scale B. This scale subjectively included loss of environmental contact and meaning, an impaired sense of identity, feelings of having lost control, and paranoid ideation. Some of the correlates of Scale B, particularly those from the overall summary scores, resemble those of Scale A but they assume a somewhat different meaning. Scale B, like Scale A, is associated with an increase in Level 1 formal features, an increased defense demand, and a drop in form quality. Peculiar verbalizations, incoherence, images of inappropriate activities, and affective contradictions are also associated with high Scale B scores. These therefore represent breakdowns in ego functioning which are in keeping with the psychoticlike effects of Scale B.

Scale B is not, however, associated with any of the imaginative effects that we found to be related to Scale A. It is associated instead with an increase in Level 1 content, images that express drives in a blatant, unmodulated form. There is also a significant increase in subjects' self-references in their responses, and a striking use of denial once a primary-process response has been given. This is the most primitive kind of attempt at defense and in fact is essentially a failure of defense.

The psychoticlike effects of Scale B are correlated in the drug day Rorschach, then, with a breakdown of ego controls and with a loss of distance shown both in the self-references incorporated in the subjects' responses and in the eruption of uncontrolled primary-process content, which subjects with high scores on Scale B attempt to handle with simple denial, if at all.

Scale C. There is only a chance number of significant relationships between Scale C (body image changes and somatic symptoms) and Rorschach test changes under LSD. Scale C effects, being largely noncognitive in nature, are apparently not manifested in a perceptual-associative test such as the Rorschach.

Scale D. Scale D effects, which include fear of losing control and associated somatic symptoms, are unrelated to the amount of formal or content primary-process manifestation, either on the pretest or under the drug, and they are also unrelated to the effectiveness of defenses under the drug. High Scale D scorers, however, gave pretest Rorschachs characterized by verbal slips and other verbal peculiarities of the kind suggesting disturbance, but not psychoticlike intrusions, and by poor defense effectiveness, including poor form level and the use of intellectualizing contexts of poor quality. They expressed at the same time criticism of the quality of their responses.

Thus we find that the subjects who most fear loss of control while under LSD are those who, when confronted with the unstructured task of the pretest Rorschach, showed signs of tension, tried rather unsuccessfully to deal with its disturbing elements by intellectualization, and were aware of, and critical of, the inadequacy of these attempts.

Under LSD their intellectualizing attempts and verbal difficulties dropped to an average level, but two new features appeared. They showed a marked increase in images depicting the results of aggression, such as damaged objects or injured creatures. This apparently reflects their great fear of damage to themselves, although it may also be related to the intense somatic symptoms they reported in that state. They also showed a marked increase in the use of color (both *FC* and *CF*), suggesting a "flight into reality," possibly as a way of avoiding an influx of threatening fantasies.

We find, then, that subjects whose drug reaction is characterized by a fear of losing control are those who are made anxious by the pretest Rorschach and try to put its disturbing elements at a distance with largely unsuccessful attempts at intellectualization. Under LSD their Rorschachs include many images of damage and suggest a flight away from fantasy into external reality.

Conclusions

Our findings amply confirm the expectation that the Rorschach test and, in particular, its analysis in terms of primary-process manifestations and their vicissitudes, would provide a sensitive instrument for demonstrating some of the important effects of the states of consciousness produced by LSD. First, we found, although we have not presented the evidence in full detail, that the predrug Rorschach predicted important aspects of the drug reaction. This was best shown by the high correlations between the predrug and drug scores for many of the measures, and by the pretest correlates of some of the empirical scales. Second, as for the general effects of LSD states on Rorschach test responses, the major finding is that these states affected the formal properties or mode and manner of thinking and perception, rather than creating an increase in instinctual drive content. In general, the adequacy of intellectual controls was impaired under LSD, and there was an increased fluidity of the percepts, along with more inappropriateness, arbitrariness, and vagueness. Denial became a prominent defense, while more sophisticated and conventional controls were used less often. There was also a drop in reported responsiveness to color in the inkblots. The main change in content that was found—more percepts of the results of aggression—apparently reflects the helplessness and passivity of the drug experience. Put another way, the altered states involved notable changes in ego functions and little change in id expressions.

Finally, the relationships between drug state effects on the Rorschach and the empirical scales of subjective LSD effects demonstrated the sensitivity of the Rorschach test responses to the different forms the drug states may take. Specifically, Rorschach responses reflected the loosening, expansiveness, and imaginativeness of Scale A; the primitivization of Scale B; and the fear of the emergence of instinctual drive derivatives and fantasy of Scale D.

Drawings of the Human Figure[31]

Our chief interest in the human figure drawing was in its presumed ability to reflect the nature and adequacy of a subject's self-concept and body image. These drawings may also reflect a person's idealized self-image; his concept of others; manifestations of drives such as hostility, sexuality, and dependence; and something of the nature of his controls over these drives. They are also influenced by pictorial skills and cultural factors.

While there are gifted clinicians whose ability to interpret human figure drawings is impressive, there is no standard, well-validated scoring system. In this study we used the set of variables developed by Karen Machover for the investigation of psychological differentiation (Witkin et al., 1954) and examined other aspects of the drawings as well. Our interest here is in the changes that occurred under LSD and their correlates in our subjects' drug experience and behavior. Our expectation was that under LSD there would be an individually determined regressive shift toward primitivization of these drawings.

The subject was given a sheet of paper and a pencil and asked to draw a whole person. After the first figure, usually a male, was drawn, a figure of the opposite sex was requested. The subject was then asked to tell something about each figure, including the age and the kind of person it represented.

Drawings were scored for the presence or absence of a number of specific indicators, as well as for four scaled variables: sophistication of body concept, activity-passivity of posture, sexualization, and size of figure.

Results—General Drug Effects

First, one of our staff members assessed whether each set was drawn by a drug or placebo subject and, then, the order in which the drawings were made. He correctly identified 17 of the 20 drug subjects ($p = .001$), but only 9 of the 16 placebo subjects (at chance). As for order, the pretest

[31] See Appendix 4, Note 9, for the details of the procedure. We wish to thank Dr. Norman Reiss who assisted in the scoring and preliminary analyses.

and drug day pairs of drawings were correctly identified for all 20 drug subjects; rather surprisingly, the order was also identified correctly for 13 of the placebo subjects (.01 level). These findings show that drawings made under LSD were obvious in most cases. The placebo situation, however, also led to changes in the drawings which, although less blatant, were often identifiable (primarily through less detail and altered line quality); in some cases they were mistaken for drug effects.

Sophistication of Body Concept. The overall score for the level of sophistication of the body concept dropped markedly for the figures of both sexes in the LSD states; there was no change in the placebo group. A number of the specific indicators of this dimension also changed significantly under LSD.

In the male drawings closure difficulties (breaks in the outline), missing or distorted feet, and undifferentiated waistlines increased, while there was a drop in overall organization, amount of detail, and conventional attire (nudes and costumes were drawn more often under the drug). A significant number also described the male figure as older than the pretest male. Of the elements showing no consistent change, the most important are facial expression and secondary sexual characteristics. These changes in the same-sex figure[32] seem to indicate a sense of insecurity, loss of ego boundaries, feelings of passivity, and impaired impulse controls in the drug states.

Significant changes in the female figures included sketchier outlines, missing hands and weaker arms, mouth disturbances, missing or distorted feet, heavy waistline emphasis, less organization, and less detail. These changes, while also indicating passivity and insecurity, seem in addition to reflect a fear of women and hostility toward them that were revealed in some subjects under LSD.

Size of Figures. The average size of the male figures did not change significantly under LSD. The average female figure, however, became larger, but this increase occurred only for those who drew notably hostile-looking female figures under the drug; in all cases their female figures became larger than the male under LSD. As we shall describe below, the shift to an overpowering and frightening female figure was not primarily related to the drug reaction per se but rather reflected long-standing conflicts that became manifest under LSD.[33]

[32] The same-sex figure is considered to be the most direct expression of feelings about the self and, as we shall see below, it reflects the ongoing drug state more directly than does the female figure.

[33] Since the subjects include many overt homosexuals, we investigated whether it was they who produced this effect. Surprisingly, all of the subjects showing this effect were heterosexual. The male drawings of the homosexuals became both much larger than the females and more highly sexualized under LSD.

Sexualization.[34] While, as expected, the average female drawing was more sexualized than the male for both groups under all conditions, the drug group's male drawings tended to become somewhat less sexualized under LSD, while their female drawings became significantly more sexualized. Under placebo conditions no such shift appeared.

Representation of the genital area, however, was affected somewhat differently under LSD. We studied Machover's "indications of disturbance in the sex area," as shown, for example, by erasures, transparencies, or excessive shading (Witkin et al., 1954). Under the drug this dropped out entirely in the female drawings and tended to drop out in the male drawings. This finding, however, results primarily from the marked avoidance of *any* portrayal of the genital area in subjects under LSD, either by means of an enveloping gown or through the posture of the figure. In the drug group virtually every pretest male drawing had some indication of the genital area, usually appropriately drawn. Under LSD half of the male drawings lacked any such indication. Their pretest female drawings, however, generally either lacked indications of the genital area or showed disturbed features; under LSD almost every female drawing lacked genital portrayal. The majority of subjects under LSD showed a shift away from any representation of the genital area, while no such change occurred in the placebo group.[35]

Other sexual areas, such as breasts and buttocks, did not change in any consistent way under the drug. Emphasis on the mouth, however, increased significantly in the female drawings under LSD, while becoming less prominent in the male drawings.

Thus we find that while the female drawings generally became more sexualized under LSD there was a marked avoidance of the genital area in the drawings of both sexes in the drug states. We have already seen, through the sophistication of body concept scale and certain specific indicators, that the drug states produced a regression to a less mature concept of the body. The retreat from genital representation shows that, while the identification of the sexes through secondary sexual characteristics was not impaired in some ways, psychosexual regression did occur in other forms.

Activity-Passivity. Activity level, as measured directly in the ratings of

[34] Sexualization was scored on a 5-point scale ranging from 1 (primitive or no sexual features), through 3 (adequate but not emphasized), to 5 (extreme sexual emphasis). Except for a few drawings given high scores, the sexual features present were secondary sexual characteristics.

[35] Avoidance of the genital area was not necessarily related to the sexualization scale, which was scored primarily on the basis of secondary sexual characteristics. As an example, two overt homosexuals drew male nudes under LSD, but both were rear views.

posture on the 5-point activity-passivity scale, did not change significantly in either figure.

Figure Drawing Correlates of Drug Effects[36]

Because figure drawings have such a manifest focus on the body, we compared changes in these drawings with somatic and body image drug effects in some detail. While such relationships were found, they were not the most impressive correlates of the figure drawing changes. We did find, for example, that subjects who drew figures with missing or misshapen hands were more likely to report that their hands were numb, and that those whose male figures had missing or distorted legs were more likely to report numbness in the torso or stomach cramps. Such isolated findings, however, reflected broader changes in self-concept, rather than essentially bodily changes. In another vein, while impairment in the sophistication level of the male figure was strongly related to alterations in the self, it was primarily related to psychoticlike thought disorder (Scale B) and was unrelated to bodily effects. Similarly, while an increase in the size of the male figure was associated with the report of feeling lighter or as if floating, it was unrelated to other bodily effects; rather, these somatic effects were part of a more general manic, expansive reaction.

As with the Rorschach, we can best understand the maze of specific relationships by looking at the figure drawing correlates of the major LSD state measures, particularly each of the empirical scales.

Scale A. The most important correlates of the Scale A drug effects (loss of inhibitions, elation, and feelings of new insights) are an increase in the size of the male figure and missing hands on either figure. The size increase was related to the maniclike effects in Scale A and, behaviorally, to silliness. In contrast, behaviorally manifest anxiety was related to a reduction in the size of the male figure.

Since hands were more likely to be missing in the drawings of those with strong Scale A effects, it seems likely that their omission implies loss of contact in a maniclike, elated sense (absence of hands was most closely associated with the a priori scale of elation).[37]

Scale A was also associated with drawing nudes under LSD and with transparencies in the female figure. It was significantly associated with more sexualized female drawings under both pretest and drug conditions, although

[36] The figures drawn by three subjects are reproduced in Chapter 5. Each set shows the effects of a different kind of altered state.

[37] It can apparently also represent the loss of contact associated with more profound ego impairment, since missing hands in the male figure only (which is the more direct representation of self-attitudes) were also related to the psychoticlike effects of Scale B and particularly to the a priori scale of loss of contact.

not with an increase in this under LSD. Thus it appears that a strong Scale A effect is more likely to occur in subjects who are usually open to sexual feelings, an openness that is accentuated under LSD.

Scale B. Scale B, which represents the most profound and psychoticlike alterations in the subject's state, was associated with the most striking changes in the Human Figure Drawings, virtually all of them in the male figure. Subjects with a strong Scale B effect drew male figures under LSD that were more primitive (i.e., lower body sophistication scores), older (both in appearance and as stated by the subjects), sometimes without hands, and less likely to include any representation of the genital area. The increase in the age of the males drawn by these subjects does not mean that their drawings conveyed a sense of greater maturity, but rather depletion and loss of virility.

Of the a priori scales, loss of reality contact was related consistently to these drawing changes, as were ego change or alienation and visual distortions; also related were the behavioral measures of regression and visual distortions. The questionnaire report of being suspicious was specifically and strongly associated with drawing older or more primitive figures.

The striking ego breakdown represented in Scale B, then, was reflected in the drawings of the male figure, which became regressed under LSD, both in the overall level of sophistication of the body concept and in the level of psychosexual maturity.

Scales C and D. Scales C and D, which include the somatic and body image effects of LSD, had very few correlates in the figure drawings. The only drawing change significantly related to Scale C was a lack of normal attire (nudes or costumed persons) in either figure. The a priori scales show that this relationship stems entirely from the body image effects in Scale C and not from the somatic symptoms.

The Scale D correlates are primarily reflections of the fear of losing control rather than direct reflections of somatic symptoms associated with this fear. Under LSD, subjects showing a strong Scale D effect did not represent the genital area in their female drawings and used less shading in their male figures than they had on the pretest. Since shading is sometimes considered an expression of sensuality, we may conclude that the fear of losing control under LSD is associated with an avoidance of sensual feelings. This interpretation is in keeping with the Rorschach correlates of this scale.

Figure Drawing Correlates of Personality Dimensions

The entire set of personality assessment variables was examined in connection with only one figure drawing effect, the emergence under LSD of a hostile, overpowering female figure. This occurred in the drawings of subjects whose pretest assessments revealed paranoid tendencies and much conflict over aggression. This suggests the possibility that the drug day female figure served as the vehicle for the emergence of long-standing unconscious conflicts and defenses.

The drawing change correlates of the Ego Adequacy personality assessment scale were examined. Subjects with inadequate egos were more likely, under LSD, to avoid representing the genital area in their female drawings and to have less shading than on the pretest in their male figures. More competent and autonomous subjects were more likely, under the drug, to draw male figures with missing hands but more shading and to represent the genital area in their female figures. This suggests that the relatively adequate subjects were more likely to give themselves up to the drug experience, particularly its sensual aspects, while poorly integrated subjects were particularly threatened by their sexual stirrings under LSD.

Summary

Under LSD the most prominent shifts in the human figure drawings included a primitivization of the body concept and changes in sexual qualities, particularly an absence of specific representation of the genital area. The alterations under the drug of male and female figures had different implications. Drug changes in the male figure reflected the ongoing LSD state most directly, particularly the profound mood changes and impairments in ego functioning. As for changes in the female drawing, the acceptance of sensual feelings (as in the Scale A effects) or the fear and avoidance of them (as in the Scale D effects) were reflected rather directly in the sexual aspects of the female figure. Furthermore, hostility and paranoid tendencies, suppressed in the normal state, appeared openly in the drug day drawings of some subjects. These were projected onto their drawings of the female, who appeared hostile and overpowering, while their male drawings were more likely to reflect their fear of these feelings.

Finally, although LSD producd a wide variety of somatic symptoms and body image changes in our subjects, the figure drawings did not, by and large, reflect these specific bodily alterations. They reflected, rather, more basic changes in the self and in the concept of the self, such as disturbances in the sense of identity, breakdowns in ego functioning, loss of contact with reality and with the environment, and the vicissitudes of certain drives.

CHAPTER 5

LSD States and Personality

We have described, in a broad and general way, the altered organismic states that we call "the LSD effects," and distinguished them from the normal state. One of our clearest findings, however, is that there is no single altered state, but considerable individual variation. That different people react very differently to the drug is most evident in the sizeable variance and range in the scores obtained on most of the questionnaire and behavioral scales.

The next question must then be: Do the individual variations in the altered states of consciousness form coherent and meaningful patterns? To observe that a given subject experiences a particular drug effect is an isolated fact of some interest. If, however, we consider the total pattern of effects he experienced, we can then define in an integrated way the specific state of consciousness he experienced under LSD. It is conceivable that many variations would occur, with no two subjects alike, but it is more likely that certain patterns would characterize groups of subjects, while other clusters of reactions might not be found at all in this sample. Each of the patterns that emerges can be viewed as representing a particular kind of organismic state induced by LSD.

We shall demonstrate that we do in fact find recurrent patterns of reactions to LSD within this sample of drug subjects. Once this has been established, we turn to the question whether each specific altered state occurs in a particular kind of person. We then demonstrate that this is the case; that is, that the different states induced by the drug are, indeed, personality-linked and can be understood in terms of the subject's personality.

The Identification of Drug Reaction Patterns

Each subject's reactions were defined by eight scores, four from the questionnaire on subjective reactions and four from the observations of behavior. The four empirical scales (see Chapter 3) were used as the measures of questionnaire response. The four measures of behavior were obtained by combining scores with high intercorrelations (see Table A3.3).[1] Person clusters were then obtained by grouping subjects so that those in the same cluster had similar patterns of scores, while those in different clusters (or groups) were dissimilar.[2] Seven groups of subjects were identified in this way, each with a specific altered state; they included 26 of the 30 drug subjects.[3] There resulted one group of 7 subjects, three groups of 4 subjects each, one of 3 subjects, and two groups with only 2 subjects each. The reaction patterns found in each group are summarized in Table 5.1.

Consistency between Drug Reaction and Personality Attributes

The 93 Personality Assessment measures (see Appendix 2, Note 3) were used to determine whether the different groups of subjects, created in terms of different altered states, also differed from each other consistently in personality dimensions. Using both the 93 separate items and a set of 14 personality factors derived from them by combining highly intercorrelated items, we found that the drug reaction pattern groups are indeed internally consistent in their personality attributes; as compared to chance expectancies, each group has a significant number of personality items that characterize it and also distinguish it from the other drug groups (see Appendix 5).

We may therefore now consider in some detail six of the seven reaction types we have established,[4] secure in having demonstrated that they are internally consistent in both their altered-state reactions and predrug personalities. First, the predrug personalities typical of each group are described, using primarily the Personality Assessment items that characterize

[1] The first measure combines Regression, Visual Distortion, Inappropriate Affect, and Silliness; the second combines Depression-Elation, Motility, and Withdrawal-gregariousness; the third combines Anxiety and Bodily Preoccupation; and the fourth combines Hostility and Suspiciousness.

[2] A modification of the D^2 technique was used. The D^2 method measures the distance between any pair of subjects in the eight-dimensional space represented by the eight scores. The modification (Gardner et al., 1959, pp. 164–167) takes into account not only the absolute distance between any two subjects, but the direction of their deviations from sample means as well (i.e., the closeness of their vectors).

[3] Three subjects had patterns that could not be placed unequivocally, and the data for a fourth were considered inadequate for this purpose.

[4] Since groups of two cannot establish a pattern with any certainty, only Group III is included in the detailed study because the two subjects in that group resemble each other to a striking degree in many aspects of their altered-state experience not included in the criteria for clustering. They also exemplify an altered state that readily lends itself to interpretation. Such was not the case for Group VII and therefore presentation of this group is omitted.

Table 5.1. Seven Types of Reactions to LSD[a]

	Person Clusters						
	I	II	III	IV	V	VI	VII
Questionnaire							
A. Elation, expansiveness, disinhibition	*High*	*High*	Average	Average	Low	Low	Average
B. Contact loss, ego change, suspiciousness, loss of meanings	Low	*High*	High	(High)	Low	Low	Low
C. Body image change, inhibited, slowed, some somatic change	(High)	(High)	(High)	High	*High*	Low	*Low*
D. Anxiety, fear of losing control, some somatic effects	Low	Low	High	*High*	*High*	Low	*Low*
Behavior							
E. Regression, silliness, inappropriate affect, confused thought, contact loss, visual distortion	Average	High	*High*	Average	Low	Low	(High)
F. Elation-depression, motility, withdrawal	Average	Elated	Elated	Depressed	Average	Depressed	Elated
G. Anxiety, bodily preoccupation	Average	Average	*High*	High	Average	Low	Low
H. Hostility-negativism, suspiciousness	Average	(Low)	High	High	Low	Low	Average
Total questionnaire	High	High	High	High	Varies	Low	Low
Total behavioral effect	Average	High	*High*	High	Low	Low	(High)
Number of subjects	4	4	2	3	4	7	2

[a] Italicized entries indicate extreme effects, while those in parentheses are minimal effects.

them, and drawing additional data from the results of specific psychological tests wherever they are illuminating. After presenting the personality findings, we will describe the altered state of consciousness that characterizes each group using not only the 8 broad criterion measures but also the 16 more specific a priori questionnaire scales, the 11 behavioral measures, and the group's performance on the experimental tasks. After an attempt to integrate the personality and drug reaction sets of data, a typical subject from each group is described.

GROUP I

With respect to their usual personality attributes, the subjects in Group I are very open in expressing their emotions and revealing their thoughts. They have high self-esteem; they are rather narcissistic and exhibitionistic; and they tend to be cheerful rather than depressed. They do not defend themselves against feelings but rather accept their own impulses and express them openly. They are emotionally impulsive and spontaneous, and have a genuine interest in other people.

They are also intellectual, sensitive, introspective, interested in knowledge and understanding, and have strong creative strivings. Their thinking is clear and not inhibited; they use words in a colorful manner, and give the impression of having vivid imagery. They are not orderly, very punctual or well-organized in their use of time, and dislike having to wait. They report a high capacity for involvement in their work, and are notably independent of parental figures.

The clinical analysis of their Rorschach records confirms their narcissism and also indicates a strong reliance on isolation as a defense. Their pretest Rorschachs appear schizoid in that they have many primary-process manifestations in both form and content, but they successfully control such material through humor and intellectual contexts, or by identifying the percept as a fictional or fantasy character. These subjects are also particularly likely to reflect on their own responses, either introspectively or critically. Thus their Rorschachs may be described as adaptively regressive, showing a readiness to use primitive modes of thought creatively.

Their conscious values are in keeping with this picture of controlled openness. In their Paths of Life preferences, they emphasize self-knowledge, going it alone, and sensuous and self-centered enjoyment of what life has to offer, with a minimum of entanglement or active striving. They reject group belongingness and working together for common goals as an ideal. Their clear and adaptive thinking is confirmed by the Color-Word test, in which they show notably little interference, indicating a flexible style of cognitive control.

The altered state experienced by these subjects under LSD was characterized by many subjective changes which were primarily expansive in nature; their overt behavior, however, was much less affected. Subjectively, they were elated, lost their sense of time, and reported various disturbances in thinking, body image changes, and some visual distortions. More striking were the frequent reports of the emergence of new meanings in experiences and of improved functioning. While they reported some inhibitory effects (especially in thinking), disinhibitory effects were greater. Yet they did not fear losing control, and in fact they did not really do so on any level.

The content of their ideation under LSD emphasized the feeling of having acquired new insights into themselves and the world: "I feel more mature"; "I understand more about myself"; "I realize that a childhood experience had more bearing on my life than I realized"; "Overall glittering generalities, . . . life, beauty, beauty and life, and there is nothing else"; "I felt omnipotent at times, as if I understood truths I'd never be able to communicate to anybody"; "I keep seeing people in terms of their essence"; "A face becomes a concept of a face." The feeling of new powers extended into the physical realm: "I felt tremendously strong, as if I could lift enormous weights." This is the only group of subjects in this study whose subjective experience as reported bore any resemblance to the expansive, psychedelic LSD effects so widely discussed among lay persons.

Their behavior, as observed by the experimenters, was affected somewhat less than the average; most notable was the absence of marked regressive behavior. The most consistent behavioral effect was reduced motility and a tendency to be somewhat withdrawn, perhaps because of their intense ideational activity. This occurred in three of the four subjects in this group; in two of them it was associated with anger (particularly when the tasks interrupted fantasy), and in the third it was accompanied by depressive feelings linked to the recall under LSD of a previously forgotten adolescent experience he viewed as crucial in his life.

As for the experimental tasks, performance on the cognitive test battery was unimpaired on the four subtests that were affected by LSD in most subjects. In the Color-Word test, interference with color naming by the words was unaffected (they showed the normal test-retest effect of marked improvement) and, unlike most drug subjects, they did not become more variable in their reading times. On the Theme Lists their learning ability was superior to the others on the pretest, and under LSD it remained excellent on both drive and neutral lists; they also showed excellent recall of the pretest lists under the drug. Thus we find that their cognitive ego functioning, in terms of their ability to assume a stable task orientation and their capacity for mobilizing and maintaining focused attention when required, was extremely well maintained in their particular altered state.

As we would expect from the expansive nature of their drug reaction, their reliance on color, rather than form (a regressive trend), in the Color-Form test increased substantially. As for their Earliest Memories, Group I showed no clear trend; two reported the same memory given on the pretest day, one reported a more regressive memory, and the fourth was the subject just mentioned who reported the same first memory but later recalled an adolescent experience he felt had been crucial in shaping the subsequent course of his life.

Only two of these subjects were asked to draw human figures under LSD. Their male figures had no striking common features except for missing hands and failure to indicate the genital area (one was highly sexualized, the other completely desexualized). Their female drawings were both highly sexualized nudes (the only two nudes drawn in this study in which the genital area *was* represented), with missing hands.[5] The emergence of heterosexual drive material in these subjects (one of whom was a homosexual) is quite unusual in this study and may be related to their expansive feelings. The missing hands on both the male and female figures may indicate a withdrawal of interest in the environment.

In the Rorschach test their primary-process content actually decreased under the drug; it had been unusually prominent in their pretest Rorschachs, although in a well-modulated form (i.e., Level 2). The decrease was most striking with respect to the results of aggression, such as blood or damaged creatures, which generally increased in other subjects under LSD. In contrast to their reduced primary-process content, there was an increase in the formal manifestations of primary-process cognition, but only in certain respects. The outstanding features of their drug state changes in this regard were an increase in fantasy, loosening of reality ties, and a marked diminution in the use of color.

Under the drug these subjects lost distance from primary-process content to some extent, not by expressing it crudely, however, but by increased expression of it through humor, fantasy, and both fictional and esthetic justification. It is striking that the quality of their fantasy and esthetically expressed responses actually improved under the drug, in spite of an overall drop in the form quality of their responses as measured by the weighted average form level. The drop in overall form quality was the result of fewer superior (complex and integrated) images and more vague forms but not of any real breakdown in form perception (that is, *F*— did not increase notably). There was also an increase in their symbolic use of color and imagery, mostly idiosyncratic in nature but with rather appropriate and original symbolic meanings.

[5] The drawings made by one of these subjects, Arthur, are reproduced in this chapter.

The formal manifestations of increased primary-process functioning, in addition to idiosyncratic imagery, included autistic logic and arbitrary linkages, but not affective contradictions, self-references, or denial of responses, which were seen in subjects showing marked ego breakdown under LSD. Introspection and criticism of their responses actually increased (for most subjects they decreased), both tendencies reflecting their continued capacity to achieve some distance from their responses and to reflect on them.

They displayed an introversive shift in experience balance resulting not so much from their increase in human movement responses (*M*), which was slight, but more from a reduced use of color as a determinant, indicating less involvement with the external environment.

Thus both the formal and content changes in their Rorschachs under the drug represent a loosening of adherence to reality and purely intellectual controls, an outpouring of fantasy, and more idiosyncratic forms of expression. Nevertheless, their continued capacity for self-observation and the absence of a true breakdown of form perception (i.e., *F—*) support the evidence from the cognitive tests that their capacity for secondary-process thinking was not really impaired by their LSD state.

Both their Rorschach protocols and their drawings of the female figure reflect an expansion of instinctual drive expressions and emotion; they were more fantastic and free, in an enjoyable, comfortable, and potentially creative way, emphasizing libidinal rather than aggressive drives.

In summary, then, of the five groups with a substantial reaction to LSD, this is the group whose altered state was most like an extension and disinhibition of their usual mode of experiencing.[6] It is not surprising, then, that theirs was the most enjoyable and least threatening LSD experience. These subjects are usually quite open to fantasy and readily accept their impulses and their inner life, valuing them highly and taking a lively interest in them. They are literally "self-centered" in a rather engaging, unhostile, unthreatened, and not unpleasant way. Thus under LSD they made ready use of their drives and fantasies, which became more available through the altered state, in which their openness is exaggerated but handled well. They also experienced an enhancement of their "understanding" (whether valid or not) of themselves, others, and the world. The slowed motility and moderate social withdrawal therefore seem to be the behavioral expressions of their preference for immersing themselves in the drug experience without resistance.

The well-maintained overt behavior and cognitive performance of these

[6] This could also be said of Group VI, but only in the sense that their drug reaction was so minimal that it was the closest to a waking state.

subjects indicate that their usual defense of isolation continued to serve them well. On the drug day their ability to shift comfortably from rich inner fantasies to experimental tasks and then back again (with some complaints but minimal strain) was remarkable in comparison with other subjects. An important factor in this was their lack of anxiety in response to the influx of instinctual drives and fantastic ideation. This suggests that the anxiety that such material produced in other subjects was at least partly responsible for the deterioration in their cognitive functioning. Distracting inner fantasies do not, per se, impair cognitive performance when subjects are well defended.

The subjects in Group I, although they experienced an altered state of consciousness, are apparently people to whom this state is quite congenial and who can adapt to it readily. They may have comparatively ready daily access to the kind of material that unfolded in the drug state and to somewhat altered states themselves, without recourse to a drug. If this is true, it may be that they are in a sense experienced in handling such states (or muted versions of them) without any lasting or uncontrollable disruptions of their ego functioning. Further, their existing defenses against such cognitive disruptions continued to operate adequately under LSD and enabled them to maintain their equilibrium in the altered state.

We can see from this group that the totality of the altered-state experience is based on a balance between instinctual drives and fantasies derived from them on the one hand, and defenses and coping abilities on the other. Regressive experiences may be well tolerated if a subject has an ego that can deal with them. Let us now turn to one of the subjects in this group for a closer look.

Each case study was carried out by the same two researchers working entirely independently of each other and without knowledge of the subject's LSD experience. One used the verbatim assessment interviews and the subject's own autobiography, while the other made an intensive study of his pretest, waking-state Rorschach test responses.[7] In describing each of our representative subjects, we include the summary prepared independently by each experimenter, trusting that they complement each other and form a blend which yields a relatively complete picture of the subject from many vantage points.

The Case of Arthur

Arthur's interviews and autobiography provided the following picture of this subject. Arthur is a gifted young man with many pervasive anxieties

[7] The authors wish to express their gratitude to Dr. I. H. Paul, who analyzed the Rorschach material for the six subjects.

and a wide range of capacities with which he attempts to maintain his precarious equilibrium. He was among the younger of several children in a family in which the father was a strong, community-minded person who held many responsible civic positions. Although they moved often, his parents created strong family ties with many family meetings and discussions.

Arthur describes the home of his childhood as a kind of castle where he played "Jack and the Beanstalk," with himself as Jack and his father as the giant. He also took great pleasure in playing "Superman" and in reading and playing imaginative games with his mother. Yet, despite this involvement, Arthur felt chronically alone and afraid, and seemed to be struggling against an intense sense of depression. For example, he recalls, at the early age of 3 or 4 years, being frightened and alone with his dog while his family was at a neighbor's house where a violent death had occurred. He mastered much of this anxiety, which also included a dread of monsters, through his own vivid imagination and playacting. As a child, he developed a serious interest in magic and by adolescence was unusually adept at it.

Arthur openly hated his older siblings because of their teasing, critical, and bossy attitudes. As a preschool child, he reacted to the birth of a younger brother initially with indifference and depreciation, but then with acceptance; these feelings are attributed by him, however, to his dog. In what became a repetitive pattern, feeling the loss of his mother at this time, he turned immediately to a substitute in a maid and drew close to her through sharing his stories and tales with her.

In grade school he was very bright but also very provocative, enraging older students to the point where they once tried to smother him. Poor controls over his own aggression, and self-destructive provocations of this type, occurred often throughout Arthur's life. He engaged in sexual explorations with boys in grade school but stopped because of intense guilt. He played hooky often, feeling bored and disillusioned with his teachers.

In high school he was active socially and in the student organization and yet spent much time alone, reading and writing. He masturbated excessively and felt very guilty. He consciously felt that he was competing with his father for his mother and withdrew. His mother, at this time, was seen as warm and interested, and his father as a hard worker.

Once into adolescence, however, Arthur became disillusioned with both parents and took to raging against them openly but hating himself for these outbursts. Petting now caused guilt and anxiety which disrupted his school work, but despite this he graduated from high school and received a scholarship for college.

While Arthur was in high school, his father was killed in an accident. Arthur was full of guilt, feeling that he could have saved him, and upset that he had quarreled violently with his father before the accident happened. Despair followed, as did replacement via an intense relationship with a religious adviser.

In college Arthur had several tempestuous affairs. He set himself up as the girls' lover and healer, but often felt that they were trying to destroy him. He felt guilty and disillusioned when these affairs took a traumatic turn and left school to return to his mother and younger brother in an attempt to expiate his guilt. He has now married, however.

He was the protege of the dramatics teacher at his college and worked under him in summer stock, but found the pace taxing, having always resented responsibility. He has not completed college and is currently on a leave of absence to work in the theater; he has had some success in this endeavor.

In summary, Arthur's life history shows him as a young man with many facets. His anxieties, guilts, and depressions are multiple and very much on the surface. He has poor controls of both sexual and aggressive impulses. His conflicts are also multifaceted and openly expressed: ambivalence, with love and near-conscious death wishes, toward both his father and his mother, psychopathic acting out followed by much guilt, and open oedipal fantasies with guilt, to name but a few. He aggrandizes adult figures only to depreciate them and narcissistically attribute to himself the sense of omnipotence and magical power he initially projected onto them. When he acts on this grandiose basis, he ultimately finds himself in a crisis and retreats passively, seeking care from others. However, if on the verge of success, he often undoes the situation and flees. A paranoidlike sense of persecution is present as well. He often turns aggression against himself as readily as he expresses it toward others.

Yet, in the face of this pathology, Arthur can function creatively and effectively, although not without pain and disruption. In all, he seems to have considerable pathology but many resources with which to struggle against his inner turmoil.

The separate and independent assessment of Arthur's personality structure as reflected in his Rorschach test responses led to the following description of him. Arthur is an intense person, given to strong feelings and to wide mood swings. Although they are quite deeply felt, his affects tend to be amplified or attenuated in the service of his histrionic fantasy life which is rich, complex, and sometimes even exciting. While he is quite creative and can probably use his imagination adaptively, his productions nevertheless tend to be overly flamboyant and merely showy.

There is sometimes a current of stark melodrama in his fantasies, and he has a penchant for grappling with the apocalyptic and the extremes of life and death. At times his productions can become so idiosyncratic and far-fetched as to appear rather autistic. In part these fantasies reflect an underlying phobic streak in him, and in part they reflect an important streak of grandiosity; both tendencies are quite childlike in quality.

The test suggests that Arthur's grandiosity is largely a reaction to underlying feelings of weakness and vulnerability in the face of the all-powerful male (father figure). He seems to feel vulnerable to stimuli in general, and this may take the form of his feeling that he is the passive victim of mysterious, awesome, and inexorable forces (e.g., "The whole idea of fate, luck, chance"). This in turn is associated with the fact that he probably often experiences anxiety in the form of vague forebodings and worry.

Arthur is an ambitious person with the capacity to work hard. Although he has fair intellectual abilities, his thinking tends to be somewhat erratic, scattered, and without much discipline. He is tense and nervous, and this often interferes with his ability to concentrate. Instead of deliberating much, he tends to plunge ahead impulsively and uncritically. However, he generally has good common sense and a perceptive eye. On the whole, he is not psychologically minded or reflective. Instead, he is prone to rely on repressivelike defenses, such as avoidance and denial, and generally prefers the childish position. His perception of people and of interpersonal relationships is apt to be weak; he is likely to be quite naive and pollyannaish. Angry feelings in most forms are intolerable to him and, while he may use mockery in his humor, it tends to stay gentle and without much anger or bite. He shows a striking tendency to idealize others, especially adult figures, and thereby to exclude any ambivalent feelings. He may also idealize his past and yearn for it nostalgically.

The test reveals a self-image as a precocious but isolated child—the lonely little misfit who is weak, somewhat ridiculous, and quite helpless to resist parental pressures. There seem to be important feelings of inadequacy as a male, and he seems to fear masculinity. This may take the form of anxieties about competition with men and worries of being attacked. He is also apt to experience an acute need for support and nurturance, although he is not very comfortable with such feelings. His test responses also suggest the presence of an underlying feeling that he is somehow evil, and there appear to be some important feelings of guilt. He may also occasionally experience an overwhelming sense of responsibility and blame, but this feeling alternates with the feeling that he is wrongly blamed and really innocent. Like all his feelings, his guilt is genuinely felt but also heightened for effect and attenuated by grandiosity; he enjoys assuming a tragic pose.

Despite his feelings of inadequacy and his fears of aggression and competition, there is a prominent streak of self-confidence in him. To an extent this is based on some well-integrated counterphobic defenses that reflect his long-term struggle against the feeling that he is impotent, insignificant, and ridiculous ("not usable, good for nothing, decorative"). His strong need to entertain others, for example, may be based on these counterphobic tendencies.

In summary, the Rorschach test responses indicate that Arthur has a fairly well-integrated, although rather immature, personality. He shows significant obsessive-compulsive features along with some schizoid tendencies in an hysterical character. Narcissistic tendencies are also present, but secondary.

By and large, Arthur's LSD reaction followed the pattern typical of his group. His fantasy productions and imagery were the richest in this group, and reflected themes going back to his childhood, some of which occurred repeatedly during the LSD day. He was the most remarkable subject in the entire study in his capacity to produce free, exceptional, and extremely interesting material without becoming at all disorganized. Strong intellectual control and vivid imagination occurred together when the task permitted it. In his Theme List performance his recall of the themes was as good as on pretest and there was no drop in the cognitive battery. He had, in other words, a striking capacity for what seems best viewed as "regression in the service of the ego" (Kris, 1952) despite his apparent personality difficulties.

He felt that he was "spontaneous, fresh, as if seeing things for the first time; felt them actually as a child would." Several of his images were extremely vivid and in more than one modality: "The image of that prehistoric swamp . . . seemed to be so totally there sensorily—smell, etc., seemed so real to my senses. I remember the rest of the afternoon trying to go back and see what it was all about." (He did in fact return to it repeatedly.) Two years later he said, "It was a marvelous experience, clarified a lot of things . . . came out of it with a lot of loose ends tied up. I saw that, basically, things that are important to me now are a result of my earlier years. The fact that I respect and value children, I had a happy life. Temperament—I began to see where I got certain elements of my own temperament, mother and father." Regarding his interest in the theater, he stated: "How I've always been fascinated with the difference between reality and illusion; to be able to conquer illusion gives me a stronger sense of reality."

He was the only subject in Group I who did not appear at all withdrawn. This may reflect his lifelong history of using fantasy to establish his sense of self and his place among others rather than to avoid contact. The participation of his parents in his youthful playacting may be a factor in this. When asked 2 years later whether he talked more than usual under LSD, he said, "Compulsively, sometimes, to get things said seemed very important . . . in life, most of us have lost the real connection between words and what we mean; under the drug, thoughts, attitudes and feelings were more bonded to the words; words were more full . . . I saw the connection between words and what we are. Communication is something I've been obsessed with anyway . . . the reason society is so off; we can't get back to sane values because of the way we misuse language—advertising, etc. . . . very few people can connect something vital with the word and transmit it." Since his drug experience, he has begun to write poetry: "I write every day. One thing the drug did, I became aware of the importance in my life of the darker, more elusive things, those were important for my art. I saw the depth of the well . . . the importance of images, which were so real and intense. They are what we live by anyway."

In the Rorschach his pretest primary-process material was abundant and read like many LSD protocols, and these trends increased under the drug where he also showed some impairments (e.g., in form quality). Nevertheless, his attempts to intellectualize, particularly through esthetic contexts, expressed his striking need in the LSD state to integrate and conceptualize the Rorschach cards in a symbolic, organized way. A good example of this was his characterization of the entire drug experience as a fugue with intertwining repetitious themes.

His figure drawings (see Figure 5.1) on both days express his feelings of inadequacy and childishness as a male, contrasted with a powerful, sensual female figure. Both drawings, while much freer and looser under LSD, accentuate the differences between the sexes that were visible on the pretest day. It is also notable that, while the LSD day female is much more potent than the male, she is appealing rather than frightening.

The remarkable control that Arthur maintained together with his openness to rich fantasy and memory material, and absorption in important personal themes, apparently took its toll. He became exhausted and somewhat flat toward the end of the day and on the following day he was irritable, depressed, slowed down, groggy, and hypersensitive to light and sound.

Arthur was also a subject in an experiment in which his dreams were monitored on several nights, including the night after he took LSD. He is an extremely productive dreamer, with a remarkable ability to recall his dreams and the physical sensations in them. His dreams are long, rich, full of color and a variety of affects, and in them he shifts roles easily. There were, however, no apparent differences on the LSD night.

Whether he gained genuine insights is open to question; his comments to us did *not* offer clear evidence of genuine insight. Arthur's own statement about the LSD state as a way to self-knowledge sums up his feelings about his experience quite well. He spoke of having had a similar experience of self-exploration and self-knowledge once in an acting class, but he found the latter preferable because the drug effects felt synthetic and not self-controlled.

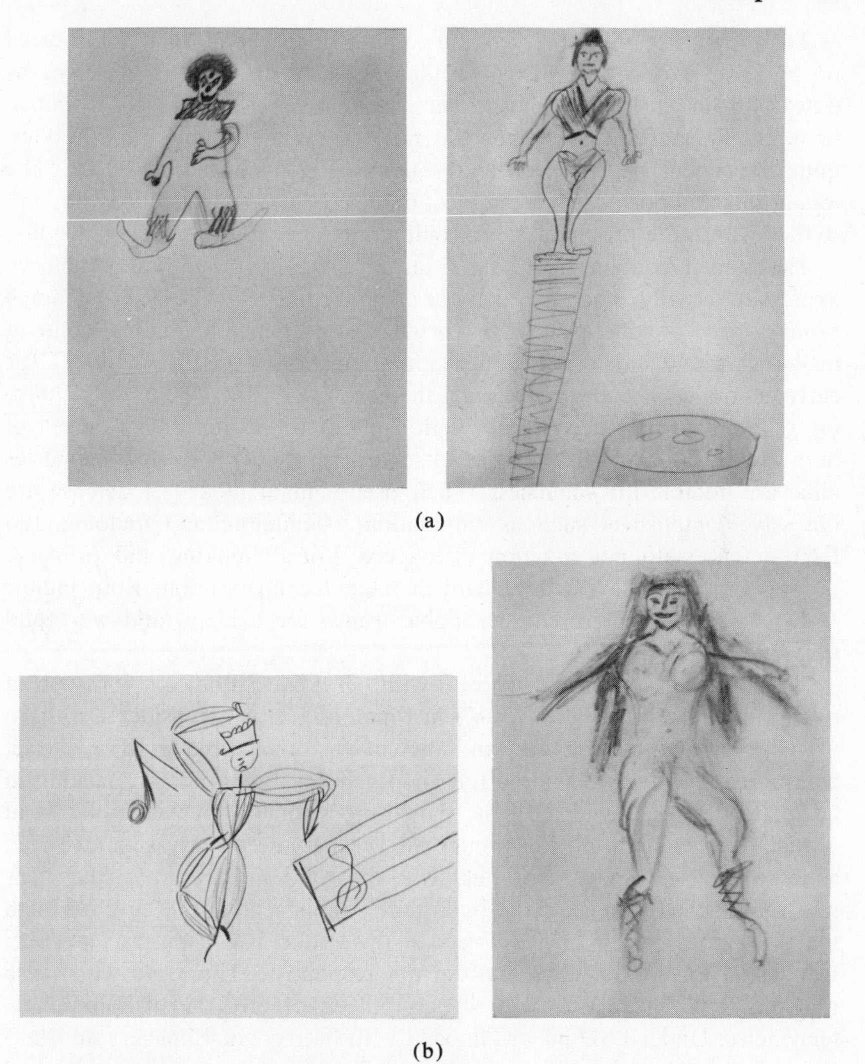

(a)

(b)

Figure 5.1. Arthur's Human Figure Drawings. (a) Pretest Day; (b) LSD Day. The left-hand figure of each pair was drawn first.

GROUP II

The subjects in Group II are all persons with poorly integrated personalities, predominantly schizoid and narcissistic in character, who have a tendency to regress to a childish, dependent passivity under stress. They are in many ways inadequate and poorly defended, giving up their goals in the face of difficulty. Their self-esteem is poor and they are rather depressed and self-abasing, feeling incompetent and expecting failure. They also expect to be exploited.

Their identities are unfocused and conflicted; they tend to be homosexual or to have strong homosexual tendencies, and they see themselves as outcasts or in a helpless childish role. Their earliest memories, for example, featured illnesses in which they did not receive adequate care. They are quite dependent on parental figures (especially male ones) and fear the loss of their support. They are subject to diffuse anxiety, which they attempt to deal with quite primitively by avoiding introspection and their inner life.

These men contain their anger inside themselves and are unable to express it verbally. They are likely to somatize under stress. There is much primary-process content in their Rorschachs, particularly libidinal content, including sexual, homosexual, and exhibitionistic-voyeuristic images. Their early memories also emphasize anal themes. Yet on the whole, their thinking is inhibited and stereotyped, with signs of repression and a dearth of both imagery and fantasy. Their Rorschach responses and early memories alike are notable for vagueness. Their predominant modes of defense are obsessive-compulsive, such as rumination, vacillation, and undoing, but their defenses do not function effectively. Loose thinking and primary-process intrusions reveal the extent of their decompensation. Both phobic and, to a lesser degree, counterphobic trends are evident, and we found paranoid tendencies as well.

This is, then, a group of subjects with pervasive pathology. It is one of two groups (the other is Group V) in which no one was considered to have a well-integrated personality, and two of the four subjects were in fact considered to be on the borderline of psychosis. Being notably lacking in adequate defenses against stress, they were strongly affected by LSD in virtually every area of functioning and experienced pervasively altered states of consciousness. Not only was the total impact great, but their reaction reached its peak early, by 2 hours, and stayed at that level through the 8 hours of testing. One subject in this group had a protracted effect that lasted for several days and did not respond to Thorazine. He was a religious, inhibited person with strong, but unaccepted, latent homosexual tendencies. Under LSD he was flooded with heterosexual imagery and fantasies that he found both pleasurable and reassuring, and which he had difficulty giving up.

This group reported great loss of control and loss of inhibitions in many areas of functioning under LSD. They felt that their thinking and sense of time were impaired, and they reported visual distortions and changes in the meanings of their experiences (both loss of meaning and new meanings). They also experienced loss of contact and feelings of alienation, along with suspiciousness. In spite of their extensive loss of control, they were elated (or perhaps somewhat manic) rather than anxious, seeming to give themselves up to the experience. They also had fewer somatic symptoms than average.

Their comments convey some of the quality of their experiences: "Feel very disconnected at various moments"; "What real world?" "Trying to come back to reality seems meaningless to me. I'm just zooming—it's great!" "Certain sort of realizations which you have known before take on more meaning, you feel you can express them more, not suppress them"; "I'll get into a climax of feeling, so that the body is continually changing, changing in its tensions . . . intensification of all sorts of things, warming up now, general feeling of . . . I can't describe it; but I still feel almost detachment from the body." The feeling of detachment from the body was typical (sometimes with somatic delusions): "Feel like it [body] doesn't belong to me any more; . . . everything tingling [as though] plugged into electric currents and everything beyond my control, floating, *no responsibilities, I'm a child*—I'm so light." Some of the changes in meaning had a paranoid tinge: "Some of the things the experimenters do [are meaningless], shutting the door, shuffling papers, arranging the tape machine, things of that nature."

Their visual images were very vivid and very absorbing. Some were well-worked-out scenes, but more often they were abstract images or intensifications of real stimuli: "Colors are really something, the patterns, certain feelings or senses that you must have experienced in a wonderful way, somehow"; "The inkblots . . . many more vivid impressions, texture hopped right out on one of them"; ". . . [see connections between] objects that have similar background." The pseudohallucinations were experienced as both fascinating and potentially frightening: "You just want to pay attention to your own experiences, which are more interesting than anything else. I have had some strange experiences. . . . I suppose it could be terrifying, if it got more ominous, or if you treated them as if they were more ominous."

The experimenters' views of their overt behavior agreed closely with their self-reports. They were seen as very regressed, silly, childish, and in a maniclike state, but not withdrawn. Anxiety and bodily preoccupation were, however, rated as only average, and they were not at all hostile.

Their performance in the experimental tests of cognitive functioning was strongly affected in the altered state, but the nature of the effects suggests that their comprehension ability was much more impaired than their ability to mobilize and focus attention. Their recall under LSD of the previous day's theme lists was at an average level, and their Color-Word reading times did not become more variable, indicating that their attention was not seriously disrupted.[8] This is in keeping with the fact that they did not become especially anxious. They were strongly affected, however, on the measures that we have interpreted as the result of comprehension difficulties;

[8] Unfortunately, none of the subjects in Group II took the cognitive test battery.

Color-Word interference was much greater under LSD, and their learning of the neutral theme lists was very poor in this state.

In the Color-Form test, their reliance on color increased considerably, indicating a shift away from the more reality-oriented, secondary-process use of form to a more emotionally determined basis for perception.

All of these subjects gave new earliest memories under LSD, although the changes in their recollections accentuated themes already apparent on the pretest day. Their concern with damage to themselves and view of the environment as hostile and nonnurturant were the same on both days, but these themes, vague in the nondrug state, became more vivid and explicit under LSD.

Their male figure drawings deteriorated in quality and became larger, older, weaker, and more passive in posture under the drug. Their female figures also became larger, but not notably weaker, so that under the drug they were more active and generally stronger than the male figures.

Their Rorschach responses, quite poorly controlled and with much vagueness on pretest, showed striking changes in the LSD state. Primary-process content increased and became more blatant (shifting from Level 2 to Level 1); aggressive images changed from those of perpetrators to those of objects of aggression, reflecting their passivity and difficulty in functioning under the drug. While they resembled Group I in showing a tipping of the balance toward movement responses, more formal features of the primary process, and poorer form quality, the nature of these changes was different. They produced fewer superior forms under the drug, but differed from Group I in that vague forms actually decreased while misperceived forms increased. As for formal features, under LSD there were more fluid transformations of percepts, inappropriate activities, affective contradictions, self-references, incoherence, and peculiar verbalizations. Pathological defenses also appeared, especially denial and projection. Thus their Rorschach protocols revealed an extensive failure of ego functioning, showing loss of control, passivity, and primitivization of percepts.

The connection between their predrug personalities and their LSD state seems straightforward. Their inadequate defenses and poorly maintained modes of thought readily collapsed under the drug, so that primary-process intrusions emerged in full force. Impaired reality contact and manic behavior followed. Their extremely regressive behavior, passivity, and poor coping abilities made it impossible for them to maintain any semblance of control under LSD.

While their functioning under the drug was, from the clinician's point of view, more pathological than that of any other group, we must keep in mind that these subjects did not find the drug experience very threatening. In a sense, they enjoyed it. Subjectively, as the quotations cited indicate, they reported a heightening of experience which was in marked contrast to the mental confusion and diffuse anxiety that they usually suffer. In neither the Rorschach test nor their Earliest Memory report was there any essential change in content from pretest to drug day, although the form altered in a regressive direction. On the pretest day, the inadequacy of their defenses was obvious, and their typical way of handling pathological ideation was with vagueness and inhibition of fantasy. Under LSD not only did the pathological content emerge more vividly, but their defenses became more pathological as well. There was also a general heightening of sensation: touching, tasting, and smelling, as well as seeing. At the same time their anxiety was either reduced, largely through denial, or became focused on delusional content.

It may be that the fact of having taken a drug and being in the protected environment of the laboratory gave them a feeling of safety. They felt relieved of personal responsibility, utilizing their passive dependency and regression as protection: ". . . no responsibilities, I'm a child," as one subject put it. Two of these subjects in fact felt physically like children under LSD; one felt like a fetus, seeing the experimenters as much larger than himself.

Despite the lack of anxiety, these subjects' disturbed thinking and damaged defenses led to severe impairments in their cognitive test performance. Their pretest functioning, which showed considerable vulnerability in this regard, clearly deteriorated in the altered state. It seems likely that this group represents a type of subject for whom LSD is particularly dangerous, not merely because it produces a pathological state, but because it offers a feeling of relief from the confused, anxious state in which they normally exist and creates an intensity of sensory experience and a sense of self that are usually not available to them. The pleasurable flood of fantasy seems to have produced a maniclike elation which extended to feelings of power and impaired their reality testing. Thus, both the altered state itself and the extensions of these feelings into subsequent days are potentially dangerous for such persons. Two of these subjects continued to experience effects for several days. One, whose influx of heterosexual fantasy has been noted, reported that 2 days later, when playing ball, ". . . my reactions were very quick to sense what my opponent was doing . . . could read from their eyes what the other players intended." Grandiosity and tenuous reality testing is implied here. Another reported 2 years later, in great detail, the sensory experiences he had enjoyed (e.g., ". . . in the washroom, a little blue plastic soap case, boy, I jumped at that thing, it was so beautiful, and the colors were so vivid, exciting"). He felt that his senses were heightened and his imagination much more creative: "Things much more clearly in focus, things that happened when I was a child came back much more clearly, the drug allowed me to relax and become much more subjective, *not have a conscious block, objectivity, that hampered it.*" The danger of LSD for these subjects is highlighted by his opening comment after a 2-year interval: "I thought the drug was great, I'd like to get a supply of it."

The Case of Bert

Bert's autobiography impresses one as a narrative of homosexual relationships to the virtual exclusion of all else. He was the youngest child in a large family and his earliest recollection is of climbing to kiss a chalk-like statue belonging to his grandmother and crashing to the floor with it. This is in keeping with the few early life events that Bert mentions, most of which reflect considerable castration anxiety and fears of bodily harm. Bert's favorite childhood game involved castles and queens, and their beheading, the latter associated with fear of the dark. He was a "sissy" and preferred to play with girls. His attempts to join boys in sports and games (i.e., his attempts to become a man) were marred by an experience in which he was struck by a stone thrown by one of these boys, opening a wound over his eye. He recalls the doctor injecting his leg (sic) and stitching the wound; later, his mother bought him a huge baton as compensation. The sense of anxiety, strangeness, and obvious symbolism are striking.

Beyond these experiences Bert recalls fighting with boys and a brother helping him with battle tactics. He remembers his first day at school with a sense of loss, accenting his separation from his mother, but he tells us virtually nothing about his parents or siblings. The little he does say about them deals with parental pressure to work early in his teens, rather than complete school. They also failed to protect him in those years from trips he took in search of an acting career, some of which entailed very clear exposure to possible physical harm or death. They did, however, insist he make good a theft of money from his first job, which they learned about from a friend whom he had told about it.

Inquiry in Bert's interview added some information about his childhood and family. Bert was a late bed wetter and shared a room with several siblings. There was an atmosphere of overstimulation in the family; his mother had a male visitor whom his father suspected of being her lover, but Bert suspected he was a homosexual; his father was flirtatious with other women. To Bert his parents were remote; his mother disciplined him harshly at times, encouraged an interest in housework, and was an anxious, tearful woman who was often ill with both surgical and medical problems. His father was a laborer, seldom present, who hardly spoke at all. Bert enjoyed being with his sisters and felt distant from his brothers.

A friend of one of his brothers was the object of Bert's first homosexual experience when he was about 11 years old; Bert suddenly approached him in his own house, fondled his genitals, and performed fellatio. This experience was associated with a dream from that time: Bert is in a factory and a man is going to—or does—hang him up, possibly by the penis.

This was a "satisfying, frightening" dream, and Bert's association to factory is castles (large, stone-walled, bleak places).

Bert describes his life from his early teens onward, both in the theatre and socially, almost exclusively in terms of a series of homosexual relationships. The men were usually older, and he related to them and viewed them openly as father figures. In these relationships Bert saw himself as a helpless, needy child to whom his partners offered care, security, money, and love. Ultimately, they all quarreled with Bert or abandoned him. Once, he contracted venereal disease in a brief affair, and he now fears sexual contact and further harm.

Currently, Bert is often overtly anxious and is worried about failing as an actor. He seems depressed and full of doubts about his future.

In summary, Bert appears to have a very pervasive sense of castration anxiety and fears of bodily harm which seem based in part on an overseductive family situation, even though relationships in his family seem largely distant and empty. Bert apparently protects himself from his overwhelming anxieties through denial of his masculinity by establishing both a feminine identification and one of a helpless boy. He flees heterosexuality and becomes homosexual, thereby also seeking, no doubt, further phallic reassurance.

The corruption of his superego, the inadequacies of his controls, the poor quality of his object relationships, the intensity of his anxieties, and the openness of the symbolism acted out in his life experiences all indicate that Bert suffers from rather severe pathology.

He has a pervasive sense of inadequacy, anxiety, and depression. Bert seems to have few resources with which to deal with these problems. He clearly senses this and characteristically hopes for help from somewhere or someone but is quite pessimistic about finding it.

The Rorschach provided this picture: Bert is an immature and quite seriously unstable person (he describes himself as "very nervous"). Although he is an egocentric and detached young man who rarely feels things deeply, he is subject to acute feelings of insecurity and he sometimes feels genuine hopelessness and despair. This is over and above his long-standing and deep-rooted feelings of vulnerability and weakness, and his strong need for support and rescue. His relationships with people are likely to be highly passive and dependent as well as quite tenuous, and he may periodically withdraw altogether into a detached shell.

The test gives evidence of considerable intellectual capacity which, however, he is unable to put to much adaptive use. There seems to be some important interference with his cognitive functioning; he is currently having difficulties paying attention and his thinking is marked by blocking and groping. Moreover, even in his best state, his thoughts tend to be idiosyncratic and even peculiar, his reasoning overly concrete and uncritical, and he is prone to loose associations and a kind of arbitrariness. He is not psychologically minded; in fact, he is rather simple-minded and naive. Further, he is not very reflective and tends instead to fall into empty obsessional stewing and unproductive doubting. He tends to vacillate a good deal and is extremely passive; he also lacks much drive or ambition.

Bert's fantasy life, like his affects, seems to be quite stilted and constricted; there is often a labored and stereotyped quality to his productions. His major yearnings have to do with being protected and safe, and this is associated with a marked detachment from others. He also yearns to be alone and "inside" where it is safe, longing for a past when he enjoyed maternal nurturance. He is the kind of passive person to whom things happen without his seeming to play any active part at all.

Bert describes himself as an overt homosexual with no conflicts or misgivings about it. He appears to have an openly feminine identification, probably with the mother figure whom he views as omnipotent ("a queen") and he tends to court the protection of older men. The only thing that seems to trouble him about his passive, dependent relationships is the sadomasochistic aspect, of which he remains largely quite unaware. However, he may from time to time experience some anxiety having to do with his inability to maintain autonomy from an older man.

The test points up some marked distortions and confusions connected with sexuality. Bert probably has some conceptions of sex that are bizarre at worst and childish at best. The female is feared, perhaps because the vagina is viewed as an engulfing organ that opens directly into the stomach; he regards the penis as a sadistic weapon. An anal conception of intercourse, and also of birth, are implied as well.

The test suggests that Bert is often under the pressure of unmanageable impulses. Aggression is typically masked and disavowed, and he is prone to protest his innocence. To a moderate extent he may also project hostility and then react with some fearfulness. This propensity is part of a mildly paranoid streak in him, which is based also on his pervasive egocentricity. He is prone to see meanings and connections where they don't really exist and to see them in reference to himself. While he can be very perceptive of external stimuli, he frequently becomes overalert to them. For the most part, however, this aspect is based on important voyeuristic impulses that take the form of a need to look as well as to be looked at.

es in sudden outbursts during which they are experienced as ego-alien
obic manifestations also appear at times.

These men have, however, certain strong assets. They have considerabl
elligence (IQs of 134 and 144) which they use effectively. They have
de intellectual and creative interests, are good at solving problems, inter-
sted in knowledge for its own sake, and sensitive to minimal cues. As
xpected, intellectualization is one of their most often used and most effec-
ive defenses, often used in conjunction with isolation. Obsessive-compulsive
rends are prominent; they are orderly and thrifty, and their thinking is often rigid, overly planful and ruminative. We saw evidence of undoing, as well as denial, in their personality assessment. They also seemed lacking in imagery. Reaction formation is apparent, and they are conventional and conscientious, with a strong need to be helpful to others. They are deliberate, prefer routines, and dislike adventure. In their conscious values moderation, balance, and control are emphasized.

They also consciously disapprove of a passive-receptive, inward-turning, contemplative attitude toward life. At the same time, a streak of passivity and yearning for comfort comes through. We got the impression of strong underlying passive tendencies which are defended against by reaction formations. In regard to their LSD state, it is of special interest that their Rorschachs indicate that they tend to regress to a passive position under stress.

Their relationships are marred by anxiety and are not smooth; they also tend to somatize. By and large, however, they function rather effectively, although not comfortably, by means of their rigid controls and by relying on their skills, competence, and knowledge, in a seemingly independent manner.

The effect of LSD on these subjects was cataclysmic. Their total questionnaire score was very high, indicating a most pervasive and overwhelming altered state experience. Three other groups (I, II, and IV) reported about as many subjective effects as this group (although the patterns were different in each case), but the disruption of overt behavior in these subjects exceeded by far that of any other group.

The most remarkable thing about their reaction, however, was its course over time. While their peak effect, 2–5 hours after drug ingestion, was greater than that of any other group, their reaction was minimal during the first hour (the lowest of any group) and declined sharply by 8 hours to one-third of peak level. The other three high-effect groups, in contrast, reached about one-half their peak effect within the first hour, and remained at about two-thirds of this peak level at 8 hours. Groups I and II also reported more LSD-like effects than average on pretest and posttest days, while the Group III subjects reported virtually none. For this group, then,

Bert therefore has a poorly integrated personality, with noteworthy borderline schizophrenic features. Basically, he is a narcissistic character with schizoid features, along with some hysterical and weak obsessive-compulsive tendencies and some mild paranoid tendencies.

Bert's LSD state was in most respects typical of Group II, with extensive loss of control and contact, thinking difficulties, visual hallucinations, and experiences of altered meanings. His behavior was more regressed than that of any of the others in Group II and was described as "grossly psychotic." Body image changes were extreme; he became very anxious, rather than manic, with a marked loss of motility. He felt that his arms were useless and his legs paralyzed, cut off, or numb from the waist down (which made him think of a childhood figure with whom he identified himself), as if he were old or, at the same time, like a baby. He also felt "like a little ball floating in space, while you're talking to me as a man possessing arms and legs and a body."

At times he felt smaller: ". . . as you mentioned it [i.e., asking if he felt like a child], I thought of being all curled up, womblike." The childlike feeling was pervasive: "The reason I want to give up cigarettes—now, I'm a child—the connection with guilt, legs, school teachers—I never saw a teacher smoke." This relates to the way he viewed one of the female experimenters while she was asking him questions: ". . . enormous, towering like a queen, enormous breasts getting bigger and bigger, undulations of legs and skirt. Very seductive, also forbidden, like a prison warden, or teacher." This of course concretizes the conception of women that was apparent in his pretest projective tests. He also felt that the desk at which she was sitting became bigger and in fact that "everyone was much bigger than I."

He saw well-worked-out scenes from the past, including long-repressed recollections (a funeral procession, for one), in the folds of the curtains and said, "I seemed to be drawn into them." The loss of boundaries was evident in many ways. He was the subject already quoted who felt as if his body were beyond his control, plugged into electric currents, ". . . floating, no responsibilities, I'm a child—I'm so light." As this suggests, the drug experience was by no means totally unpleasant for him, but in his case an early elated mood was succeeded by a flat depression during the latter part of the day.

The effect of the drug on his performance in the experimental tasks was, as we would expect, very great, particularly in the projective tests. His loss of reality contact was reflected in a very marked shift to perceptual organization on the basis of color in the Color-Form test, and extremely poor learning of the neutral theme lists under LSD. It is noteworthy, however, that although his behavior was noted as anxious he, like the other subjects in Group II, did not exhibit the cognitive disruptions that stem from anxiety.

Under the drug his recall of the pretest theme lists was excellent, and his Color-Word reading was very stable, without the increased variability usually shown by more anxious subjects (he was not given the cognitive test battery).

His Rorschach test performance which, as we have seen, reflected severe pathology on the pretest day, became grossly psychotic under the drug. His previous vagueness and obsessional vacillation vanished; there was a great loss of distance, with an eruption of oral, anal, and sexual material. The fit between the blots and his percepts became grossly inappropriate, and both his use of color and the links between the parts of his images were often arbitrary. His verbalizations became at times bizarre, and self-references were prominent. Projection became apparent, and his use of the primitive defense of denial was extreme.

The change in his figure drawings was equally extreme (see Figure 5.2). Both the male and female figures became larger, less organized, and fragmented. The regressive emergence of blatant homosexuality was expressed through an extreme emphasis on the buttocks, and his loss of reality testing, evident in the missing parts of both figures, was most marked in the male figure which, after an abandoned attempt in the center of the page, ran off the page and was drawn too large for the entire figure to fit had it been centered. While the pretest male and female figure drawings were identical with each other except for hair and clothing, the male figure drawn under LSD was, despite its musculature, depleted and unsupported, and dominated by the potent and seductive-looking female figure. (The fact that the female was drawn first on both days is an expression of his homosexuality.)

Under LSD he recalled a more regressive Earliest Memory, which had been repressed until that time. We may note that when the Earliest Memories given on the two days are compared, the one reported on the pretest is seen to be a screen memory for the one that emerged under LSD (see Langs, 1971, where they are presented in detail).

To summarize his pretest personality and his drug reaction: Bert typifies this group of borderline subjects with impaired defenses and poor ego functioning in the waking state who experienced under LSD a pervasively regressed altered state, with markedly impaired cognitive functioning, loss of ego boundaries, and altered reality contact and testing.

GROUP III

Since Group III consists of only two subjects, its status is more dubious than that of the other groups, and the presentation of data is therefore limited to those features in which these two men are both extremely deviant from other subjects and are very similar to each other.

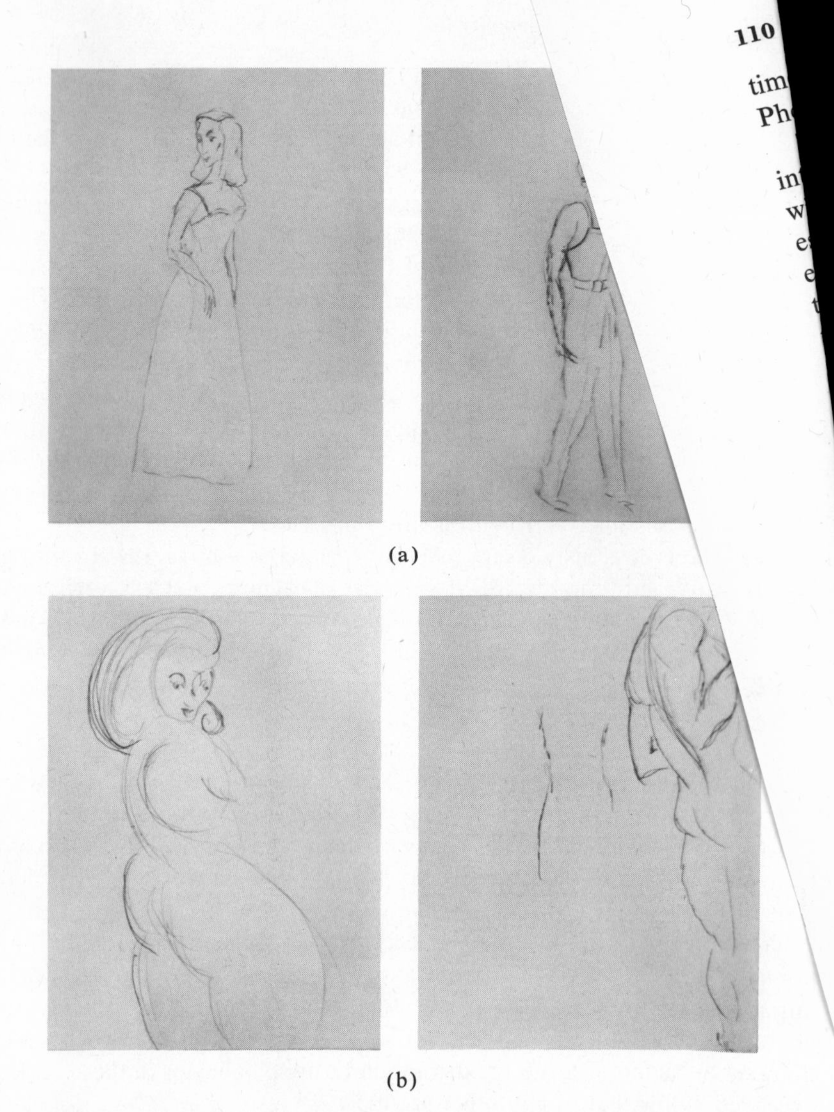

(a)

(b)

Figure 5.2. Bert's Human Figure Drawings. (a) Pretest Day; (b) LSD Day. The left-hand figure of each pair was drawn first.

These two subjects are characterized by a good deal of inner turmoil, much of it within awareness, against which they exercise strong controls that normally operate fairly well. They are notably prone to depression and disillusionment and often experience anxiety. They suppress their anger rigidly, expressing it only in the form of passive aggression. Some hostility to women is evident, but they have a marked tendency to submit to paternal figures. They feel sexually inadequate and suppress sensuality. Thus their emotions and impulses are generally inhibited but do break through at

the effects of the drug erupted suddenly, for a brief time, and in marked contrast not only to their everyday experience but also to the controlled state they managed to maintain through other parts of the LSD day.

Under the drug they reported that both their thinking and sense of time were very much slowed down. Loss of contact and feelings of alienation were also prominent. They experienced changes in the self, but with a marked sense of standing aside and looking at themselves. There were many body image changes and somatic effects, and they reported feeling both suspicious and extremely anxious, particularly with the fear of going crazy.

Behaviorally, they were extremely regressed, silly, inappropriate, and maniclike. The last-mentioned behavior, marked by uncontrolled laughter at times, was in marked contrast to their failure to report feeling elated or silly. There was behavioral evidence of visual distortions and concern with the bodily effects they were experiencing, and motility changes were very marked, fluctuating between lethargy and hypermotility. Experimenters reported hostility and suspiciousness. Most striking of all was their extreme anxiety.

The conjunction of bodily changes and anxiety is very striking in these subjects. One, who experienced many changes in the size and color of his face and hands, reported: ". . . there's this feeling in my stomach, do I become a different person? This physical discomfort, as if there's something on the tip of my tongue, in my mouth, a gnawing, hungry sensation that I think I ought to be able to fill by sucking on candy, but I won't. There it comes again, first in my stomach, then on the tip of my tongue. *I just wanted to find reality* . . . so many different solutions." The same subject said at one point: ". . . [my body] doesn't feel as if it belongs to me, not getting satisfaction texually (sic)—texturally, that I should; as if somebody else were chewing my food." He felt at one point divided into three selves: "a little me inside enjoying all this; the rational one outside, helpless, deprived of sensory pleasure"; and a third self who criticized. His fear of losing control was great; among other things he was afraid he might "burn myself and not know it."

The experimental test data for these subjects are limited because their extreme drug reaction made it impossible to carry out the complete testing schedule with either of them. In the tests of cognitive functioning, attention was grossly impaired, undoubtedly because of their extreme anxiety. Their performance on the first three cognitive tests (Word Naming, Serial Sevens, Robinson Numbers), and their recall of pretest Theme Lists were markedly disrupted. One subject took the Color-Word test and his reading time became much more variable. In contrast, there was no indication that the comprehension of either man was impaired. Color-Word interference decreased (the normal retesting effect) and Theme List learning, which was superior on the pretest day (as we would expect from their high intelligence), was rather well-maintained. Finally, the one subject who took the Color-Form test under LSD showed the greatest increase in color determination (emotionally dominated perception) found in the entire study.

The projective material from Group III, unfortunately, is virtually useless. Only one gave a drug day earliest memory; it was the same as in the pretest. While both made figure drawings, one was tested late in the day, after his brief and acute drug reaction was over, so that his two sets of drawings were virtually identical. The other drew figures that showed a clear loss of motor control but little else. Neither was scheduled for the Rorschach test under LSD.

In spite of the limited experimental task data available for these subjects, a clear contrast with Group II is evident. While both were impaired in cognitive functioning, the disturbance was completely different. Group II experienced a grossly psychoticlike LSD state, with impairment in ability to comprehend the meaning of verbal material. This was related to the massive failure in ego functioning, including the breakdown of reality testing, that these subjects experienced (seen, for example, in their Rorschach responses and figure drawings). Group III, however, showed no such loss of comprehension in the cognitive testing under the drug; instead, they had extreme fluctuations in attention. This supports the interpretation that their very marked behavioral changes under LSD represented a panic state, associated with extreme and frightening somatic reactions, rather than a psychoticlike break with reality.

These two subjects, normally rigidly but fairly well controlled, were, before taking LSD, afraid of emotions and prone to depression, anxiety and somatic symptoms. The drug apparently released a flood of unacceptable emotions and extreme bodily reactions. Their fear of losing control made them hold on as long as possible and then experience extreme anxiety when this was no longer feasible. Their ability to reinstitute control unusually quickly indicates their great dread of regressive material, but also the strength and resiliency of their defenses, in contrast to Group II. Here again is a group of subjects for whom LSD can be extremely dangerous, especially in large doses that might more seriously breach their defenses.

The Case of Calvin

Calvin's autobiography and interviews reveal that he is from a small-town, religious family. His father provided the family with a strict moral code, yet was warm and effective and is viewed as the source of considerable strength. There are threads of a strong positive identification with him on Calvin's part throughout his life. Early memories of his father center on many mutual activities, notably related to music and to building things together. The image is marred somewhat by the feeling that his father was too remote and not successful enough financially.

Calvin seldom mentions his mother. He turned to her for advice in his father's absence, but beyond that nothing is said about their relationship. There is indirect evidence of a strong, displaced desire for her (e.g., Calvin's rather early attraction to older girls) and repudiation of this desire (e.g., memories of being repelled by the embraces and odors of perfume from older women who consulted his father professionally).

An older brother is also not clearly portrayed. Sports and illicit activities (e.g., smoking) were shared with him. There is evidence of wanting to imitate him, but there is also a sense of competition and hostility in which Calvin feels he is inferior.

Calvin's memories of his early years feature games and sporting activities, with efforts to achieve a strong masculine identity, and haunting concerns about being a sissy. At five he underwent surgery which he recalls with mixed feelings, and there are many other recollections that indicate intense castration anxiety and related fears (e.g., of his bicycle being stolen; later, of his ducks being killed and devoured by dogs). In general, as his story unfolds, we hear of many attempts to alleviate his sense of castration and his feminine identification, most of which were successful. In school, for example, he was very bright and a leader; he was also creative, outstanding in sports, enterprising, and strongly interested in girls. Yet, despite his many successes, he had a sense of falling short. His bike gets stolen or a business venture he cleverly undertakes fails because his ducks are killed.

Later in life Calvin married somewhat prematurely and risked his education by losing his college scholarship, although he finally did complete college. His marriage does not appear entirely gratifying to him. Despite his advanced education, he has held a variety of odd jobs and has not yet established a career for himself.

A major theme in Calvin's life is that of morality. In his early years he did many forbidden things such as smoking and playing with toy guns. In school he was often late and teased the girls, disrupting class. Yet when severely reprimanded, he established controls and, particularly in adolescence, gave up this kind of misbehavior and worked seriously.

There are virtually no direct expressions of aggression in his autobiographical narrative; he was, instead, a nail biter.

Calvin reports what may have been phobias, such as a fear of water and dogs, but these were overcome in puberty with "the help of God." He also tends to somatize. An early example of this was his reaction to smoking; he became nauseated and vomited, and he still becomes nauseated when exposed to cigarette smoke. Thus his guilt over the forbidden gratification finds somatic expression, possibly as a punishment and also as a form of undoing or repudiation. A current example is associated with his dissatisfaction with his present life, along with hints of impulses toward acting out which he must repress; these conflicts seem to be associated with frequent minor illnesses.

Calvin has a good, though limited, capacity for sublimation; he identifies with the interests of those who are important to him and develops such activities constructively for himself. He constantly battles his feminine identification through masculine work endeavors, and he also receives considerable reassurance through performing.

In summary, Calvin's central anxieties appear to be phallic-oedipal castration anxieties. He is able to handle them through his career and through phallic fantasies and activities which are not, however, entirely successful. His feminine identification appears to be in part a feeling of being castrated, but it also seems to be defensively related both to a flight from oedipal wishes and to unconscious pregnancy fantasies as a means of repairing the damage to himself. He has a severe, strict, and rigid superego which in his youngest years allowed forbidden actions and now holds them firmly in check. Finally, he has a strong ego which succeeds in alleviating much of his anxiety. Some unresolved conflict remains, however, and he has not reached a level of optimal functioning.

On the Rorschach, Calvin appears to be an altogether boyish person: somewhat flighty, very wide-eyed, utterly nonrebellious and good, and also quite egocentric. His preferred self-image is as the harmless and funny one, the young boy without much masculinity or power. The test indicates that he has a strong oral orientation, including, for example, an overriding optimism, and that his oral needs are quite well integrated. Passive yearnings are apt to be quite conspicuous, and he seems to believe that the father figure can solve all problems. At present, however, he is likely to feel quite lost and alone and in some danger at times; he yearns for others (e.g., an all-powerful "Daddy") to come to his rescue. Ordinarily, his fantasy life is taken up with boyish dreams of glory, and his ambitiousness is partly based on a need to emulate others.

Calvin is a very intelligent person. He places high value on skills and achievement, as well as on efficiency and dutifulness, and he emphasizes carrying on in the face of difficulties and frustration with a minimum of complaining. He also has the tendency, however, to become too cautious and deliberate, and he easily falls into empty meticulousness and fussiness. At such times his judgment may become somewhat impaired, but it is mainly characterized by a kind of overweening naivete and simple pollyannaishness. He tends to minimize all strife and unpleasantness, especially conflicts with others, and he glosses over difficulties and tensions. This can result in some degree of poor social judgment and insensitivity to people and situations.

At the present time, Calvin seems to be struggling with feelings of despair that are quite unfamiliar to him. He typically brushes away such unpleasant feelings in a rush of disavowals. His repressive defenses currently may be under too much strain, however, and he may be experiencing some anxiety and worry. The test suggests that he is struggling with angry feelings that are directed mainly toward women. He may resort to some externalization of blame and responsibility in order both to maintain his passive posture and to protect his self-image as the pure and good one. The only form of anger acceptable to him is verbal aggression in the form of mockery and scorn; but such mockery is probably never more than mild.

The test also indicates that sexuality is regarded as taboo and is the focus of some phobic reactions. He may be prone to feelings of disgust with himself (perhaps having to do with early masturbation) and is likely to attribute sexual impulses to "devilish instincts" of an ego-alien kind.

Calvin is, in summary, a relatively inhibited, obsessive-compulsive character with conspicuous hysterical features. Despite some immaturity, he is on the whole quite well-integrated. At present, some tension and some depression are indicated.

The effect of LSD on Calvin was minimal during the first hour, although nausea and dizziness are reported. By the end of the second hour, however, he was so overwhelmed by massive physical reactions and anxiety that testing had to be temporarily discontinued: "At one time I felt like I could hardly breathe, and several other times I was asked to stand up out of the chair or to get up off the cot, and I just couldn't do it at all." Several times he felt that he was dying. His nausea became extreme and, 4 hours after taking LSD, he vomited. After this he regained control fairly rapidly and, although he felt rather weak, he was able to fulfill the demands of testing adequately during the last 2 hours of experimentation.

As we have already noted, his experimental test data were rather limited.[9] He did very poorly on the three tests of the cognitive test battery that were affected by anxiety (Word Naming, Serial Sevens, Robinson Numbers), but was at the average of the drug group in learning the new Theme Lists, supporting the view that the massive effect of LSD on Calvin represented a panic state rather than a true loss of reality ties. His figure drawings were made toward the end of the day, after he had regained control, and were indistinguishable from his pretest drawings.

[9] Neither the Color-Word nor the Color-Form test could be considered valid (although he actually took the Color-Word test) because he is color-blind. As already noted, the Rorschach test was not scheduled for him.

Thus Calvin had an acutely catastrophic altered-state reaction to LSD. What is particularly interesting is that his actual functioning was quite adequate (compared to Groups II and V in which this is not the case) largely because of strong but rigid and inhibiting defenses. The regressive pressures created by the drug were fended off for a brief period and then erupted, creating a severe disorganization which precipitated a panic state. With the support offered by the experimenters and the passage of time, a safe reintegration quickly occurred. We certainly cannot be confident that the outcome would be as favorable for such seemingly healthy subjects were they to take LSD without professional supervision.

GROUP IV

These three subjects are all obsessionals, with weak interpersonal relationships and a good deal of manifest hostility. They tend in particular to be verbally aggressive and, at the same time, they are afraid of their aggressive impulses. They rebel against authority and convention. Blame is externalized and some projection appears; they anticipate being exploited and are highly sensitive to evidence that might be so interpreted. Ruminative, obsessional thinking characterizes them.

The subjects in this group have difficulty in forming warm personal relationships or lasting emotional ties, and they fear loneliness. Emotionally they are bland, uncommunicative, and defensive. Their feelings they conceal not only from others but basically from themselves; they avoid introspection. They are, however, very open to sensual impressions of many kinds, including sexual ones; fires, storms, and the like, are vividly imagined and fascinating to them. Their consciously preferred life style is one of sensuous enjoyment without entanglement.[10]

Not surprisingly, their self-concept is an inadequate one. They have little self-esteem; their sense of identity is conflicted or unclear, with impaired unconscious body images; and an air of disillusionment surrounds them, along with hints of depression. They are also sensitive to exploitation and tend to project blame onto others in what may be a paranoid interpretation of their feelings of inadequacy.

[10] It is of interest, in this setting of sensuality combined with emotional detachment, that in the Rorschach, Color-Word test, and Color-Form experiments they were notably inhibited in their responsiveness to color. This fact implies that they are unresponsive to emotional challenges from other people. They are also the only group whose pretest male figure drawings were more highly sexualized than the female drawings; the subsequent collapse of their male figures under LSD (see below) suggests that the sexualization of the pretest male figures reflects a rather fragile defense against a basically weak self-image.

As we might expect, their attitudes toward work and responsibility are poor. They readily give up their goals on encountering difficulties and resort to substitutes in fantasy.

Under LSD these subjects reported severe reactions, but the pattern of altered state was quite different from that of the previous groups, centering on bodily symptoms and unpleasant emotions. They reported many somatic symptoms (although only an average level of body image change), and more anger, anxiety, and fear of going crazy than any other group. They also reported changed meanings in experiences, sometimes with a paranoid tinge, and both losses of meaning in events and new interpretations of them. Inhibition of movement, speech, time, and thinking were also apparent. One specific response is noteworthy; each reported feeling like a child in the sense of feeling helpless and incapacitated.

The behavioral effects noted by the experimenters corresponded to their self-reports. Anxiety and hostility were the strongest effects, with suspiciousness, depression, and bodily preoccupation also above average. One of the three vomited.

Their cognitive performance under LSD showed extreme impairment in the directing of attention. In the cognitive test battery, their performance on all four tests was markedly disturbed, particularly on the three tests that depend most strongly on the capacity for sustained and focused attention. Recall of the previous day's Theme Lists was very poor, and their reading of the Color-Word page was highly variable. Comprehension was not notably affected, however; their learning of the Theme Lists, which had been rather poor on the pretest, was not much worse under the drug, and they did not become more interference-prone on the Color-Word test.

On the Color-Form test, they were the only subjects who did not respond more to color under LSD. This should be considered together with the Robinson Rhymes subtest of the cognitive battery, in which this was the only group that consistently performed poorly under the drug. The ability to solve the rhyming problems and an increased reliance on color in perceiving apparent movement both benefit from a playful, open attitude. This was completely impossible in the depressed, anxious, hostile state these subjects experienced under the drug.

The Earliest Memory data are inconclusive (one changed regressively, one did not change, and one was not tested) and none was scheduled for a drug day Rorschach. Their figure drawings, however, showed some striking common effects (see Fig. 5.3). While their pretest male drawings had been well-drawn and sexualized, under LSD they became more poorly drawn and smaller, appearing weaker, older, and quite desexualized. In marked contrast, their female drawings became more active, acquired hostile facial expressions, and were reasonably well drawn. Thus under LSD their poor self-concept was expressed directly through their inadequate male drawings, while the female figures looked as if they could dominate the male figures and served as a vehicle for the projection of their hostility.

Their comments under the drug convey the quality of their bodily sensations and the emotions associated with them: "Felt more sensitive, raw, as if the body was an open wound. Burning feelings inside my mouth, pains in my leg, like electric shock. Very painful most of the time. . . . waves of heat over my whole body as if I'd been popped into an electric toaster. You logically know what's happening to you, but emotionally you can't do anything about it. Feeling of fear, realizing it was the effects of the drug, but I couldn't do anything about them . . . hopeless."

Fear of their own hostility, as it became more openly expressed under the drug, was also evident. One of these subjects kept asking the experimenter whether others became so angry under the drug. When answered with the platitude that different people react differently, he said, "No, I mean has *anybody* felt this way. If one other person felt this way, then it's all right." When assured that such a reaction was not unheard of, he became markedly, although temporarily, less anxious.

The most direct connection between their personalities and drug reactions was in their hostile and paranoid tendencies, which became directly evident in their behavior under LSD, although expressed less openly in their self-report.[11] Their weak self-concepts and, in particular, their damaged body images erupted into their LSD-altered consciousness through a storm of unpleasant physical reactions so that they felt that their bodies were seriously threatened. Their usual blandness failed them; they felt an infantile helplessness and were flooded by anxiety over both the bodily threat and the consequences of the hostile feelings that came to the surface under the drug. Their figure drawings under LSD reflect in a striking way both their own collapse (male figure) and their feelings of threat and fear of retaliation (female figure).

It appears, then, that LSD broke down the defenses these subjects usually apply against their hostile and paranoid tendencies. Here the danger of the release of unmodified aggression in the altered state is striking; we cannot tell whether its potential effects would be limited to the subjects' own intense anxiety, or whether it would pose a threat to others as well.

The Case of David

Through David's autobiography and interviews, we learn that he is a college graduate, interested in becoming either an actor or a psychologist.

[11] As noted in Chapter 3, such feelings are, for evident reasons, among those most likely to be consciously suppressed in the questionnaire responses.

He appears to be very introspective and even obsessionally self-conscious in this regard (for example, in writing his autobiography, he frequently includes thoughts on the task itself rather than confining himself to his life story).

David is the oldest of several children. His early memories cluster around his mother who was chronically ill with a gastrointestinal ailment which eventually required surgery, and whom he remembers as a beautiful, aggressive woman. She worried that David might not be able to care for himself if she were to die and therefore taught him many household chores. She was harsh at times and he remembers her hitting him on the buttocks and hurting her hand on his wallet! Other memories of her suggest a strange and erotized relationship between mother and son, for example, overhearing her discuss a man whose penis became stuck in his wife's vagina. Anxiety in response to other memories suggesting primal scene experiences is also present, with anal features again notable (e.g., a fire necessitating the evacuation of his building; gas escaping from a stove, the latter memory accompanied by guilt because he had hit the stove with a stick).

While David aggrandizes his mother, he ridicules and fears his father; "Now, you take my father please!" is his introduction to the relevant section of his autobiography. His father was an obese, angry, critical, and apparently primitive man who fought with his wife; it was not a happy marriage. He also criticized his children relentlessly, especially about cleanliness. David has some positive feelings about him, however; his father took pride in David and often brought home gifts, notably tricks which David used to fool his friends, allowing him to feel superior to them.

One brother, who is described as bright and effeminate, is also belittled. David was surprised at his arrival and called him "Stinky." They shared a bedroom and often quarreled. David, who was asthmatic and allergic as a child himself, mothered the younger boy who also had asthma; the brother would vomit and David would clean it up.

David says little else of his early years other than that his family moved often. David was an average student in school, acting for the first time in grade school and recalling it as a performance full of errors. Later, acting was also marked by a mixture of simultaneous success and failure.

David seems to have an unconscious identification with his mother in his exhibitionism and in his sense of narcissism and grandiosity, which he shares with her, apparently to compensate for his feelings of physical and emotional inadequacy.

Although he is a college graduate, his autobiography is full of the simplest spelling errors (e.g., "are" for "our," and "incert" for "insert"), which suggests some type of learning block.

Socially David has many male friends but describes no overt homosexuality. He dates, but seems distant in his relationship with girls.

In summary, David seems to be a man who has a strong feminine identification with an overvalued, somatically damaged mother, along with a great fear of his critical, anally preoccupied father. There is an air of flamboyance and grandiosity about him, and hints of magical thinking. He is capable, but is in conflict about his career and success, undermining his abilities with simple errors which invite ridicule. He is making an apparently marginal heterosexual adjustment; he seems more like a frightened child than a man. Finally, much of the material suggests poor defenses, primitive and terrifying sexual fantasies with fears of losing control, a tendency to erotize relationships, and a rather unstable ego organization.

Through the Rorschach David appears to be a sensitive and bright person who can be witty and amusing. At the same time, he is somewhat guarded and in certain ways rather evasive. His favorite posture is that of a disarmingly self-effacing person, given to irony and self-derogation, who entertains others with his ready wit and coyness. Through all of this it is apparent that he is hiding behind a shield of humor, deflecting attention from his true feelings, and also warding off intense feelings that embarrass him. He is an emotionally labile person, prone to wide mood swings, and he frequently has trouble controlling his feelings. At times he may feel overwhelmed with affects and confounded by them; he experiences periods of anxiety and worry, and may also become somewhat depressed and fearful.

David's main defense against strong feelings as well as strong needs is to minimize them, disavow them, and somehow to deflect and transform them. Maintaining control seems to be one of his overriding concerns. He views self-control as the only road to success; one must hide and suppress one's feelings, one must carry on bravely in the face of loss, and one must never give in to grief and despair. He may therefore be rather slow-moving and dry, and he readily becomes overcontrolled and guarded. Moreover, he is seemingly free of any ambitiousness and appears undemanding. It is also characteristic of him to maintain control by simply ignoring unwelcome stimuli and disavowing unwelcome thoughts. This may make him seem evasive and even somewhat slippery or elusive. Although his evasions can at times be rather clever and ingenious, at other times they can be naive and ingenuous and may make him seem like a pollyanna.

David is an intellectually gifted person and often resorts to intellectualizations. These are not usually very successful, however, because of a tendency to become overly concrete in his thinking, as well as a bit arbitrary. He may sometimes fall into a fussy and unproductive kind of rumination, and he may have difficulty making any decisions. He has a strong wish for decisions to be made for him by others, and he also shows a tendency to externalize responsibility. He probably enjoys a quite rich fantasy life that is taken up mainly with simple dreams of glory and heroism.

The test suggests a preoccupation with punishment that is partly associated with underlying retaliatory impulses and hostility toward his father. He abhors both hostile and aggressive feelings, and his experiences of anxiety are probably associated with his struggles to ward them off. One of his ways of avoiding anxiety and depression is to try to laugh them off, and at such times he may become somewhat silly and maniclike, showing a degree of inappropriate affect. This inappropriateness, along with his strained denials and minimizations, is quite prominent at times and contributes to an autistic streak that may reach borderline proportions. The tests also hint at a sadistic conception of sex that is connected with his abhorrence of aggression. He may harbor some autistic fantasies about sex, centering on a fear of being damaged by sexual intercourse.

David has, then, a relatively inhibited obsessive-compulsive character with prominent hysterical features and some schizoid tendencies. Currently he is quite anxious and mildly depressed. Overall, his personality integration is moderately good, although under some strain at present.

In his altered LSD state, David experienced a wide range of disturbing somatic symptoms and became very anxious. He is the subject cited above who become anxious about his emerging angry feelings and was somewhat reassured on being told that other people also had them. He then seemed, in a sense, to take advantage of an implied license to be hostile under the drug: "In a way it reminds me of my grandfather, in that he is very blunt and speaks his piece, and this is not right, it shouldn't be that only an old person should speak as they think, be as harsh as they want—it should be for the young, too. That's why I'm interested in doing this experiment." He said afterward that the drug "brings out what I depress (sic): aggression, harshness, distortions."

The identification with a hostile old man appeared in his figure drawings (see Figure 5.3), which showed a dramatic shift from pretest obsessional defenses to an eruption of hostility under LSD. His pretest drawings were made painstakingly, slowly, and very well, with much detail. The male, "a young salesman," stands rigidly, carrying a briefcase on which are the subject's initials; the female, wearing a bathing suit and standing tightly erect with a pool of water at her feet, was characterized as a "bathing ugly." The loose, wild, and very expressive caricatures drawn under LSD were a "sly, tricky, old man of 80 or 90," wearing a formless robe, and a woman of 75, described by David as "kindly, generous, pleasant, happy, and proper," but in fact with a rather triumphant expression and much more vigorous-looking than the old man.

His behavior was both more depressed and more suspicious than that

(a)

(b)

Figure 5.3. David's Human Figure Drawings. (a) Pretest Day; (b) LSD Day. The left-hand figure of each pair was drawn first.

of the others in Group IV. Clearly, the sense of impairment and catastrophe that he usually worked so hard to disavow in the waking state became compelling under LSD. The pretest earliest memory was of traveling in a train with his mother and running to a strange man, who was "polite" to him, while his mother slept (perhaps a muted version of maternal abandonment). The drug day memory was of a fire in his house, a mad rush in which everyone was fleeing and during which he was carried downstairs but then left in the hallway crying, "Why don't they take me out?"

While he gave the clinical impression that paranoid ideas developed under the drug, these were not openly verbalized at the time because he was very guarded about revealing them. Afterward, however, he reported that he had refused to shake hands on being introduced to a new experimenter because he noticed a red mark on the other man's hand and knew it meant that if he accepted the outstretched hand he would be revealed as a homosexual.

David's performance in the experimental tasks under LSD confirms the impression gained from the qualitative material. His extreme anxiety was reflected in poor performance in the cognitive test battery, poor recall of the previously learned Theme Lists, and a sharp increase in the erratic variability of his Color-Word reading. His inability to give himself up to the LSD experience enjoyably was shown in his poor handling of the Robinson Rhymes test but even more strikingly in the Color-Form test; he was one of the two subjects in the entire study whose perception of movement relied on form more under LSD than on the pretest day. It is possible that his increased use of form represented an attempt at defense against the emotions aroused in him by the stimulation of color under the drug.[12]

His ability to comprehend was not as strongly affected, as shown by the fact that in the LSD state both his learning of the new neutral Theme Lists and the interference effect in the Color-Word test were at the average level for the drug group.

To summarize, what LSD did to this anxious, obsessional, defensive young man, with his latent hostile and paranoid tendencies, was to concretize his conception of his body as quite damaged; to bring his hostilities, suspicions, and anxieties into the open; and to bring into consciousness some of his worst fears of helplessness and abandonment. The altered state apparently weakened his defenses and brought out his autistic, paranoid thinking, which was of course potentially quite dangerous.

GROUP V

All four subjects in Group V have very poorly integrated personalities, and their IQs are the lowest of any group; in both respects their less adequate functioning differs significantly from that of the remaining subjects. Furthermore, three of the four show schizoid manifestations in their Ror-

[12] This interpretation is supported by the fact that on the LSD day his use of color on the first trial was only slightly below average; it dropped drastically on the second trial, however.

schachs. These facts should be kept in mind in considering a peculiarity in the personality assessment descriptions of this group. While they deviate from average on more items than any other group, they are below the mean on most of the assessment items that characterize them.[13] In other words, they are described in terms of what they are not.

Thus they were rated as notably lacking in hostility of all sorts, as not rebellious, sensitive to threats, nor afraid of being exploited, and as not experiencing their impulses as ego-alien or fearing the loss of control over them. They are not depressed or angry with themselves, and they do not feel unloved or identify with outcasts. They are not introspective, sensitive, intellectual, or interested in creative pursuits; their interests are narrow and they are poor at problem solving. They are also not anxious, tense, restless, defensive, or withdrawn, and they are not given to undoing, isolation, or ruminative thinking.

The only positive statement about these subjects from the personality assessment concerns a hypomanic kind of role playing, shown in their propensity for clowning and a changeable, chameleonlike quality of fitting their behavior to any setting. This is reinforced by some of the ancillary test data, which identify them as exhibitionistic, interested in social activities, with a need for guidance and a clinging quality, but quite lacking in intellectual or artistic interests. They are also given to avoiding solitude, feelings, speculation, and introspection.

A closer look at their pretest Rorschachs helps to clarify the picture. Their protocols are long (the average number of responses is 49) but of poor quality, with many $F-$ scores (concepts that fail to fit the forms in the blot). While primary-process manifestations occur in many responses, they are unusual in that the bulk of it emerges only on inquiry. These subjects use obsessional defenses, but rather primitive and ineffective ones; they avoid recognition of the implicit primary-process elements in their percepts until queried and also find fault with their responses and make unsuccessful attempts to rationalize them through humor or intellectualization. There are, in addition, notable verbal peculiarities and failures of logic. The overall impression is one of very poor ego functioning in a setting of decompensated or more fully developed obsessional tendencies.

They give the impression of a lack of identity or sense of self, rather than an inadequate or conflict-ridden one. In keeping with this impression, we find that their pretest male figure drawings were quite poorly drawn, and the female figures were in costume, sometimes explicitly related to a role in a play, and rather faceless. One described his female drawing thus:

[13] All other groups are above the mean on a half or more of the items that characterize them.

". . . just a clothes horse, to style clothes around; I don't see her as a person, just a mannequin." Their drawings thus use clothing in the service of role-playing, reflecting a lack of individual identities.

An additional finding of special interest, in view of their drug reaction, is that on a specially constructed MMPI scale of bodily concern and symptoms all of the subjects in Group V had extremely high scores, particularly in regard to worry about their bodies and their state of health.

To understand their personality pattern we may contrast them with Group II, also schizoid and poorly integrated, but of average intellectual functioning and characterized as narcissistic, regressive, phobic and counterphobic, somewhat paranoid, and with much open disturbance. Group V subjects show none of these features and are in fact quite guarded. They may best be viewed as very constricted, schizoid people who show little sign of either open disturbance or struggle against inner turmoil. They are limited in their intellectual functioning and inner life; their preferred way of getting along in the world seems to be through a shallow sort of social interaction in which they mold themselves according to the immediate demands of the situation, lacking any clear direction from within. At times, they also appear somewhat manic.[14] The facade of cheerfulness probably hides an underlying diffuse depression. The one clear channel for the discharge af anxiety for these subjects is through somatization and worry about their bodies.

Under LSD these subjects varied widely in the extent of the total reactions they reported in the questionnaire, but all showed comparatively little effect in their overt behavior. The subjective effects that characterized their altered state were concentrated in their bodies, both as somatic symptoms and as body image changes. There was a loss of body boundaries; they felt as if they were merging into their surroundings and they felt heavy and old. They reported more bodily effects than any other group. A slowing down of movement and thought was also reported, as well as anxiety and fear of losing control. They did not, however, report any marked thinking disorder, meaning change, suspiciousness or visual distortions. In other words, psychoticlike ideation was not evident.

As to their overt behavior, the only trend was some evidence of depression, but in no case was it extreme. Observers saw less anxiety than would be expected from their self-reports. When it was noted, it tended to be relatively short-lived.

It is also noteworthy that their pupils were significantly ($p < .01$) more dilated than those of other subjects. Thus the only objective measure

[14] These qualities may be quite adaptive in an acting career. It is striking that some of the subjects whose subsequent careers have been most successful are in this group.

available of a somatic LSD effect confirms their self-report of a massive physical reaction.[15]

Group V may be contrasted with Groups III and IV, both of which had an altered organismic state with strong ideational and bodily reactions. The Group III subjects experienced, for a brief time, extreme regression and a massive breakdown of defenses, and they were flooded by anxiety; their bodily reactions were an inseparable part of their panic state. Group IV subjects had impaired body images to begin with which became accentuated and conscious under LSD. Their somatic symptoms were also used as a defense against the hostile feelings that came to consciousness as their obsessional defenses were weakened in the LSD state. Group V subjects, in contrast, seem to have an unusual investment in their bodies, and under the drug their altered sense of self and a wide range of fantasies were expressed through their bodily symptoms and changes rather than ideationally. Psychoticlike ideation was virtually nonexistent, and although they reported feeling anxious it was not notably evident to the experimenters.

The experimental tasks did not yield much in the way of clear trends for Group V, except to indicate that LSD did not interfere very much with their performance on the cognitive tests. Their pretest cognitive performance was, as we might expect, not very good, but clearly the drug state did not *disorganize* their normal intellectual processes, as it did in other subjects. The most striking change was that they reported new earliest memories under LSD, more regressive than their pretest memories, with a marked increase in oral content and emphasis on the body and on clothing. They also showed a strong "rub-off effect" in the Uloomoo-Takete experiment, that is, a fusion (or failure to differentiate) between the attributes of a pictured face and those of its assigned name. On the Color-Form test, they showed only a minimal shift toward greater reliance on color.

Their figure drawings under LSD, as on the pretest, tended to be nude or costumed rather than in normal attire. The changes from pretest to drug were not great, and the figures were not more poorly drawn on the experimental day. The one point of interest is that, while their male figures tended to be as well-constructed or better drawn and somewhat more sexualized under LSD, their female drawings became smaller and less sexualized; in all cases the shift in the relative sexualization of the two drawings was toward a more sexualized male figure and a less sexualized female. This may be another manifestation of their heightened concern with their own bodies in the altered state.

The drug day Rorschachs of these subjects were in many ways similar

[15] In addition, one of these subjects vomited. This happened, in fact, to one subject in each of the three groups reporting the strongest somatic reactions (III, IV, and V).

to their pretest records and, in contrast to the usual effect of the LSD states, certain pathological features of the pretest record appeared less often under the drug. These were obsessional defenses, delayed expression of primary-process elements, verbal peculiarities, logical contradictions, self-criticism, and the unsuccessful use of humor, intellectualization, and esthetic contexts. Thus their rather primitive and ineffectual attempts at obsessional control through various forms of avoidance and intellectualization were utilized less under the drug, and there was less need for them because less primary process came through. This was also the only group to use color more often as a determinant of their Rorschach percepts under LSD. This finding suggests that these subjects turned away from introspection under the drug (this may be related to their reduced use of their obsessional defenses). In all, these findings suggest that in their altered organismic state these subjects expressed both impulses and defenses more on the bodily level than on subjective and ideational levels.

Their form quality on the Rorschach, which had been poor on the pretest, became worse under the drug, primarily through a marked increase in vague forms, although there was also an increase in their already high use of poor forms ($F-$). Two types of condensation or contamination produced by these subjects are of special interest even though they involve only a few responses. These are fusions of two competing percepts and images of composite creatures combining parts from different animals to form unreal hybrids. Both kinds were more common than usual in this group's pretest Rorschachs, and they increased further in the LSD state. Such responses represent a clear abandonment of the attempt to rationalize or rule out inconsistent percepts, calling to mind the fact that these subjects, in the Uloomoo-Takete experiment, failed to maintain clear-cut boundaries between the usually separate schemata of the face and its name.

There was a noteworthy shift in the aggressive content of their Rorschach responses from pretest to drug. These subjects saw more objects or victims of aggression than agents of aggression on pretest (the reverse of the usual balance in this total series), but dropped references to such victims under LSD, thereby shifting toward the more usual balance. Outweighing this shift, however, was a striking increase in images related to the results of aggression, such as damaged or maimed creatures or blood. An increase in this type of percept is associated with a strong somatic component in the LSD state and apparently is related to the experience of bodily impairment experienced by these subjects under the drug.

To summarize their Rorschach changes in the LSD state, these subjects used their usually ineffective ideational (obsessional) defenses less often, and the forms of their percepts became more vague and fused. The experienced assault on their physical identities, expressed both in powerful bodily symptoms and Rorschach images of destruction, then emerged in full force.

While there are puzzling elements in the personalities of Group V subjects and in their LSD state, both their personalities and their drug state have a common focus—their bodies. Their sense of self, or any verbalized sense of personal identity, is undeveloped and may exist in largely nonverbal bodily schemata. They avoid awareness of inner life, and their primary defenses against anxiety take place on the somatic level. Their propensity for role playing and their interest in costumes and clothing may be seen as attempts to compensate, through external substitutes, for a poorly formulated sense of identity.

It would seem that the body itself has assumed a major role in their definition of themselves; thus a threat to the integrity of their bodies constitutes a threat to their sense of self to an unusual degree. For these subjects the drug state is just such a threat, so that their bodies become the focus of their drug reaction. Perhaps it takes place in the following manner. Since these subjects are relatively more alert to physical symptoms than to their psychic life, it may be that a given degree of physiological drug effect, such as moderate dizziness or nausea, seizes their attention more than it would that of other subjects. However, their greater pupillary dilatation suggests the possibility that they may in fact suffer stronger somatic reactions as well. The nature of the connection between their bodily symptoms and their anxiety is unclear. It may be that they tend to defend themselves against anxiety, from whatever source, through somatization, or that bodily symptoms are particularly threatening to them; both seem likely to be true for these men.

In any event, the bodily changes and the accompanying anxiety *are* the essential characteristics of their LSD altered state. Defenses against anxiety are often classified into two broad types: defense through denial, repression, avoidance, or constriction; and defense through ideational elaboration or rationalization, for example, by handling the anxiety through paranoid ideas or by attaching it phobically to a specific object. Normally, these subjects rely heavily on the first kind of defense, but the increase in anxiety and physical symptoms that develop under LSD makes denial of the sources of anxiety much more difficult to maintain. They do not, however, seem to have elaborate ideational defenses readily available to them, and therefore they do not develop delusions, hallucinations, or their nonpsychotic variants under the drug, but simply endure the anxiety and physical distress.

There remains the question of why their behavior did not reflect anxiety and bodily concern to as great a degree as did their own report on the questionnaire. We can approach an answer in two ways: in terms of the general problem of assessing anxiety in the entire group of drug subjects, or in terms of the personalities of the subjects comprising Group V.

Taking all the drug subjects together, we find that the behavioral measure of anxiety correlates .46 with Scale D, which is the best questionnaire measure of anxiety. Thus while the correlation is statistically significant, it is far from perfect; the self-report accounts for only a modest portion of the variation in overtly anxious behavior. Scale B, however, which represents the most psychoticlike aspects of the self-report, has a comparable correlation with anxious behavior, even though Scales B and D are unrelated.

Examination of the actual patterns of scores is more illuminating: extremely anxious behavior occurs only when both Scales B and D are high, while experimenters reported little manifest anxiety when either or both were low. In other words, a subject who by his own report is anxious loses control over his behavior only if his drug reaction includes the more psychoticlike drug effects; this did not occur in Group V.

Another interpretation of these same data begins with a recognition that anxiety is an extremely elusive and controversial concept. The assessment literature is divided between proponents of behavioral measures, based on external observations, and advocates of subjective measures, based on self-report—a phenomenological conception as compared to a behavioristic one. Our data support the interpretation that what the experimenters *called* anxiety was sometimes the agitation accompanying a subjective state that was not actually experienced as anxiety but as any of various pathological types of ideation.

There is another factor that may contribute to the limited expression of anxiety in the overt behavior of Group V subjects. These subjects typically use external sources of role definition to guide their behavior, and they modulate their actions freely and appropriately when given a stage role, a social situation, or some other prop. Without such guides, however, they are not very expressive, particularly where their own feelings are concerned; this may account in part for their limited expression in behavior of the anxiety they report as subjectively experienced.

The Case of Eugene

As seen through his autobiography and interviews, Eugene is the youngest of several children, most of them girls. His autobiography is striking for its almost total concentration on himself, with others appearing only as shadows who crossed his path.

As a child, he was pampered and yet felt lonely, creating imaginary companions and animals to share the hours with him. He was gregarious and very active, and successful in sports. Yet he sees these activities as having made him ill, although he envies his sisters because they could do exciting and dangerous things such as climb roofs and eat green apples; he was not permitted to do such things.

His preschool years are vague in his memory. His report of the grade school years is notable for his lack of controls. He would have temper tantrums and hit his schoolmates. He was sexually very curious, and explored first himself and then both boys and girls at an early age. He felt that his parents expected too much of him, yet they did not encourage his education. He was repeatedly concerned with competition which for him had elements of attempting to survive against his adversaries. He recalls bullies who wanted to beat him up and girls who were brighter than he. In this competition he often cheated and, although he was caught at it and felt guilty, he continued such practices. His temper particularly upset his mother, and in his later teens he tried to control it.

In high school he was active in sports and organizations and had girl friends who were "available" to him as conquests; his father bragged about his son's prowess. He felt hemmed in by parental curfews, however, and disillusioned by his parents' financial limitations; he took advantage of them when he could.

In college, sports lost some of their value as a provider of power when his team did poorly (losing a stuggle with death, as he put it) and, after failing to be accepted in a professional school, he decided to teach. He was interested in acting, but felt it was too closely identified with femininity and homosexuality. Yet in the end he refused a job as an athletic coach for fear of depending on the skills of others, and chose to act so that he could gain the recognition of the "masses" and be "unlimitedly creative."

Once he had completed his education (as he put it, after the "college and academic old hen had put me out from under her wing"), he encountered many obstacles to success and considerable pressure from his family's expectations. His present goals are to "satisfy the basic urge of mankind—that of picking a partner in life to reproduce life," and to rise above the masses by expressing himself as an actor; but he is full of fear of not reaching these goals.

Eugene appears to be a very narcissistic man who, while having had many relationships, perceives them in remote, impersonal terms. He has struggled all his life with envy of women (viewed as more powerful and creative, particularly in their birth-giving capacity) and with his own strong feminine identification. He seems to have feared annihilation, and he attempted by counterphobic means to deny his feminine-homosexual longings through sports and other stereotypically masculine activities. As of now, however, these measures seem to have failed him and he is caught in a conflict between masculinity and femininity.

His early years were lonely and he may have been quite depressed. The death of a sibling may have been important in stimulating pregnancy fantasies in him. There are signs of sexual overstimulation in an otherwise barren home setting, and his sexual and aggressive controls were poor, with an autoerotic component. Despite some intellectual deficiencies, he was generally a capable and adequate person. The intensity of his need for repair of his damaged self-image led to a corruption of his superego and psychopathic features in the form of an amoral seeking of success through any means.

Eugene has not resolved his conflicts and remains anxious, somewhat paranoid, and still in the midst of a struggle against annihilation; he has somewhat grandiose hopes that exhibiting himself to "the masses" will provide him with an identity and the protection he so desperately seeks.

The Rorschach interpretation portrays Eugene as an unstable person, subject to sharp manic-depressive mood swings, who is currently depressed. He appears to be slowed down in his actions and thought, and he may at times feel rather immobilized. At such times he may also be troubled by a sense of confusion that he calls "distraction," when he cannot think clearly or communicate with others and is overwhelmed by a rush of feelings and sensations. It is difficult for him to acknowledge these problems, and he is prone to dismiss his fears and anxieties in a way that may be strikingly incongruous. Similarly, he tends to minimize and disavow the significance of his actions in a way that is quite inappropriate, showing poor judgment and resorting to strained and sometimes peculiar rationalizations. All of this, together with evidence of a noteworthy thought disorder (the ease with which he tolerates loose thinking and far-fetched associations, and the degree to which he perseverates and ruminates) raises the question of a borderline schizophrenic picture. Yet he is not without significant strengths and adaptive resources, and indications are that his current unstable and depressed state is being exacerbated by the fact that he is struggling with an acute crisis having to do with his identity and his career.

The Rorschach points up a probably long-standing and prominent streak of egocentricity that combines with grandiosity. There are also indications of a serious problem over autonomy. Defining and maintaining his separateness from others has probably been a major issue for Eugene for a long time. One way in which he seems to have resolved the problem is to regard himself as special, and combined with this is a striking tendency to regard himself as an object. However, there are indications that he is troubled by the idea that he is so different from others. For one thing, acceptance and recognition by others (adulation) is really very important to him, and he must therefore avoid being at odds with them. He is also preoccupied with competition; but it is more comparison-oriented than achievement-oriented, as it is based on such concerns as whether he is bigger and better than others (how does he compare?), and motivated by a need to be the superior one in all respects.

Eugene's egocentricity, grandiosity, and weak judgment may combine to form a paranoidlike orientation. He often shows a need to integrate everything into a grand scheme as well as a readiness to distort or to slight reality in order to fit things into his plan. Moreover, he is ever ready to feel tricked, taken advantage of, and trapped. There is also an indication of some preoccupation with "evil" that is mainly associated with masculinity and the father figure, as well as with a sadomasochistic conception of sexuality. He appears to have important underlying fears of punishment for sexuality. At the same time, indicators are that he has long had difficulty dealing with any angry and hostile feelings.

Among his assets is the fact that Eugene is an open and unguarded person with some noteworthy capacity for rather well-integrated emotions. He seems to have the capacity for some genuine reflectiveness and sensitivity. For example, he may at times deal quite insightfully with his problems concerning automony. To some extent, this is possible for him because he has recourse to the defense of isolation of affect along with a propensity to intellectualize. One of his favored roles at present is that of the philosophical man, the one with an all-embracing imagination and far-ranging ideas. He uses this self-image to deal with his doubts and insecurity about his career as well as about his adulthood. The big drawback for him is the fact that he lacks sufficient intellectual strength and psychological-mindedness to support these intellectual pretensions. Therefore he readily becomes overly pedantic, stilted, and given to empty and pretentious displays of affectations and mannerisms. Moreover, despite the fact that he does have the capacity for a reasonably well-modulated fantasy life, his fantasies at present are liable to become vivid flights that can be quite bizarre and overly idiosyncratic.

In summary, as seen in his Rorschach, Eugene has noteworthy borderline schizophrenic features[16] along with manic-depressive tendencies; he has a poorly integrated, but not constricted, obsessive-compulsive character. There are narcissistic features and some paranoid tendencies.

Under LSD Eugene's reaction was characteristic of Group V: that is, concentrated almost entirely on his body, with extreme feelings of anxiety. He expressed the interweaving of emotions and bodily feelings quite artic-

[16] As a note of caution, it is noted that persons with strong tendencies to use somatization as a defense often give schizophrenic-appearing Rorschachs although their behavior may remain free from any psychotic symptoms indefinitely.

ulately: "At one point my entire body was shaking, a state of feeling like laughing and crying. A tingling sensation through my body. I almost released laughter, but the minute it would start, it would go into sobbing. I imagine it comes from the dislike and fear of unknown feeling. Like a balloon near the bursting point, body and mind felt like a balloon, and if it should break, my body and mind would go into a thousand pieces—disintegrate." Asked if he felt he had lost control he said, "Nearly, first physically, then mentally. On the threshold of loss of control of the body, and because of that possibly also my mind."

Ths dependence of his self-concept on the integrity of his body was verbalized in a follow-up interview 2 years later: "The first time I've ever accepted and thought that I was going to accept complete defeat. I came in with a very strong ego that the drug wouldn't hit me too hard. I've always been most confident of my physical being, and that's where it attacked me—at my strongest points." What Eugene calls his "strongest points" are in fact his most vulnerable under LSD, perhaps because of their very importance to him.

His fear, of course, was of annihilation—losing his "self" entirely: "If the drug is so strong the thought of brain damage did enter my mind." He reported that the anxiety and fantasies of destruction were overwhelming: "The anxiety was terrific, it was on the threshold of insanity. At one point I thought, if I go much further I'll froth at the mouth and run, if I start running I won't stop. I knew that if I ran through the wall, and a couple of other walls, and into the street, and in front of a taxicab, and I was lying in the street, I still wouldn't get rid of that anxiety. It was an internal thing." He stopped smoking for a year afterward, "using the thought that the anxiety of not smoking was so small compared with that experience; like comparing a scratch to an operation."

Nevertheless, the experimenters did not note any substantial loss of control in his behavior, except for his evident physical distress; he was noted at times to be shaking, and he vomited. It is also noteworthy that the paranoid tendencies inferred from his Rorschach did not produce any paranoid interpretations of his distress. These trends in his personality are expressed primarily as simple grandiosity, with little tendency to project blame. The impact of the drug demolished his grandiose notions about himself, but compensatory paranoid projections did not develop. Rather, he felt more helpless and immature, suggesting a regression to a more primitive state. Most striking was the new earliest memory that he reported. This was of someone looking down on him, wearing a lavender shawl. He checked with his mother, who told him that during the first 6 weeks of his life his nurse had always worn such a shawl.

Both his figure drawings and Rorschach test under LSD corresponded to the pattern already described as typical for Group V. The male and female drawings on both days were rather abstractly drawn figures in Elizabethan costumes; they became even more featureless in the drug state, resembling dolls for displaying the costumes rather than real people. On the pretest Rorschach test both the formal features and content of his responses showed much evidence of the primary process. There was an extreme amount of oral and sexual content, with strained attempts to rationalize this libidinal material through intellectualization; form quality was poor, and there were many self-references and verbal peculiarities. Under LSD the oral and sexual content, as well as the strained intellectualization, dropped to an average level, and there were fewer peculiar verbalizations, although still more than average for subjects in the LSD state. There were still many self-references, and form quality remained poor, with an increased use of vague forms. The one notable increase was in the images of damage (results of aggression). Thus both the influx of libidinal material seen on the pretest day and his relatively ineffectual obsessional defenses against it fell away under LSD, and his experience of potential bodily destruction was expressed directly; compensatory ideation did not appear.

The effects of the LSD state on his experimental test performance were very similar to those seen in David in that they reflected mainly his pervasive anxiety. Recall of the previous day's theme lists was poor, and his Color-Word reading became much more erratic; his use of color in the Color-Form test, in contrast to that of most subjects, did not increase. In new learning of neutral theme lists and Color-Word interference, however, his performance was similar to that of the average drug subject. He was not given the cognitive test battery.

Understandably enough, he felt for some time after taking LSD that he wouldn't do it again "for a half million dollars." Eventually, however, he felt that he had more empathy with others and that he could understand the terror that an insane person goes through. He was also impressed by the splitting of his viewpoint: ". . . the feeling of part of the brain being perfectly rational, and the other part going off on a wild goose chase." He was still not eager to take LSD again, but he had at least found some compensation and felt that having lived through it once he would not be as anxious again. He had thus mobilized some resources for dealing with the experience, at least in retrospect.

GROUP VI

The seven men in this group are strikingly independent, assertive and hard-headed. This is the largest single group in our study. They are active, cope well with the problems of life, and act on their own initiative, pushing their goals with persistence, even against opposition. They see themselves as practical and realistic, and in fact show good common sense and judgment. They prefer action, including physical activity and adventure, to feeling or speculation. Their thinking tends to be rather literal and they are notably not intellectual, intuitive, introspective, or ruminative. They are given to acting out their conflicts, rather than experiencing them consciously.

Both fantasy and sensuality seem shut out from these men's experience. Their figure drawings were particularly lacking in sexuality; one subject even drew stick figures. The lack of primary-process material in their pretest Rorschachs was also quite striking. The constriction of their inner life can also be seen in their earliest memories, which were quite detached and lacking in warmth. Themes of dependence and orality were lacking in comparison with other subjects, and the subjects tended to appear in the memories as observers. The recollections were strongly embedded in reality and also showed concern with ego boundaries. They stressed themes of identity, independence, and freedom from controls. Insofar as they were active in these memories, they behaved aggressively toward others, often losing control.

Their need for independence and self-assertion is tinged with mistrust and a fear of being controlled. They tend to be defensive, manipulative, and ungenerous; they feel unloved, and hostility colors their relationships. Positions of authority and status are important to them, and they emphasize discipline; some insularity and social prejudice are evident. They are clearly heterosexual and have few conscious conflicts or feelings of inadequacy in regard to sexuality.

In all, the personality picture of these men corresponds to the stereotype of the masculine role in our culture and, by and large, they fulfill this role rather successfully, although at the apparent cost of considerable constriction and inhibition.

Their reaction to LSD was minimal; of all subjects, they gave the fewest indications of an altered state, in both their self-reports and in their overt behavior. Thus while there were several different types of strong LSD reactions seen in our study, there was only one kind of weak reaction. Both their total questionnaire score and total behavioral change were significantly lower than those of Groups I through IV; Group V had significantly higher questionnaire scores than Group VI, but also showed minimal behavioral changes. In view of Group VI's apparent resistance to the psychological effects of LSD, it is of interest that their pupils were significantly less dilated than those of the other drug subjects.

It is well to keep in mind, however, that these subjects *were* affected by the drug. Minimal though their reaction was, it was significantly greater than that of the placebo subjects, more so in their self-report (.001 level) than in their behavior (.01 level).

Their altered state was, however, limited to certain kinds of effects. They reported feeling and acting silly, difficulties in concentration, impaired judgment, and a variety of somatic effects (dizziness, numbness, nausea, and feeling weak, hot, and cold) as often as did the other drug subjects. Behaviorally, they showed fluctuations in affect (mostly depressive) to about the same degree as other drug subjects. They were also observably anxious and preoccupied with their bodily symptoms (significantly more so than the placebo group, although significantly less than the other drug subjects).

Their questionnaire responses indicated that their moderate degree of anxiety was focused on the concern that they might lose control of their bodies or their emotions but did not involve fear of going crazy as was evident in Group V. They reported virtually none of the more bizarre features of the altered state seen under LSD, however, such as changes in meaning, perceptual distortions, changes in self or body image, and loss of contact with reality.

In keeping with Group VI's minimally altered state, the cognitive test battery showed no impairment in directing and focusing attention; the first three tests in the cognitive battery were completely unimpaired; Color-Word reading did not become more variable; and on the Theme Lists, although their pretest learning was poorer than average, their recall of the pretest lists under the drug was good. They did not do quite as well, however, on the tests of comprehension, although they did not do very poorly either. There was a moderate increase in interference proneness in the Color-Word test, and the learning of new Theme Lists under LSD was also moderately impaired, but less so than for the average subject in the study.

Both the Color-Form test and the Robinson Rhymes test showed some drug effect but, again, it was not extreme. The impairment in Robinson Rhymes is of interest, in view of these subjects' excellent performance in the other three tests from the cognitive battery. It may reflect the fact that, to the extent that these men showed mood changes, depression was more typical of them than was a maniclike reaction (the latter aided performance on this test under LSD).

As for the projective tests, each of these subjects gave essentially the same earliest memory under the drug as he had on the pretest. Their figure drawings under LSD became larger and somewhat more poorly drawn, especially the female figure, which probably reflects some impairment in motor control, but they were not very different from their pretest drawings. Male figures remained adequately sexualized, including a clear representation of the genital area, but the female figures were less sexualized under the drug. The latter figures did, however, acquire a hostile expression in several cases; this may be a projection of their attitude toward women, rather than a generalized expression of hostility as it seemed to be in Group IV.

The subjects in Group VI showed virtually no change in their Rorschachs in the altered state except for some improvement in the form-quality of their percepts. This resulted from an increase in superior forms and a decrease in vague forms (they did not produce any bad forms on either day), an effect also found in the placebo group and thus probably a test-retest effect.

These men, then, normally so hard-headed and in control of their lives and themselves, were strikingly resistant to LSD, and resisted most strongly the primary-process and altered state effects of the drug. Their usual bent for acting out and focusing on the "real world," their guardedness, and their inhibition of fantasy and inner life in general, continued to operate strongly and effectively under the drug, so that only somatic effects, some report of difficulties in concentration, and some silliness appeared. These symptoms indicate very minimal alteration in their state of consciousness.

These men were quite successful in avoiding any really disturbing drug effects, however. They would perhaps not feel that they had missed out on an interesting experience, since they lack the taste for such experiences that we have found, for example, in Group I.

The Case of Frank

As seen through his autobiography and interviews, Frank is a young actor from a broken home who feels that he is a child of doom, frustrated by fate, and who steadfastly attempts to avoid the ultimate defeat he seems to arrange for himself unconsciously.

Frank is the younger of two brothers. He describes his childhood in terms of the great depression in the country at the time, yet avoids focus on the suffering and disruptions within his family. He describes his personal suffering without notable emotion, although an underlying air of hopelessness is readily detectable. In this world "bent apone (sic) destroying its self (sic)," his father was an alcoholic who frequented the local bars where he seldom heeded the pleas of Frank and his brother to come home. As a result, his picture of his father is quite remote. His image of his mother, however, is just as empty; we are told little about her, simply that she had her ups and downs. Frank's closest family relationship was with his brother, with whom he shared a room and played games into the night, but even this brother seems but a shadow who eventually left home.

Frank's early years were spent on the move; there were no friends and no stability. Before Frank reached adolescence, his parents were divorced; Frank says virtually nothing about this event. His mother eventually married and had more children. Frank began to make his ties to friends outside his home.

Before puberty, Frank had several homosexual experiences which he discontinued quickly. Then, very early in puberty, he turned to girls and began a long series of sexual relationships. At first many of these girls were closely identified with his mother, and one senses a great struggle with incestuous feelings toward her, heightened by the absence of his father and by the stimulation of his mother's many suitors. In this pubertal period he tended to act out (for example, by refusing to do school work) and to somatize. A feeling of great struggle with murderous rage also pervades this period; Frank used much denial and impersonal projection onto the world about him to cover these feelings.

Frank's main area of achievement was athletics, through which he became a hero and developed many friendships. As an adolescent, Frank developed a bone ailment which was at first frightening but was treated quickly without sequelae. He became a high school athletic star, only to injure his knee in his senior year. Surgery failed to correct the problem, and he never played again; he feels that he has been on the decline ever since.

He went to college for 2 years but did not do well. His mother was killed in an accident, and he stopped school because of lack of funds. He writes: "When I first learned that my Mother had been killed it felt like a hammer had hit me, but I soon got over it, and we bureid (sic) her two days later." This passage typifies his momentary feelings of being overwhelmed, followed by flight, denial, and the discarding of the affect. After his mother's death he turned to acting for admiration and compensation, but he describes little success and great hope (which has a hollow ring). He ends his autobiography by claiming strength through suffering and disclaiming any wish for pity.

Frank seems to be a person who turns away from his inner feelings and fantasies, on the one hand, and from the painful realities of his life, on the other. He seems to feel overwhelmed and depressed, yet he tries almost desperately to deny it. He is frightened of emotions, of defeat, and of loss, and seeks restitution through exhibitionism, counterphobic actions, and a flight into reassuring sexualized relationships. Projection, externalization, somatization, and denial are also prominent among his defenses. There is some identification with an apparently psychopathic father. His central conflicts, however, seem concealed, possibly because his primary concern is still that of finding stable objects with which to relate and through which he might find an identity of his own. He denies anger and maintains a heterosexual orientation but does not convey a sense of warmth or closeness to anyone. He seems headed for further unconsciously self-inflicted defeats, and an air of hopelessness pervades his communications.

The pretest Rorschach test indicates that Frank is deep in an identity crisis, and he seems to be quite depressed. It is difficult to separate the effects of his current difficulties from his more long-term characteristics. He seems to be a stiff and rigidly defended person, who can become so defensive and guarded that he may also become quite detached and aloof. Much of this is probably in the service of his current need to maintain a tight control over his intense conflicts and turbulent feelings. Underneath his almost masklike exterior, he seems to be worried, and is struggling to suppress anxiety and apprehensions (his wish to smooth over problems is expressed in his Rorschach image, "oil on water") that are largely related to his career as well as his self-image.

Frank seems to be a rather pretentious and pompous person, prone to an exaggerated self-confidence that can look like cockiness. He has intellectual pretensions that outstrip his limited abilities. For example, he may sometimes try hard to be witty and sardonic but cannot really bring it off. His intellectual abilities are quite spotty; his thinking tends to be concrete, inflexible, and rather conventional. He is not reflective; in fact, he seems to avoid strenuously any psychological-mindedness or any confrontation with his feelings. He tends instead to externalize blame and disown responsibility. What he seems to be struggling most against at present are feelings of resentment and impulses of retaliation. His responses imply a good deal of bottled-up rage and fury, along with a potential for explosive impulsivity.

Frank's current identity crisis centers around a long-term need to be strong, successful, and manly, without soft feelings that might imply femininity. He seems to dread any weakness and, for him, to have problems is to be weak; to be a failure is unmanly. There are indications that he punishes himself for feeling his needs and frustrations, readily falling into despair and self-recrimination. At the same time, however, he also tends to fall back on facile excuses and externalizations. For example, he may excuse his own opportunism by viewing others, and the world at large, as corrupt. He places a high value on success and esteem but is currently experiencing considerable conflict over it. At times he will disavow any ambitiousness; at other times he will feel trapped in his ambitiousness and corrupted by it. He seems generally subject to feelings of guilt, for there seems to be a strong, although poorly integrated, streak of morality in him. Indications are that he can be tyrannized by pangs of conscience and at the same time experience them as quite ego-alien.

Certain aspects of the test suggest important depressive features that take the form of feelings of abandonment and preoccupations with loss. Along with his despair over achievement and success, there is a view of interpersonal relationships as being unstable because others are unreliable.

The theme of being abandoned (particularly by the fickle woman and mother figure) is quite prominent.

In summary, then, Frank has a rather poorly integrated personality with a strong element of depression. He has some inhibited obsessive-compulsive features along with some hysterical tendencies set in a narcissistic character.

Frank's reaction to LSD was striking in its reflection of his need to shut out anxiety-producing experiences, particularly any hint of weakness; it also reflected the generalized constriction of his inner life. By ½ hour after taking the drug, he accepted 12 questionnaire items, slightly above the average for the entire group of drug subjects, but twice as many as the others in Group VI. At that time his body was tingling; he reported a funny feeling in the pit of his stomach, he felt that his hand was shaking although he could see that it was not; he had difficulty in concentrating; and his hearing was hyperacute. These are reactions typical of the onset of an altered LSD state. Instead of intensifying and spreading to other areas of functioning, however, his drug responses subsequently became sharply curtailed. At 2 hours he accepted only 8 items; at 5 hours, which is the usual peak period (sample mean = 28 items), he was down to 3, and at 8 hours he reported none.

Behaviorally, he seemed quite depressed, and was one of the subjects most consistently so rated in the study; he also showed some anxiety, about average for the sample, but high for Group VI. These effects, particularly the anxiety, were also most evident earlier in the day, although they continued somewhat longer than his subjectively reported symptoms.

His performance in the experimental tasks showed little change under LSD, except for a marked drop in the Robinson Rhymes test undoubtedly caused by the depression he experienced in the drug state. His Rorschach test, like that of other Group VI subjects, had few manifestations of primary process in either form or content on the pretest day and was practically unchanged under LSD, except for a slight improvement in form-quality.

Thus, in his reaction to LSD, Frank demonstrated his need to deny weakness in himself and to maintain his defensive denial at the expense of inner life and fantasy. His initially rather strong reaction, his depression, and his anxiety suggest that he is, in fact, vulnerable. His remarkable reinstitution of controls, however, shows not only his great need for defense and constriction, but the impressive strength of his defenses. It also suggests that in Frank's case the threat posed by experiencing an altered state induced by LSD actually reinforced, rather than weakened, his on-going defenses. From this we can infer that subjects with strong defensive needs and capacities can successfully limit the pressure toward regressive experiences created by LSD, at least when the drug dosage is not too great.

CHAPTER 6

Conclusions

The researches described in this book are obviously subject to a number of limitations; they are also provocative of considerable thought. In this chapter we review and discuss the results of our various explorations into the altered organismic states produced by LSD and the personality factors that seem to be related to them. After touching upon the limitations of our study, we consider its implications on a theoretical, clinical, and practical level, summarizing our major findings.

LIMITATIONS

The limitations of this research and the restrictions on the generalizations we can make from it are many, and we will briefly mention some of the most apparent of these. The study is confined to men, and in many respects to a rather select, relatively homogeneous group of men: actors, mostly unemployed ones at that. This is more of a limitation than would have been suspected only a few years ago because of repeated empirical demonstrations that primary-process thinking—particularly in adaptive regressive states—seems to be organized quite differently in men than in women (Pine and Holt, 1960; Holt, 1970; Shorr, 1971). Further, our subjects were screened so that persons with severe pathology, particularly those with well-defined psychoses, are not represented. For these reasons, but mainly because of their occupation and the high incidence of homosexuality, our sample of subjects must be considered quite selective and limited.

One important consequence of the small size and relative homogeneity of our sample of subjects is the distinct likelihood that an unknown number of other, distinctive patterns of reaction to LSD may exist. The reader should keep this limitation in mind constantly throughout the rest of this chapter. Nevertheless, we are confident enough of the theoretical meaningfulness of our findings to hypothesize that most of our conclusions apply in a general way to unsampled types of persons and altered states.

Our experimental method and procedures also introduced certain limitations. The lengthy testing of our subjects throughout the drug day, and the particular setting of our experimental room, made their experience a special one that limits generalizations about nonexperimental situations in which people take the drug. Further, while we did have a control group, it was not always well matched with the experimental group, sometimes in regard to pertinent variables. With almost all of our subjects, it became apparent quite early to both the experimenters and the subjects themselves whether the subject had received the experimental drug or the placebo. We used only a single dosage and a single administration; there is good evidence that many more psychoticlike reactions may be obtained by the considerably larger doses that have been used subsequently, and that the same person may have at least superficially quite different reactions at different times. Our data tell us nothing, of course, about the effects of long-term, repeated taking of LSD, such as is reported in contemporary clinical literature (see, for example, Blacker et al., 1968). Last, many of our observations and substudies must be considered exploratory or preliminary in nature, limited by the relatively small number of subjects, and they thus require validating work. In all, then, our research must be viewed as a limited venture into previously unexplored aspects of the effects of LSD. Our results and conclusions are therefore offered as tentative and as hypotheses that require confirmation and validation.

One special feature of our work has both negative and positive aspects. The experimentation was carried out before the effects of LSD were popularly known and before its illicit use had become widespread. Thus our subjects were not familiar with its effects and none of them guessed the drug correctly either during the experiment or during the follow-up period, so that their reactions were probably relatively untainted by specific expectations. It is, of course, no longer possible to find a group of equally intelligent young New Yorkers who are naive about the effects of LSD.

On the specific issue of generalizing from our results to the probable effects of LSD bought on the street and taken by an "acid head" in a crash pad in the East Village area of New York City or the Haight-Ashbury section of San Francisco, we want to point out a number of caveats. First, pharmacological studies of materials illicitly sold as LSD (Cheek, Newell, and Joffee, 1970; Krippner, 1970) have shown that the substance is generally adulterated, often by harmful drugs such as 2,5-dimethoxy-4-methylamphetamine (STP) and that the actual content of lysergic acid is generally smaller than the alleged amount (which is often 250 μg). The chances are very slight, therefore, that an illegal user would get a dose of LSD comparable in size and purity to our experimental potion. The body of information, misinformation, observations of drug use by himself and various others, mystical lore, and other sources of expectations about the kind of "trip" the acid dropper was about to have would be a great deal richer than, and almost entirely different from, the meager anticipations of our naive subjects. The contemporary user might feel a good deal more anxiety because of the knowledge that he is taking an illicit drug, for which he could easily be arrested, and because of the lack of supportive authorities on whom to depend. Our subjects, in contrast, were aware that two of the staff who attended them were physicians and that many of the others were more-or-less learned university professors. On the other hand, a present-day user might take the drug in a somewhat ritualized context, with the quasi-religious intent of giving himself over to an intensified experience of hidden aspects of himself, which might give the whole episode a more positive cast. Finally, we have the unsubstantiated impression that in the time that has passed, young men under 30 (as most of our subjects were) have become quite a different breed than our actors, who seem in retrospect astonishingly "straight" or "square." There may have been a shift in the predominant types of defenses, which might make some of our results not wholly applicable today.

THEORETICAL IMPLICATIONS

First, in looking at our data most broadly, we find that the questionnaire and testing detected shifts in dimensions of cognition and state of consciousness for every subject who received LSD. The formal characteristics of our subjects' manner of thinking and the content and form of the ideation, their general frames of reference and contexts for experiencing, their controls, their identities, and the degree of reflective awareness, as well as the range and scope of their awareness, all shifted under the drug. Such observations are by now commonplace, although the detailing of important nuances and clusters of effects had not been accomplished prior to this study. Furthermore, the individual differences in regard to such effects had not been as thoroughly studied previously in any other LSD research known to us.

There is, of course, a range of these effects among our subjects, typified by the six LSD reaction types we have described. The effects vary from a concatenation of many blatant manifestations of an altered state (e.g., Group II), through a series of specific variants of grossly altered functioning, to a minimal shift in the organismic state (e.g., Group VI). It is clear, then, that persons differ in the extent to which the usual manifestations of drive, defense, and adaptive functioning, and the balance among them within the personality, are modified under LSD. When we later review the separate reaction clusters, we will cite specific features of these individual differences. Before we do so, however, a few general comments regarding our experimental test procedures are in order.

These tests yield a rather wide range of results under the drug, from tasks that showed gross and severe impairment or alteration in performance to those on which our subjects under LSD performed as well as our placebo subjects in their normal waking state. (We did not include tasks on which improvement might have been observed, such as tests of divergent production.) The experimental tasks may be grouped into one set requiring relatively autonomous, neutralized, drive-free, and conflict-free functioning (such as the cognitive battery and the Color-Form test), and a second set (such as the Rorschach test, Earliest Memories, Figure Drawings, and Theme Lists) that more easily permit or openly invite intrusions of peremptory motivations and conflicts. We can demonstrate differences within this range of tasks in their vulnerability to disruption and change in the LSD states.

Four classes of determinants strike us as crucial to performance on these tasks—and, more broadly, to observed functioning in the LSD states: (1) *the nature of the task* and the cognitive organization of the functions that are called upon in responding to it, (2) *the nature of the specific altered state* in which a particular subject responds to the task, (3) *his capacity for attending,* and (4) *the personality of the subject.* We will discuss each of these strongly interrelated factors briefly.

1. The Nature of the Task

The nature of the task and the cognitive organization whose functioning it calls upon form a pair of complex variables in altered-state functioning. The continuum from relatively neutral to drive related is only one dimension in terms of which our substudies may be considered. Each task also calls upon different functions, such as recalling, learning, abstracting, integrating visually, and so on. Some tasks call upon and measure unconscious processes, whereas others tap only those that are easily accessible to conscious awareness.

Some general conclusions are possible, however. Simple direct learning tasks were generally minimally or not at all impaired by 100 μg of LSD. More complex learning was generally disturbed, largely (we believe) as a consequence of a disruptive form of anxiety experienced by many subjects. This anxiety in turn disrupted a number of functions, particularly attention. While the learning and recall of neutral thematic material (theme lists) was impaired by the drug, drive content diminished this effect by capturing and fixating attention more strongly than nondrive material. In such a task, then, motivational "pressures" aided the cognitive functions of comprehension and learning of new material; their role in other more personal tasks was, as we will see, different.

As for the other specific test procedures, the Color-Word task examines the capacity of a subject to maintain a set and reject extraneous stimuli intruding on a task, and these functions, which are also strongly related to that of attention, were generally impaired in the LSD states. Disruptions of the personality in the form of psychoticlike experiences were an important contributing factor here.

The Uloomoo-Takete and Color-Form tests tap still other aspects of mental functioning. The former explores the ability to maintain separate schemata; that is, the extent to which distinct cognitive organizations (roughly, concepts) are maintained as separate. In LSD-altered organismic states, schemata or the presentations derived from them seemed to merge, to be less distinct, and to be colored by the altered state itself. This indicates a change in mental organization in the direction of greater openness or fluidity of mental contents as one shifts from the normal to the altered state, an observation supporting the thesis that primary-process functioning becomes more predominant in such states (e.g., the greater use of unrealistic condensation and displacement). Moreover, presentations (brain processes on their way to becoming ideas or images) tend to be less subject to voluntary control (Holt, 1972), that is, more peremptory or intrusive (Klein, 1967). To anticipate a little, all of these changes and others to be cited may be characterized as a drug-induced shift in the direction of what Rapaport (1953) called *passivity,* or a loss of autonomy.

The Color-Form test investigates an interesting but not fully understood aspect of perception. The results may be interpreted as indicating a primitivization or regression of perceptual functioning in drug-altered states, which is in keeping with the reports of other experimenters (see Chapter 1), if a little more generalized a statement than we would prefer to make, for regression was always partial and selective in our subjects.

In the earliest memory recall study, partial regression also appeared in certain subjects under LSD. This task requires the use of personal memory schemata which are strongly relevant to important motive systems and conflicts. In certain subjects LSD led to the emergence of previously unreported and earlier, more drive-dominated recollections, which were also less attuned to reality. That is, in subjects who experienced considerable change in the self under LSD, more primitive recollections reached consciousness and such memories were striking for their condensations and symbolism (see Langs, 1971). LSD did not, then, simply produce a regression to utilization of more primitive cognitive organizations or an emergence of the primary process for every subject or on every task. The theoretically expected regression did appear in the earliest memory data but was limited to a specific range of personality types.

Results from the Rorschach test told in general a similar story. While the average production of primary-process material was not greater under LSD than in the control or standard Rorschach, the mode or manner in which it was experienced regressed markedly in many subjects, becoming more blatant and primitive. There were also many indications of impairments in defensive operations in several of the LSD states we observed, notably, diminished controls, less use of obsessive defenses, and a greater use of pathological defenses. Thus under LSD there was not a general upsurge of expression of instinctual drives, but rather an exaggeration of preexisting patterns. Subjects retained their rank orders on most aspects of primary process on the two administrations of the Rorschach, showing a general increase of primitivization in the expression of primary-process material in predisposed, relatively open subjects with, for example, more symbolic, autistic, and idiosyncratic responses, and a smaller increase in subjects with inhibitory controls. Effective controlling operations, in the form of adequate and flexible defenses and sharp perceptual accuracy, tended in general to be present less frequently under the effect of LSD, while the need for such controls and defenses significantly rose. Nevertheless, individual differences in all these effects were so great as to make general trends of questionable meaningfulness. For example, those subjects who on the pretest made good use of humor and esthetic contexts as a way of coping with their primary processes were able to maintain these adaptive controls under the drug; and although strong reactors' form accuracy declined, subjects who reacted relatively little to LSD actually improved their average form-level scores.

One of the most interesting aspects of our results is their bearing on the psychoanalytic theory of motivation. The Rorschach findings suggest, on the one hand, that the average subject's usual means of coping with, channeling, or defending himself against his instinctual drives were disturbed. According to the usual (implicitly hydrostatic) psychoanalytic conception, such impairment of the dikes holding back the somewhat variable but essentially unremitting pressure of the instinctual drives should result in some kind of uncontrolled emergence of drive derivatives into awareness or behavior or both. Classical theory would predict, therefore, that if LSD impairs controls and defenses, Rorschach responses would be much more dominated by relatively crude images of a libidinal and aggressive kind. Similarly, it leads to the prediction that when drive-relevant information is to be learned, as in the Theme List task, there will be even more of an eruption of unneutralized ideation and thus poorer performance than in the case of neutral test materials. As we have seen, both of these expectations were decisively contradicted by the findings of this study; LSD did interfere with the workings of cognitive controlling structures of various kinds, but the amount of drive material did *not* change significantly and drive-relevant information was *easier* to learn.

These findings are entirely consistent with data adduced by one of us (Holt, 1965, 1967b) in support of the contention that the classic psychoanalytic theory of motivation has such a poor fit to the facts that it needs to be drastically revised. Thus, for example, sensory deprivation or perceptual isolation—a drastic reduction in external inputs that support usual, "neutralized" kinds of secondary-process thinking—does *not* result in a regular increase in drive-dominated ideation. It is becoming clear that human motivation is a complex matter in which inner biochemical (e.g., hormonal) states, conscious and unconscious anticipations of various kinds of pleasure (Klein, 1972) and unpleasure, defenses against anxiety and guilt, and a number of inner arrangements that organize and maintain orderly sequences of behavior loosely referred to as "structures" (Holt, 1967a, b), but perhaps better conceptualized as feedback systems (Klein, 1967), interact with relevant aspects of the surrounding situation—such as opportunities, potential benefits and harms, and tonic supports (Holt, 1965). Since LSD is among other things a direct influence on various aspects of blood biochemistry, and since its effects on anticipations, defenses, and controlling structures seem to vary with the personality makeup of the individual, it should not be surprising that it can have profound effects on motivation which may take quite different directions in different persons. Thus, as we have seen, one of our subjects, a moralistically inhibited young man, felt a great increase in sexual "drive"—that is, he was able at last to experience sexual excitement and arousal in the presence of attractive female experimenters and felt that he could hardly control his impulses (although he actually did so). Another subject went through a brief, critical period at the height of the drug effect in which he felt nearly overwhelmed by destructive urges and became anxious (as some of us did, too) that he might be about to attack somebody. Since he was a physically powerful person, it was fortunate that we were able to allay his anxiety and calm his irrational angry impulses. Yet other subjects' Rorschachs showed a marked diminution in sexual and aggressive imagery, and their verbalizations and behavior gave no sign that the presence either of attractive females or of frustrations and other provocations aroused either desire or annoyance in them.

At this time, all we can do is to call attention to these data and draw the rather obvious conclusion that LSD is capable of markedly altering thresholds for the arousal of important motives such as sex and aggression;

it seems to lower these thresholds in some persons and to raise them in others. Since these findings call into question the existing psychoanalytic theory of motivation, the matter demands further intensive study and promises to yield important information for any alternative, psychoanalytically based theory of motivation (e.g., Klein, 1967; Holt, 1967b).

2. The Nature of the Specific Altered State

As to the second class of determinants of performance on the experimental tasks, the nature of the specific altered organismic state, we feel more cautious in advancing any conclusions. We have the impression that test performance was to a degree indirectly affected by LSD, the drug's impact being mediated by what we have referred to as the altered organismic state; but we recognize that we have no evidence for this conclusion and that it may in fact not even be testable. It is tempting to look on the altered state as an almost concrete or tangible reality, capable of exerting effects, although such a view is clearly vulnerable to the simple fallacy of reification. Perhaps the example of anxiety and impaired attention can make our impression seem less fallacious and more plausible. It is clear that subjects who became markedly anxious under the drug were those whose cognitive functioning was most impaired. Rapaport, Gill, and Schafer (1945) demonstrated the impairment on tests of attention by anxiety, a result that has been replicated repeatedly by others. Anxiety itself is not a universal effect of LSD, however, and it seems probable that this affect itself is secondary to the immediate impact of the drug on the subject's body image and on his defenses, which can lead to redoubled efforts to make the defenses work or to their being loosened. The latter is followed by an emergence of unusual thoughts and feelings which in turn can cause either euphoria or anxiety and the impairment of certain cognitive tests—depending on other aspects of personality. We return to this topic, therefore, after considering the role of personality in the LSD effects.

3. The Subject's Capacity for Attending

Our data indicate that attention, the extent to which it is focused and maintained, the person's ability to shift it, and his ability to control it actively or to let it be passively captured, are modified extensively albeit not uniformly by LSD. Our results may be summarized as follows. First, people differ markedly in the degree to which attention changes as the general effects of LSD develop. This is to be expected from the existence of notable individual differences in the manner in which a person attends under normal conditions; these have been given considerable importance in conceptualizing cognitive styles or dimensions of cognitive control (Gardner et al., 1959). Second, we assume that the structure or structures responsible for this function are modified both directly and indirectly by LSD. In light of the close relationship between attention and concentration, it is theoretically interesting that disturbance of the latter, not the former, seems to be among the primary effects of LSD (see below). This is comparable to the symptoms of schizophrenia in which it often happens that concentration is impaired long before attention (Rapaport, Gill, and Schafer, 1945). The inner resources required to direct attention deliberately and to exclude distractions (which we call concentration) are clearly greater than those required merely to attend. When one looks at it this way, however, the dichotomy between concentration and attention seems to disappear, and the two can be seen as regions on a rough continuum. In general, when we speak about relatively brief periods of voluntary noticing uncomplicated by distraction, we are speaking of attention; the more that difficulties are put in the way of such directed noticing, the more likely we are to refer to the function as concentration. In light of this analysis, it seems reasonable that LSD, or any other interference with this generalized function, is likely to have detectable effects first on the performances that are most active and difficult (concentration) and last on those that are relatively passive and easy (attention).

A third aspect of our data in regard to attention is the observation that in the states brought about by LSD the subject matter to which a person attends also changes. Impulses to act, such aspects of self-experience as body image and bodily feelings, visual imagery, and fantasy are among the kinds of experiences most likely to be attended to in these states. Again, note must be made of individual variations, since under LSD some subjects pay particular attention to their surroundings rather than their inner world, although in a way not seen in their normal state. In all, drive-related and conflict-related contents attract attention most readily in LSD states.

Access to attention or awareness is, to be sure, a critical factor in the defense of repression. Thus another way of describing one aspect of the alterations in attending is to label it as a change in the repressive barrier to awareness. Such a conceptualization is supported by some results of the Rorschach test and earliest memory studies. Indeed, some of the most spectacular effects of LSD—both the gaining of insight and the emergence of nightmarish ideation—seem to result from a weakening of repression in some subjects.

Among psychoanalytic theorists, Rapaport (1959, 1960) has written most extensively about attention, and we had hoped that our data might interact fruitfully with his theoretical propositions. Unfortunately, however, the latter are so exclusively concerned with hypothetical psychic energies which are not measurable apart from the phenomena they are invoked to explain that we have not found it possible to make any constructive use of his hypotheses. To be sure, we could make such very general statements as "LSD brings about changes in the structural conditions of the ego that determine the dispensing of attention cathexes," or "LSD alters the availability of attention cathexes and the degree to which they can be focused." It is apparent, however, that translation into this energic language adds nothing to the preceding summary. As already noted, we find somewhat more promising his conception of activity vs. passivity (Rapaport, 1953), since a number of the findings with the experimental tasks may be summarized as indicating impairment of active functions (concentrating, directing attention, voluntarily controlling thought imagery, learning complex materials, maintaining sets, and rejecting distractions), and a general movement toward more passivity (more intrusive thoughts and images, decreased sense of being actively in charge). We believe that these findings may be relevant to the new psychology of the will—a long-neglected problem now emerging into respectability—since many if not all of the impaired functions may just as well be characterized as *voluntary*. Indeed, anecdotal clinical observations (see, for example, Blacker et al., 1968) suggest that one effect of prolonged abuse of psychedelic drugs is great passivity, an impairment of the ability to will, to exert effort, or to take active and responsible control over one's life. In fact, some persons apparently take LSD to obtain just such a release from what they experience as an oppressive sense of a responsible self into a Nirvana-like passivity.

4. The Personality of the Subject

Ego Adequacy

Perhaps a good way to obtain a first overview of the role of personality in determining the nature of the LSD reaction is to consider the correlates of the summary rating of a person's general Ego Adequacy (ego autonomy or competence). We find that over a wide range of cognitive tasks, including both neutral and drive-related tests, high ratings on adequacy are associated with relatively well-maintained functioning under LSD. Further, those subjects rated as inadequate (nonautonomous) are most prone to show the most pervasive subjective effects in the altered state, with markedly disruptive anxiety and striking impairments in the function of attention. These three dysfunctions (a pervasively altered organismic state, anxiety, and impaired attention) do not always occur together in a given subject, depending largely on the availability of a second line of relatively more primitive defenses on which a subject can fall back.

Person Clusters

Since our major findings delineate more specifically the role of personality in the drug reaction, we will now briefly summarize and discuss the main results of our analysis by person clusters. All but 4 of our 30 drug subjects could be classified in one of seven clusters, defined by major elements of their reported and observed reaction to LSD. The important overall result was that *the subjects within each group resembled one another and differed from those in other groups in the details of their drug experience and also in the nature of their personalities.* Thus there is a strong presumption that the quality and extent of a person's reaction to a standard dose of LSD can be predicted from a knowledge of certain main aspects of his personality, if conditions are held constant.

The personalities of subjects in *Group I,* under usual conditions, are marked by fluidity, narcissism, impulsivity, and a cheerful mood. They are sensitive persons who are bright and can relate themselves well to others. They are also open to primitive, primary-process thinking but are able to handle it well. Last, their personalities are moderately well integrated.

Under the influence of LSD, these subjects responded in a manner that appears to be an extension of their usual personalities. They reported primarily expansive effects, which they tolerated well. Their altered experience was striking for subjective feelings of seeing new meanings in experiences and of improved functioning, as well as body image changes, visual distortions, and changes in their sense of time. They felt quite elated and experienced no fear of losing control or going crazy. Behaviorally, however, they showed little change.

In the midst of these marked subjective effects, their functioning in response to the battery of cognitive tests and the Color-Word test remained intact. This demonstrates that cognitive functioning can remain in good order in the presence of regressions in other aspects of functioning and experiencing. Obviously, then, regression does not occur uniformly across ego functions, or across the various cognitive organizations, but is highly patterned. It is directly related to what are usually called the person's major ego structures, such as those of defense and control, and to other balances and alignments within the total personality.

When we turn to the projective tests the results for these subjects are complex, but they may perhaps be summarized as indicating an adaptive regression. There is an apparent contrast between the increased sexualization of their female figure drawings and the nonsignificant slight decrease in libidinal and aggressive content in their Rorschach responses, a change that reached statistical reliability only for images of the results of aggression.

Formal signs of the primary process did increase after the subjects took LSD, but mainly in their Rorschach responses' enhanced fancifulness and expansiveness. It is noteworthy that this was the only subgroup in which there was evidence of improvement in adaptive controls over primary-process material (e.g., increases in use of good humorous and esthetic contexts and of reflection on their responses), even though their form-accuracy declined slightly. In light of this unexpectedly positive set of Rorschach changes, the figure drawings can be reevaluated. A look at the drawings of one of these subjects (Fig. 5.1) makes it plain that what we have called increased sexualization remains within the limits of what is appropriate; the nudity is hardly pornographic, and even though the LSD drawing has no great artistic merit, it is at least less self-conscious and freer than the control drawing. It seems reasonable, then, to characterize Group I subjects as regressing selectively and in a controlled, adaptive fashion, consistent with their orientation toward creativity. This increased availability of certain aspects of primary-process thinking did not occur at the expense of secondary-process functioning, which they maintained well, shifting flexibly from fantasy to accurate cognitive performances.

Subjects in *Group II* are schizoid, narcissistic, and inadequate persons with poor defenses and unclear identities, prone to regress under stress. Overall, they have poorly integrated, vulnerable personalities. In this group the Rorschach test revealed many instances of poorly controlled primary-process intrusions in the normal state.

Under LSD these subjects showed a wide range of effects and a dramatically altered state, both subjectively and in their overt behavior. Their experiences included impaired thinking, visual distortions, feelings of having lost control, loss of contact with the environment, and feelings that the meanings of experiences had changed. As compared to their normal state, these subjects showed a marked impairment in cognitive functioning, striking interference in Color-Word performance, a marked shift to more primitive perceptual organization as shown in their greater use of color in the Color-Form test, and a deterioration in their figure drawings, which were notable for their weak male figures. Their earliest memories under the drug shifted to new and more regressed recollections than those given in the waking state. Last, their Rorschach test protocols showed comparatively more blatant primary-process manifestations under the drug, with many formal indications of peculiar, fluid thinking. Victims of aggression were a particularly frequent type of Rorschach response reported by these subjects under LSD. Yet, despite these pervasive changes, they were not particularly frightened.

How can we understand this result? Our main hypothesis is that when their usual, more-or-less adaptive controls and defenses were seriously weakened, as shown by their bad performances on cognitive tests, they fell back on two principal defenses: schizoid withdrawal from reality and paranoid projection. The fact that these are regressive, pathogenic defenses should not blind us to their effectiveness in controlling the outbreak of anxiety. Threatening impulses were pushed away from the self, and the whole experience took on a dreamlike, unreal quality for these people, which may have helped to prevent them from becoming too upset by it.

Group III was made up of bright and competent men who rely strongly on rather effective inhibiting and obsessive defenses and tight controls. These serve to cover up depressive and aggressive trends and an inner turmoil which might otherwise plague them. Under LSD, initially, they fended off the regressive pressures fairly effectively, reinforcing their usual defensive alignment to prevent extensive disruption or any breakthrough of primitive fantasies and experiences. As the hours under LSD wore on, however, the impact of the primary symptoms finally became too great for their fragile and overtaxed ego resources, and they experienced a sudden, overwhelming, time-limited breakthrough of primitive material and functioning. This experience created great anxiety and a fear of going crazy.

At the peak of the acutely disorganized altered state experienced by these subjects, their attention was acutely impaired, synthetic functioning was markedly disrupted, some of their defenses collapsed, and terrifying primary-process intrusions erupted into awareness. A paranoidlike reaction followed, along with a marked disturbance in observable behavior; they were extremely agitated. Then, in a relatively short period of time, undoubtedly aided by support from the experimental setting, these subjects reestablished their defenses and controls, mastered the terrifying eruptions they were experiencing, and reestablished their equilibrium.

It seems clear that Group III subjects share with Group II subjects a rather severe underlying personality disturbance, but differ from those in Group II in having very strong and useful defenses against it. Although these defenses failed momentarily, they were fairly quickly reconstituted. Group III subjects may also be compared to the subjects in Group VI (see below); the latter maintained their more rigid defenses throughout the period of regressive pressure and experienced little disruption, if any, under LSD.

At the height of their acutely disturbed altered state, the functioning of Group III subjects on the cognitive tests was extremely poor, and their use of color in the Color-Form test, an indicator of regression to more passive visual functioning, was more marked than that of any other group. In contrast, tests carried out at times other than that of their peak of disturbance showed little impairment.

Let us turn now to *Group IV*: withdrawn, defensive, hostile, and paranoid persons who relate themselves poorly to others and also cope rather poorly with stress. Their identities are confused and their body images are distorted, expressing a sense of impairment. They tend to avoid introspection and awareness of inner feelings.

The altered state experienced by these subjects under LSD was notable for its concentration on physical or somatic symptoms, effects that were accompanied by a strong fear of going crazy, considerable anger, and a pervasive sense of anxiety. Further, in keeping with their characteristic reliance on the defense of projection, these subjects reported under the drug many changes in the meaning of the environment which had a rather paranoid quality. Incidentally, for these subjects as well as those in other groups, projection seems to have been rather frequently a basis for the subjective experience of new revelations under the drug.

In these Group IV subjects, the altered-state experience manifested itself in the areas in which they were most vulnerable. The somatic symptoms were no doubt based on their endemic conflicts and anxieties regarding their bodies and on their preference for somatization rather than introspection. The physical symptoms (and perhaps the unconscious fantasies they covered) had a terrifying quality and led to intense anxiety. As a result, their capacity for attention and their cognitive functioning were seriously impaired. Further, the figure drawings by these subjects showed considerable bodily disturbance under LSD.

In another vein, one could detect in this group a great fear of primitive aggressive ideas and impulses in the altered state that erupted with the weakening of their already inadequate defenses. These subjects resorted to the extensive use of projection to defend themselves against this danger, which allowed them to express some aggression as well. We might speculate, too, that the somatic symptoms served as a symbolic means for expressing their underlying paranoid fantasies as well as their anxiety and aggression. These symptoms also diverted attention from inner fantasies. Thus the somatic focus may have served in some way as a defense against a more pervasive disruption. Although our data do not provide definitive evidence on these issues, we may conjecture that the bodily symptoms account for the absence in this group of a more striking regression in other areas of subjective experience and within other cognitive organizations.

Group V comprises poorly integrated, schizoid subjects of relatively poor intellect compared to the others, with a very strong facade that guards them from experiencing or revealing their severe underlying pathology. They are role players and successful at it up to a point; they also show considerable bodily concern.

Under LSD, members of this group varied in the extent of their total reaction but shared in common the almost exclusive focus of this experience on alterations within their bodies, in the form of both body image changes and somatic symptoms. In this respect they are similar to Group IV, whose subjects also experienced primarily physical symptoms. They differ from Group IV, however, in that this somatic focus occurred in the context of a minimal emotional disruption and little impairment in cognitive and other functioning.

These subjects appeared to be struggling against a potentially disruptive subjective experience, covering it over with a strong defensive facade which concentrated their awareness of the effects of LSD on bodily alterations and may have prevented any other kinds of effects from developing. The capacity to remain intact under the drug varied among these subjects. Their cognitive and other test functioning under LSD was as a result also quite variable, both within a given subject and among the different subjects in this group. By and large, their cognitive functioning (including the capacity to direct attention) remained actively controlled, in touch with reality, and intact. In contrast, their earliest memories shifted to new, regressed recollections, and they showed a strong effect on the Uloomoo-Takete test. The former suggests the emergence of primitive, usually repressed, material under LSD, while the latter suggests a fusion between usually separated cognitive organizations in the drug state.

The selectivity of effects in this group indicates again that relatively autonomous cognitive organizations may remain intact in altered states, while other, more conflict-dominated and personal, cognitive organizations, such as earliest recollections and bodily schemata, are modified and shifted in a regressive direction. The cognitive and other structures that are selectively modified are very much a function of individual differences in personality.

An interesting aspect of the Rorschach test in these subjects is the appearance under the drug of aggressive content, particularly destruction directed against the body, not seen in pretesting. In their LSD state, somatic symptoms, body image changes, fantasies and images of bodily impairment or harm all occurred together. For these subjects, the body became the focus of fantasied and subjectively experienced alterations on several levels.

In keeping with Group V's effects, their Rorschach responses in the normal and altered states suggest that under LSD they managed to make less use of their ineffective and more pathological defenses. This finding may reflect in part a consequence of these subjects' increasing somatizing under LSD, perhaps resulting in less threat of primary-process intrusions and less need to deal with them through extreme defensive measures.

Group VI, the last cluster of drug reactors, included subjects who are independent, successful in coping, assertive, action-oriented, and prone to shut out their inner life; their character structure was described as inhibited obsessive-compulsive. Under normal conditions, they showed a minimal amount of primary-process content on their Rorschach tests and in particular seemed to be guarding against the emergence of aggressive impulses.

Under LSD these subjects tightened their rigid and inhibiting defenses and experienced only a minimal effect, typically reported as some difficulty in concentrating and a series of somatic symptoms. On the various tests administered while under the drug, they showed evidence of only minimal to moderate altered functioning. In these subjects the cognitive organizations that predominate in the normal state largely continued to do so under LSD as well and were essentially comparable in form, content, and interrelationships.

These Group VI subjects can be compared with those from Group III, since both had inhibitory obsessive defenses which were generally effective in their everyday lives. Group III subjects were unable to maintain these defenses against the regressive pressures evoked by LSD and experienced an acute, short-lived, catastrophic altered state of consciousness. In contrast, Group VI subjects maintained their defenses throughout the period of the drug's effect and did not experience more than a minimal disturbance at any time. Quite possibly, however, with a larger dose, they might have responded like the subjects in Group III. The earliest memories of Group VI subjects (both on the pretest and under LSD) suggest a fear of losing control of aggressive impulses which therefore had to be strongly repressed. We might speculate that their repressive defenses were reinforced at all costs, eliminating virtually all primitive or primary-process derivatives from access to awareness.

The Empirical Scales

The four empirical scales described in Chapter 3 offer a final way of looking at the individual differences in altered states. These scales represent different kinds of effects which appear together under LSD. The six reaction type groups already discussed represent some of the possible combinations in which these clusters of effects may occur. If we briefly consider the implications that these combinations have for the meaning of each scale (Chapter 5), the relationships of the empirical scales to the experimental and projective test data (Chapter 4), and the content of the scales themselves (Chapter 3), we can bring additional aspects of the effects of the drug into clearer focus.

The assembled evidence indicates that Scales A, B, and C represent three different kinds of clusters of regressive effects, while Scale D represents the feeling of being threatened by the drug's potentially regressive effects and the struggle against that threat.

Scale A effects emphasize a lifting of the constraints of everyday reality that is both ego-syntonic and pleasurable; it includes an outpouring of fantasy, often with a humorous or esthetic coloring, and the expression of sexual feelings. This form of regression seems, however, to be under voluntary control; when focused attention is required for a task, it can be mobilized effectively. Further, the Scale A subjective effects are not associated with regressive or anxious overt behavior. This type of regression may best be characterized by Kris' (1952) conception of regression in the service of the ego.

In contrast, Scale B reflects a massive breakdown in ego functioning and a regression in the self-concept. Primitive modes of thought appear and defenses either become more primitive or fail completely. Overt behavior is strikingly altered, in two different ways, depending on whether or not Scale A effects are also present. When both Scale A and Scale B effects are present, subjects become very regressed, silly, manic, and hyperactive and appear to be reacting to visual distortions. Subjects who showed a strong Scale B effect without a strong Scale A effect experienced what is commonly known as a "bad trip." They were overtly hostile, anxious, and suspicious, and they reported fear of losing control as well as many somatic symptoms (i.e., Scale D effects). In their panic state they did very poorly in the experimental tasks. Scale B thus represents a regressive loss of ego controls and defenses.

The Scale C effect seems to represent the most general and undifferentiated of the regressive effects produced by LSD. It includes the feeling that one has slipped into a state of childhood or infancy, with its attendant helplessness and physical incapacity (sometimes also expressed as feeling old), and is accompanied by the recovery of first memories from an earlier age than those reported in the waking state. We may postulate that Scale C includes the principal regressive effects of LSD rather than elaborations of or defenses against them.

Scale D, as we have noted, seems to differ from the other three scales in representing a resistance to regression rather than a regression per se. It is expressed in fear of losing control, generalized anxiety, and somatic symptoms. Under LSD, subjects with this reaction show a constriction of both fantasy and sensual feelings.

CONCLUDING COMMENTS

These, then, are our major findings bearing on personality variables as they enter into the complex causal network that brings about the various effects of LSD. Let us consider now some of their theoretical implications.

First, we believe that we have demonstrated more clearly than ever before that the phenomena induced by LSD (and probably by any similar drug) cannot be predicted or understood in purely pharmacological terms; the personality of the drug taker plays an enormous and critical role in determining how much effect there will be and of what particular type.

Second, the results with Scale A and Group I demonstrate that LSD can indeed have predominantly positive, constructive effects, even though our study was not well designed to detect them. They occur in people who are normally open, flexible, adaptable, and on good terms with their own primary processes to begin with. With a moderate dosage of LSD (enough to produce further expansion but not so much as to overwhelm existing adaptive capacities) in a protective setting in which people with intellectualizing defenses could feel comfortable, the same drug that upset and produced intellectual impairment in many subjects left the cognitive functioning of these select few virtually unharmed. In the particular altered state that such people experienced, there was a considerable enrichment of positive affect, imagery, fantasy, and personal recollection. (We are not considering here, since it was beyond the purview of our study, the rather complex issue of the usefulness of LSD as an adjuvant to psychotherapy.)

Third, we have proposed the view that many of our findings can be subsumed under the general formulation that LSD induces a regression from what Rapaport (1953) called ego activity to passivity. We believe now, however, that we may be able to advance a step or two further toward a more differentiated account of how LSD produces its effects—an account that is both rather general and more analytical.

Let us begin with the placebo findings. To be sure, there was hardly any overlap in total questionnaire score between our experimental and control groups; qualitatively, the most extreme placebo reactors did not resemble any of the groups that we have distinguished according to their reaction to LSD. Nevertheless, there were only 10 items exclusive to the drug condition (no placebo subject responded positively to them at any time during the experimental day), and furthermore, there were five questions that drew positive responses from at least half of the placebo subjects. It cannot be denied, therefore, that whatever caused so many of our subjects to admit to a certain number of symptoms after drinking only lemon-flavored water most probably contributed in part to the endorsement of the same items by subjects under LSD.

These determinants appear to be: (1) *expectations* as to the probable effects of drugs with which psychologists and psychiatrists experiment, based on configurations of information, folklore, and wishful and fearful fantasies about the kinds of psychopharmacological experiments that go on in university laboratories, plus the specific meager bits of information we gave about the drug allegedly to be given to everyone, plus the specific suggestions contributed by the questionnaire itself; (2) *wishes* for certain kinds of experience, which can lead a person to detect minimal signs of such phenomena and to amplify them; (3) direct effects of the *situation* or stimulus field to which the subjects were exposed—the gloominess of the black room ("Have you felt depressed or sad?"); the incessant questioning ("Have you been talking more than usual?"); the constant demands to take tests, answer strange questions, perform on tasks that had no apparent meaning ("Have you felt angry or annoyed?" "Have you been feeling silly?" "Have some things seemed meaningless to you?"); and the great variety of experimenters with different degrees of skill and experience in obtaining rapport and cooperation who nevertheless asked many personal questions ("Have you felt you would rather not talk?"); (4) elements of reassurance and *support*—the presence of physicians on the experimental staff; the awareness that universities do not allow their faculties to subject people to truly dangerous experiments; and comfort or relief felt after specific reassurances and (on occasion) suggestions or other therapeutic-like interventions. On an even more general level, sociological and anthropological determinants of much that we observed are obviously relevant; our subjects were males, responding within a framework of expectations in themselves and in us as to the kinds of behavior appropriate to the male role (thus, for example, we observed very little weeping or so-called "unmanly" behavior) and to their occupational roles as actors. American culture of that era also contained a considerable body of lore about drugs and their effects and the nature and preoccupations of psychologists and psychoanalysts.

We cannot estimate the importance of the just-cited determinants merely by noting the frequency of positive responses to questionnaire items in the placebo group, or the magnitude of changes in the latter's performance on various experimental tasks. In the experimental group, the effects of the drug quite probably interacted with the above determinants, potentiating them. That is, in another culture, or in a laboratory with quite a different atmosphere, or even with a different set of experimenters, the same dose of LSD would probably have potentiated a considerably different set of experiential readinesses. For these reasons, only after a great deal of research in many settings and with many different kinds of subjects will it be possible to look for invariant, constant findings that one can begin to attribute with some confidence to the drug itself.

Further, as two of us have shown elsewhere (Linton and Langs, 1962b), the placebo effect was by no means uniform within the control group but was highly correlated with a cluster of personality variables. In other words, these nonpharmacological determinants of LSD effects interact with a number of dispositions in subjects' personalities, which can be thought of as potentiating or as having a catalytic activity.

But of course some of our subjects did actually ingest 100 μg of d-lysergic acid diethylamide, and they responded in ways that are quantitatively and qualitatively distinctive. Granted that the drug works in part by releasing a variety of preexisting behavioral, affective, and cognitive patterns, does it not do more than that? Obviously it does; but now the picture becomes even more complex.

To begin with, LSD has been reported to produce a number of effects that are usually considered even more physiological and less phenomenological than any discussed here. For example, the EEG findings tempt one to speculate, for they seem in some ways paradoxical. How is it that a state of consciousness that seems in so many ways dreamlike is induced by a drug that produces cortical activation—that is, speeded alpha and increased beta rhythms, and enhanced response to stimuli and increased variability of EEG (Fink and Itil, 1968)? We resist this temptation, however, since we lack the neurophysiological sophistication needed to pursue matters on this level, and since the crucial links between such events as desynchronization of the EEG and the effects we observed are missing.

We assume, therefore, that LSD has potent effects on many physiological functions, and that these mediate observable psychological effects in unknown ways. There is good reason to assume that even the strictly physiological effects are not uniform across persons but differ in their general intensity and in their pattern. To be sure, in a study of these factors, doses should be equivalent in some sense in relation to bodily weight or surface. The effects we observed were not, however, stronger in light subjects than in those who were relatively heavy. (They were, in fact, slightly but not significantly stronger in the heavier subjects, a finding too weak to permit speculation about somatotypes but nevertheless of interest.) The differences we observed in the relatively more physiological effects among our subjects—for example, the fact that the greatest pupillary dilatation occurred in Group V, which had in general the most marked somatic symptoms—seem more related to the general reliance on somatizing as a mechanism of defense than to any discernible physical characteristic.[1]

Here our results lead us directly into the highly problematic area of the mind-body problem, so strewn with booby traps for the unwary. We have no hypotheses to offer about how it is that some people (such as the Group

[1] Similarly, Itil (1968) found that psychotic subjects who resisted therapy and had "hypernormal" EEGs showed no change in the recorded electrical activity of their brains even after doses of 500–800 μg of LSD.

V subjects) are so ready to respond to many kinds of stress by somatic reactions, nor why the purely bodily aspects of the LSD reaction should have been so prominent in them. Our findings seem to us rather remarkable, however, since they suggest a direct link of some kind between congruent physiological and psychological reactions.[2]

We assume that LSD must affect processes in the nervous system (and perhaps other organs, such as the liver) before it can have effects on the psychological level of the organism. In some unknown way the development of physiological effects is affected by a person's defenses and other aspects of his personality. It seems noteworthy, however, that such somatic symptoms as dizziness and feelings of numbness are among the first to be reported and are almost universal.

Let us tentatively adopt the hypothesis that a certain group of effects are *primary*. These are very widespread (reported by large majorities of our subjects, and in most other studies of LSD) and appear relatively early in the course of the reaction—which, as we have seen, extends over several hours. Table 6.1 presents a proposed list of such primary effects; it includes all of the questionnaire items endorsed by 90% of our subjects at some time during the drug day plus a few other items with slightly lower frequencies which have been very widely reported by others. The distinc-

Table 6.1. Postulated Primary Effects of LSD

Effect	Frequency (%)	Scale in Which Effect Appears in First ½ Hour
Difficulty in concentrating	100	A
"Fascination" effect on attention	87	A
Sense of losing control of thoughts, body or emotions (actual or potential)	70–87	B, C, D
Feelings of impaired judgment	97	—
Visual effects (blurring, illusions, and so on)	37–53[a]	B, D
Changes in body image	93	A, B, C
Numbness or tingling sensations	100	C
Feelings of physical weakness	90	C
Dizziness or grogginess	90	C

[a] This item is included because it is so widely reported in other studies on LSD, usually along with generalized heightening of the intensity of experience (both perceptual and affective).

[2] In this connection, see Schur's (1955) report that neurodermatitis patients showed exacerbation of their physical symptoms accompanying an increase in a primary-process mode of functioning. He assumes that in general somatization is closely tied to a prevalence of primary-process thinking.

tion between primary and secondary effects is made by analogy with Bleuler's (1911) distinction between the primary (or basic) and secondary (or accessory) symptoms of schizophrenia.

A relatively plausible case can be made that most of these primary effects are relatively direct consequences of the known physiological action of LSD. The physical sensations of numbness, tingling, weakness, and dizziness (also including a fairly large number of others with slightly lower frequencies; see Table 3.1) may be either central or partly peripheral in origin. It is easy to see how this considerable disturbance of normal sensory feedback could be elaborated into some of the more colorful types of disturbed body image that have been reported, and how, by attacking one of the foundations of the feeling of self, it could participate in the sense of losing control of the body and (by generalization) of other functions.

Next let us consider the visual effects. Pupillary dilatation has been reported as a regular effect in all surveys of the LSD literature, and although it was not measured as regularly and precisely as might have been desired, it was clearly true of our subjects as well. Enlargement of the pupil directly causes the blurring of vision that is included as a primary symptom. It is possible that this loss of visual acuity helps make the other kinds of visual effects more likely to occur, but it is clearly not a sufficient cause. Perhaps the drug has the selective effect of lowering synaptic resistance in the visual system, or some other such central effect; perhaps it also operates in part by incapacitating the usual mechanism by means of which our awareness of entoptic phenomena is suppressed (Holt, 1972). The emergence of actual hallucinations is probably a much more complicated, secondary effect, involving electroencephalographic change, impairment of judgment, loss of control over cognition, and some loss in the sense of reality.

It is tempting to link the first group of effects listed in Table 6.1 to the increased mean frequency of alpha, since there is evidence that increasing proficiency in controlling thought processes (e.g., in Zen meditation) is accompanied by a decreased alpha frequency (Kasamatsu and Hirai, 1966), and LSD seems to differ from other hallucinogens in this particular aspect of the EEG (Fink and Itil, 1968). Be that as it may, we assume that the drug does act on the brain in some way that interferes with the voluntary control of attending; deliberate focusing or concentrating becomes more difficult, and attention is more easily captured by fascinating adventitious distractions. What seems to be central to all of the first four effects in Table 6.1 is an interference with the capacity for self-control and autonomous, voluntary control of one's inner processes.

As the table reminds us, there is considerable individual difference in the relative prominence of these primary symptoms, just as there is in the underlying physiological reaction. Again, we do not know to what extent such differences reflect biochemical individuality and other kinds of individual differences on the anatomical and physiological levels of the organism, and to what extent they may entail different organizations, cognitive style, and other traits on the psychological level.

It is evident, however, that the undermining of physical identity and bodily security, plus the loss of self-control, must have a strong tendency to make an LSD user feel that he is regressing, that is, that he is losing some of his peculiarly adult capacities and his sense of himself. On one level, this is what we mean when we refer to LSD as exerting "regressive pressures." At the same time, the primary effects may be looked on as involving components of several major defenses, since they constitute a diminution in a person's normal sense of bodily integrity and identity and his resources for coping with dangers, as well as a weakening of his capacity for self-control and autonomous direction of his own inner processes. Thus the term "loosening or modification of defenses" may be seen as summarizing some of the primary symptoms, or at least as being an immediate effect of many of them. We have indicated above, for example, one way in which repression may be weakened as a result of changes in attending; there may of course be other—perhaps more direct—ways in which LSD undermines repressions as well. Changes in defensive alignment of this kind merit closer scrutiny in future studies.

The majority of the other effects listed in Table 3.1 may be looked on as secondary symptoms resulting from the above changes. Alterations in the body image, for example, plus some sensory changes, could lead a subject to respond positively to such questionnaire items as "Have you felt somehow as if you were melting or merging into your surroundings?" or "Have you found it difficult to move?" or "Has it felt as if some part of your body was disconnected or somehow didn't belong to the rest of your body?" or "Have you been afraid or upset?" The experienced impairment of voluntary, adaptive capacities and/or the modifications in defenses could lead either to a relaxation of inhibitions, the experience that things are speeded up, expansiveness and elation, and a feeling of being able to see new meanings (Scale A); or to a near-psychotic breakdown of normal defenses and a coming to the fore of projection, accompanied by feelings of unreality and loss of a sense of self (Scale B); or to increased efforts at inhibitory control over ideational effects and a concentration on somatic symptoms (Scale C); or to a sense that control was being lost without even such a primitive defense as projection to fall back on, resulting in strong anxiety and the fear of going crazy (Scale D). In each instance our data suggest that (at least when the situation is held constant) the primary determinant of which of these roads is taken is the preexisting personality of the subject.

In the light of this analysis, it seems somewhat arbitrary to designate either the early-appearing primary effects or the late-appearing secondary ones as the referent of the term "altered organismic states." Clearly, both types of effects characterize such states, and we have attempted to conceptualize their interaction.

It has been maintained that LSD is a valuable research tool for the study of the psychology of personality. Many have considered that studies of altered organismic states may serve as models for understanding such diverse nondrug clinical phenomena as schizophrenic syndromes, dreams, fugue states, stress reactions, and unconscious fantasies. Studies with drugs such as LSD may therefore provide a unique opportunity to investigate problems of this kind (see Appendix 1 and Langs, 1971). While we cannot point to any specific piece of new knowledge not involving interaction between this particular drug and personality, we do feel that our research confirms the utility of a number of basic assumptions and propositions. For example, the continuity of personality; it was impressive to see to what extent each subject retained his unique individuality despite the massive intervention of LSD intoxication, and to have the statistical evidence of high test-retest correlations (e.g., in the Rorschach test) despite the fact that one administration was under normal conditions and one under the drug. Another example is the necessity to assume unconscious processes, and a great deal of the rest of the clinical theory of psychoanalysis; we would have found it impossible to make any advance toward understanding many of the phenomena we encountered without these basic conceptual tools.

Our major finding, that reactions to LSD are patterned and meaningfully related to the preexisting personalities of the subjects (thus, in principle, predictable), can in fact be viewed as an aspect of the continuity concept. In light of the contemporary attack on the concept of stable and persisting traits of personality by such theorists as Mischel (1968), it seems worthwhile to dwell for a moment on this point. It would be difficult indeed to account for our findings in terms of a theory that human behavior is largely determined by the situation and that its apparent continuity and generality may be attributed to environmental stability. We assessed our subjects' personalities by relying heavily on what they told us (in autobiographies, interviews, and self-report tests) about themselves and their usual patterns of behavior in their normal surroundings, supplementing this information by inferences from projective test responses and to a minor extent by direct observation. Even the latter took place in staff members' offices, not in the eerie black-draped room where each subject spent his experimental day. Yet despite this special and unusual setting, and despite the unique circumstance of being the focus of varied kinds of inquiry and demands from an unending procession of experimenters all day long, while under the influence of one of the most powerful psychotropic drugs known, each man reacted in ways that are highly congruent with the independent assessment of his defenses, coping resources, cognitive styles, and like aspects of personality. We believe that these findings are a real challenge to those who lay such heavy stress on the specificity and situational determination of behavior as many neobehaviorists do.

Many empirical generalizations have emerged that may apply to a broad range of psychedelic agents. Thus subsequent research may profitably inquire to what extent our findings can be replicated with psilocybin, with various other indole-related hallucinogens, and even with Δ^1-tetrahydrocannabinol, the principal active ingredient in marijuana. At the present time, it is impossible to say to what extent the contemporary "drug scene" is a passing phenomenon, or to what extent it may persist or even be the harbinger of an even more widespread use of a range of pharmacological agents in the future. The chances are, however, that there will remain considerable social as well as scientific interest in our learning as much as possible about the kinds of reactions different kinds of people have to varied doses of LSD and similar drugs.

We doubt that in the course of such research any chemical substance will be found that will correspond to Huxley's fantasy of "*soma*" in *Brave New World*—a pleasant, nonaddictive, safe retreat from reality. Most of the frightening and distressing aspects of untoward LSD reactions cannot be viewed as "side effects" susceptible to being removed by appropriate tinkering with the structure of the LSD molecule. Conceivably, some of the common somatic effects (e.g., nausea, mydriasis, numbness) might be of this type. But any drug that can alter mood, loosen repression and modify other defenses, affect many qualitative aspects of experience, produce vivid unbidden visual imagery and release imagination or fantasy, cannot be expected to produce *only* pleasant "consciousness-expanding" effects in all takers. Surely bad experiences are to be expected for the most deeply troubled and people with very fragile adjustments—those for whom psychoactive drugs must pose a great danger. Even excluding persons with such obvious pathology, as we did, a drug that is potent enough to give the kind of positive experience reported by our Group I subjects is certain to stir up trouble, and sometimes seriously upsetting trouble, in people who do not have flexible defenses and ready access to their primary processes without being threatened by their own unconscious fantasies. LSD does not work merely by lifting repression, any more than alcohol really works by dissolving the superego, but many of the effects do seem to be attributable to alterations in important defenses. If this is the case, it is to be expected that most of the time what emerges into awareness will be frightening—since it has been held back precisely because it arouses anxiety.

Consider, for example, the potential danger to persons resembling Group III. These subjects normally function effectively, using strong defenses to cover and restrain their pathological trends, and thus they may superficially resemble the Group I type, for whom taking LSD can be an almost entirely positive experience (although fears of going crazy and marked anxiety can occur in any such subject, particularly with a large dose of the drug or at a time of increased stress—which may be just when a person is motivated to seek a chemical vacation). Under LSD, the Group III subjects initially managed to restrict alterations in their organismic state to a minimum. In time, however, many of their defenses collapsed and they experienced a terrifying disruption in functioning and a nightmarish ordeal. In the safety of our laboratory and with the understanding and care they were given, they soon reconstituted themselves, but it is easy to imagine the terrible possibilities in a different situation with the wrong kind of companionship. Other, even more precariously adjusted people (of the kinds we deliberately screened out of our sample) are vulnerable to massive and even persisting collapse of defenses; psychoses and suicides precipitated by taking LSD have been reported often enough (see, for example, Ditman et al., 1967) to make us feel the urgency of warning against the grave dangers of self-administered dosages of LSD.

Our findings show a built-in danger in a drug such as LSD. It is likely to be tried first and written about by people of the kind to whom it is least dangerous, whose rhapsodic accounts of euphoria, increased insight, or experiences of great beauty make the drug irresistibly attractive to those who are most vulnerable to its harmful effects. For it is the very people whose personalities make it likely that they will *not* have such positive reactions who are likely to be allured by the promise of a quick and easy answer to their problems in living—boredom, anxiety, the feeling of being trapped in a conformist world, depression, and the like. LSD may enhance creativity in certain already creative people, but it is quite assuredly not the key that will unlock the hidden creativeness in the average man.

Undisciplined advocates have encouraged a great deal of magical thinking about LSD, which we hope our results will help to curb. As usual, such thinking is dominated by wish fulfillment. If only there *were* some easy, quick substitute for psychoanalysis as a means of self-knowledge and inner change, or for talent and hard work as a means of artistic achievement, or for disciplined meditation as a means of attaining inner serenity! If only there *were* some inexpensive means by which the poor and underprivileged, or perhaps the middle-class striver trapped in his rut, could attain a broad and rich experience of life, deep and genuine feelings, even ecstasy! It is too much to expect, to be sure, that many people will give up such a dream, especially since the mass media have promoted the ideas of so many self-appointed gurus who push LSD as the answer. Nevertheless, to all who have the capability to respond to reason and evidence, we reiterate: the reported effects of LSD are a complex resultant of the kind of person involved, the situation and the expectations it arouses, and the dosage taken. It is, for many of the reasons alluded to in this discussion, an excellent tool for research, but, at the same time, too much of a social and individual danger to be allowed to be generally available.

APPENDIX 1

The Psychoanalytic Theory of Consciousness

A prime mover of this research was an interest in clarifying aspects of the psychoanalytic theory of consciousness. We therefore reviewed the relevant literature in some detail and found that it provided us with a most illuminating and yet provocative and unsettled framework for our study. Because our research ultimately was not primarily designed to test specific hypotheses drawn from this theory but instead followed largely exploratory and descriptive lines and pursued personality factors virtually neglected by the analysts, we have not included the review of the literature in the main text.

We will, nevertheless, describe the more salient aspects of this background here because it provides the interested reader with an overview of psychoanalytic contributions to problems of consciousness and affords him the opportunity to consider for himself the scope and limitations of the explanatory powers of this theory. It also establishes the theoretical climate from which this study evolved and enables the reader to follow the ways in which our findings modify and clarify the theory. Of necessity, this review is brief and touches upon only the major highlights. It is not critical in its intent, since to do so would take us into issues well beyond the scope of this book. In Chapter 6 we discuss in a more critical vein the implications of our findings in relation to the psychoanalytic theory of consciousness.

Sigmund Freud became interested in states of consciousness of the total human organism and the special function of consciousness or attention (from the beginning associated with his changing concept of the ego) not only through his early work with hypnosis (Freud, 1891) but also because of their relevance to his earliest formulations regarding psychopathology (Breuer and Freud, 1895) and, more broadly, the nature of the mental apparatus (Freud, 1900). In fact, Freud's most extensive attention to the topic is seen in his very earliest works. These include his *Project for a Scientific Psychology* (1895), in which the primary focus was on the *function* of consciousness or attention, and the *Studies on Hysteria* (Breuer and Freud, 1895), in which he shared only to a limited extent Breuer's emphasis on the role of *altered states* of consciousness (hypnoid states) in the etiology of this syndrome.

These two uses of the term "consciousness," to refer to a total state of the organism and to refer to the attention-dispensing function of the ego, have not always been clearly separated. Nor has the latter function been clearly distinguished from the means by which we become conscious of a stimulus, the "sense organ consciousness" alluded to in *The Interpretation of Dreams* (Freud, 1900). To complicate matters even further, other usages of the term "consciousness" appeared in Freud's later writings. To mention these briefly, one was the early topographic usage in which Freud (1900), in *The Interpretation of Dreams,* proposed that the mental apparatus be divided into three systems: *Cs.* (conscious), *Pcs.* (preconscious), and *Ucs.* (unconscious). This usage proved internally inconsistent and has been largely discarded (Freud, 1912, 1923). Another usage adopts the terms "conscious" and "unconscious" as qualitative or descriptive terms, referring to whether a given mental process, content, or fantasy is within the realm of awareness or outside of it. This usage, as we will see, currently has wider implications and refers more broadly to a hierarchy of cognitive organizations of mental contents accessible at various levels of awareness (see Gill, 1963; Rapaport, 1957). Since this particular usage is related to the problem of conceptualizing mental contents at various levels of consciousness and in altered states, we will discuss it further at the conclusion of this survey.

One last usage of the term unconscious in Freud's theorizing deserves mention here. Freud used the word dynamically not solely to refer to mental contents outside of awareness in a descriptive sense but to imply that forces of defense or repression maintained barriers against the possibility that the particular content might reach awareness. This meaning is therefore related to the concept of the function of consciousness and also requires elaboration.

With this as an introduction, let us briefly trace these various usages of consciousness in Freud's writings and in the writings of others after him in order to crystallize the essential differences in their meanings.

In his *Project for a Scientific Psychology,* Freud (1895) postulated two basic, biologically determined concepts regarding human behavior: first, primary defense against unpleasure, and, second, attention. The latter was a function of consciousness, designated in this work as one of the three major systems of neurones in the mental apparatus alongside of systems related to perception and memory. This system, which he called *W* (an abbreviation for the German word for perception), was already here conceived of by Freud as a sense organ for the perception of "qualities." In this usage, consciousness refers to the apparatus or function that invests in (or "cathects") an experience with qualities that bring it into awareness. Thus Freud (1895) wrote:

> ". . . there is a third system of neurones—'perceptual neurons' they might be called—which are excited along with others during perception but not during reproduction, and whose states of excitation give rise to the different qualities—are, that is to say, conscious sensations." (p. 370)

This function of consciousness was conceived of as operating with limited, small amounts of energies or cathexes invested in perceptual stimuli entering the mental apparatus, whether from external or internal sources. These cathexes, which Freud called ego-cathexes, are displaceable or easily shifted and are regulated by the rules of attention and defense. Freud discussed several factors in this latter regard, including the needs of the organism and the availability of stimuli. He also commented upon the predisposition of this function of consciousness to explore or scan; that is, to send out its cathexes to all available perceptions or indications of quality, independent of internal needs. This idea, along with the emphasis that this function is a basic biological given, is one antecedent of the concept of conflict-free or autonomous ego functions which refers to an individual's innate, nondrive capacities and endowments which operate relatively independently of instinctual drives and the conflicts related to them (see Gill, 1963; Hartmann, 1939).

In Breuer and Freud's (1895) *Studies on Hysteria,* consciousness was used primarily as a term referring to a state of the total organism. Breuer actually wrote the sections that emphasized the importance of altered states of consciousness in the etiology of hysterical symptoms. He postulated that, in the experiencing of a trauma that causes symptoms, there is a splitting or dissociation of consciousness, one part of which he labeled the hypnoid state. The occurrence of this altered state of consciousness and the existence of an organized dissociated state within the total organism as etiological factors in the development of hysterical symptoms were accepted only reluctantly by Freud, and he discarded the concepts entirely in subsequent writings (Freud, 1905, 1926). If we examine the basis for this conclusion, we will be able to understand why Freud paid little attention to states of consciousness in his later writings.

Freud's focus was on the understanding of the basis of symptom formation. In this context, a dissociated state, as formulated by Breuer, implied to Freud the existence of ideas outside the main ego (the primary core of the personality) in a relatively fixed or static condition. This also implied to Freud that no force is necessary to keep these ideas in limbo and therefore that no resistance is met when an attempt is made to bring the dissociated contents into consciousness. These concepts were alien to Freud's emphasis on dynamics (conflicting forces) and on the active role of defenses in keeping unacceptable ideas out of awareness. In later years, Freud (1912, 1915) often reiterated his objections to such notions, stating that it implied an "unconscious consciousness." In another vein, Freud rejected the notion of an altered state of consciousness with its own set of mental contents on the grounds that unconscious ideas did not exist in a separate place away from conscious ideas. For him the emphasis was on accessibility to awareness, which in turn was primarily a matter of economics; that is, the kind of energy invested in a given idea was the critical factor, along with the forces opposing the idea's accessibility to awareness. Availability for cathexis by attention was therefore the crucial factor, not a dissociation of state of consciousness. The concept of energic investments in ideas refers to Freud's theory that ideas were invested either with freely mobile energies by which he later characterized the primary processes of drive-dominated unconscious mentation—or with bound energies, characterizing the secondary processes of reality-oriented, available-to-consciousness mentation. The only reason Freud commented on the concept of altered states of consciousness was his great interest in dreams and therefore in the altered state of sleep in which dreams occur. This leads us, then, to *The Interpretation of Dreams* (1900).

In this book, Freud expanded his discussion of consciousness, a topic to which he only occasionally returned in later works, in essentially psychological terms. His concept of the function of consciousness was stated as follows:

> "[regarding] the 'essential nature' of consiousness: we see the process of a thing becoming conscious as a specific psychical act, distinct from and independent of a process of the formation of a presentation or an idea; and we regard consciousness as a sense organ which perceives data that arise elsewhere. . . ." (p. 144). "Consciousness . . . [is] . . . a sense organ for the apprehension of psychical qualities. . . ." (p. 574)

Freud went on to explore factors relevant to the accessibility of internal and external stimulation to this sense organ and felt that this availability was under the control of the system *Pcs.*, a temporary replacement for the ego. The process of becoming conscious was associated with a specific function of the mental apparatus, attention. This function of attention has at its command energies often referred to as hypercathexes, available in limited quantities.

To anticipate and summarize several later theoretical developments, the concept of hypercathexis seems to imply a special kind of cathexis beyond the energy of a drive, one that endows a mental content with importance, and one through which conscious awareness is attained. Access to these hypercathexes of attention is limited by anticathexes, energies of resistance or of defenses such as repression. These energies oppose or defend against the allowing into consciousness or action certain stimuli or drive derivatives related to conflict and anxiety. Some ideas consequently remain unconscious and continue in a freely mobile energic condition, while other ideas are available to consciousness and are in a bound state and become part of the system *Pcs.* or *Cs.* (see Holt, 1962; Gill, 1963).

In *The Interpretation of Dreams,* Freud (1900) discussed the changes in the mental apparatus during the shift from the waking to sleeping state, thereby addressing himself to altered states of consciousness. Briefly, he postulated two major changes in the psyche in the altered state: the first is a lowering of the barrier between the systems *Ucs.* and *Pcs.*, leading to a greater availability to consciousness in the sleeping state of usually unconscious material, such as infantile memories. Theoretically, this was conceived of as a lessening of censorship resistance and a concomitant lessening of defensive anticathexes. The second major change in the sleeping state was described in terms of shifts in the cathectic charge, or investment, in the various mental systems, notably a relative decathexis or disinvestment in the perceptual and motor systems themselves which are therefore relatively inactive, and a retention of strong cathexes by the *Ucs.* (the system Unconscious).

It is unfortunate that Freud tended to neglect both the ego function of consciousness and states of consciousness in his later writings. He did so for a number of additional apparent reasons. The function of consciousness belongs to the relatively autonomous, conflict-free sphere of ego functions, and Freud's major and most exciting discoveries related to how a person deals with anxieties and psychological conflicts and their sources. The vast regions of unconscious mentation and fantasy and their role in neuroses became Freud's central interest. For these reasons, altered states of consciousness were of only peripheral interest to him, and we have already indicated that the initial conceptualization of these altered states by Breuer was not dynamic, something Freud seems never to have reassessed.

Freud (1912) did, however, make brief subsequent contributions to the conceptualization of consciousness. In "A Note on the Unconscious," he began to discuss the difficulties in his usages of the term unconscious. Since much of his thinking on this issue is well known and reviewed elsewhere by Gill (1963), Arlow and Brenner (1964), and others, we allude to it only briefly. Freud first used the term unconscious to refer to a topographic system, the *Ucs.,* and contrasted it with the systems *Pcs.* and *Cs.* Because of contradictions that followed upon this usage, such as the need to postulate unconscious resistances in the system *Pcs.-Cs.,* and contents of the system *Ucs.* which were organized in the mode expected in the other two systems (the secondary processes), Freud (1923) ultimately rejected this model, replacing it with the structural concepts of ego, superego, and id. Second, Freud defined "unconscious" dynamically, referring to repressed mental contents. This too was given up when he found that repressing forces directed against such contents could also be unconscious (Freud, 1923). What was left for Freud was the qualitative usage of unconscious, a descriptive term in which a mental content was referred to as not having the quality of being conscious.

Freud (1917) returned to the state of sleep in one further paper, "A Metapsychological Supplement to the Theory of Dreams." In this paper he related the concept of regression during sleep not only temporally to earlier modes of functioning (e.g., to the visual mode), as he had before (Freud, 1900), but also on a libidinal level (a regression to primary narcissism or to an investment primarily in the self) and to what he labeled an ego level (a regression to hallucinatory gratification). He also reviewed once more the modifications in the censorship function during sleep, referring to the diminution of its barriers, and again emphasized that repressed unconscious materials do not surrender their cathexes or energic charges in the sleeping state.

In his remaining writings Freud returned from time to time to the function of consciousness. In 1923, in *The Ego and the Id* (Freud, 1923), while defining the ego and differentiating it from the superego and id, he wrote: ". . . in each individual there is a coherent organization of mental processes; and we call this his *ego.* It is to this ego that consciousness is attached; . . . ." (p. 17).

Similarly, in the *New Introductory Lectures,* Freud (1933) stated that the ego is best distinguished from the id through its relation to the system *Pcpt.-Cs.* (perceptual consciousness). In these references, then, Freud viewed consciousness as a function of the ego, locating it on the surface of the mental apparatus, closest to reality.

In "A Note upon the 'Mystic Writing-Pad,' " Freud (1925a) utilized this device (in which one may imprint and erase, using a transparent layer which rests on a blackened surface) as an analogy to his postulate that the function of consciousness is solely as a receptor of sensations (a sense organ) which does not itself retain these impressions. As is true of such a pad, it is a second system that registers these sensations and retains them in memory, whereas the first surface is readily erased by lifting it away. In a rare moment Freud also reflected here on the function of attention and returned to his first formulations, set down in the *Project for a Scientific Psychology* (Freud, 1895). The dispensing of attention was viewed as a function of the system *Ucs.* (although later, in "Negation," Freud (1925b) amends this idea and describes it as a function of the ego), operating via the system *Pcpt.-Cs.* This system sends out and withdraws cathectic innervations periodically in order to receive perceptions; that is, it has a scanning function.

In *Moses and Monotheism,* Freud (1939) illuminated one aspect of the problem of accessibility to consciousness or awareness by describing three conditions under which repressed material becomes conscious: a decrease in the anticathexes of defense or a variety of shifts in cathectic investments, an increase in instinctual pressure, and a reawakening caused by recent experiences.

In *An Outline of Psycho-Analysis,* Freud (1940a) emphasized that consciousness as a function operates via hypercathexes, a special added investment of energies. Further, such an investment brings about a synthesis in the cathected mental contents and a binding of free energy. Last, in "Some Elementary Lessons in Psycho-Analysis," Freud (1940b) remarked that an idea becomes conscious only after a long process of selection, rejection, and decision, processes that are themselves unconscious.

It was from these propositions that Rapaport (edited by Gill, 1967), Klein (1959a), and Gill (1963) moved forward. Rapaport (1951) followed Freud in defining the function of consciousness as a "superordinate sense organ" and "an apparatus in the service of the ego." His first efforts in clarifying this function stemmed from observations of various states of consciousness (Rapaport, 1951), observations which raised an important conceptual issue as to the relationship of the specific ego function of consciousness to the broader concept, states of consciousness of the total organism.

The function of consciousness, as Rapaport (1951) first conceived it, is both organized and selective. Rapaport explored alterations of this function and, in addition, explored the dimensions of states of consciousness through a study of amnesias; of dreams, reveries, and related states; and of Korsakoff's syndrome. He reported that in a fugue state, consciousness of the total organism is altered by an overwhelming wish and the threat of losing control over the impulses to enact this wish. As a result, the range of awareness and the degree of reflectiveness are restricted.

From Rapaport's exploration and discussion of varieties of conscious experience, we have culled a series of parameters of states of consciousness (see Table A1.1). These may also be used as descriptive characteristics through which such states can be defined. In Rapaport's discussions conflicts and drives

Table A1.1. Rapaport's Major Parameters of States of Consciousness

Waking State	Altered State
1. Thought: controlled, specific, verbal, and differentiated	1. Ideation: images, undifferentiated and peremptory
2. Reality oriented	2. Drive dominated
3. Single meanings	3. Multiple connotations
4. Secondary-process mode	4. Primary-process mode: condensations, displacements, symbolizations
5. Explicit meanings	5. Implicit meanings
6. Can turn around on itself—one can be aware of being aware	6. Cannot reflect on itself
7. Can separate: fact-assumption, memory-percept, hope-actuality, certainty-doubt, reality-fantasy	7. Impairments in these capacities
8a. Frames of reference clear 8b. Judgment intact	8. Impairments in these capacities
9. Full, adequate controls of drives with a full sense of control	9. Altered controls—excessive or insufficient
10. Full range of awareness	10. Limited range of awareness
11. Clear personal identity	11. Altered personal identity
12. Willed control over thoughts	12. Decrease of voluntary control over thoughts
13. Can reflect on contents and/or modify them	13. Awareness without reflection or modification

emerge as important influences on both the state and the function of consciousness.

Rapaport (1951) concluded his first presentation in this area with a highly personal summary of what he had gathered from Freud's writings as they related to a theory of states of consciousness, stating in part:

"The gradual development from thought as hallucinatory gratification to thought as experimental action reflects the gradual development from monoideic consciousness of the drive gratification to polyideic consciousness of the relation of perceived external reality, internal need, and memories of past experiences. The gradual development corresponds to varieties or forms of consciousness in which various balances are struck between perception of internal and external reality, in which internal experience is to various (ever-decreasing) degrees experienced as external reality and in which internal and external perception (thought and perception of reality) are differentiated with increasing clarity. Correspondingly, the thought forms consciously experienced change gradually from prelogical to logical, from syncretic to abstract, from idiosyncratic to socialized (Werner . . .). . . . This gradual development is reflected in those forms of conscious experience which I have described. . . ." (p. 402)

In his next major paper in this area, "Cognitive Structures," Rapaport (1957) further refined his thinking on states of consciousness. He defined cognitive structures as:

"Those quasi-permanent means which cognitive processes use and do not have to create *de novo* each time and more quasi-permanent organizations of such means that are the framework for the individual's cognitive processes." (p. 631)

These cognitive structures include memory organizations, modes and styles of functioning, and the like. Memory, for example, may be organized around drives or, at the other end of the continuum, around concepts. That is, cognitive organizations range from drive-dominated, condensed, and illogical (primary processes) to goal-directed, ordered, and logical (secondary processes).

Rapaport reviewed his observations of various states of consciousness, referring to his parameters in this paper as the objective criteria of the form of cognition that predominates in a given altered state. The clinical phenomena studied by Rapaport (1957) demonstrate:

"Distinguished forms of cognition . . . [and] cognitive organizations . . . [which are] . . . accompanied by varieties of awareness (that is, consciousness) that appear to be specific to them. This suggests that varieties of consciousness are themselves organized means of cognition . . . we are dealing here with quasi-stable cognitive organizations that use different tools or mechanisms of cognition, and are themselves organized means of cognition." (p. 648)

Here Rapaport uses awareness to refer to the function of consciousness as one aspect of the cognitive organizations that characterize various states of consciousness, thus distinguishing more clearly the two usages of the term consciousness and the relationship between them (see also Rapaport, 1960).

Gill and Klein (1967) summarized Rapaport's theory of states of consciousness and we will paraphrase them to briefly conclude our survey of the latter's contribution. Rapaport conceived of a state of consciousness as an organization subserving cognition, not as a unitary phenomenon; he conceived of a continuum of states from waking to dreaming, differing in kind and extent of prevailing reflective awareness, voluntary effort, forms of thought organization, and the like (see Table A1.1), each corresponding to a specific cognitive organization. He considered states of consciousness to be structures of control and "organized means or tools of cognition." Of the array of cognitive structures involved in states of consciousness, such as memory organization, cognitive style, grammar, and syntax, Rapaport focused on two: first, those structures that preserve distinctions in *modes of experience* (e.g., capacity to distinguish fact and assumption, memory and percept, and so on; see Table A1.1); and second, those higher-order structures that are formed by the organization of these varieties of experience into states of consciousness (Gill and Klein, 1967, p. 26).

Rapaport (1959) later studied in detail the concept of attention cathexis, and we return to his paper on this topic after dealing with the work of Klein

(1959a) and Gill (1963), which preceded this last of Rapaport's contributions to the subject.

Klein, in his paper "Consciousness in Psychoanalytic Theory" (1959a), presents a concise presentation of the central issues in this area. He focuses on the economic or energic aspects of the problems, the aspect Freud himself thought was the key issue. Klein therefore first defined the function of consciousness as the "cathexis or attention-dispensing function of the ego system" (p. 15). Second, he defined states of consciousness in terms of the patterns of deployment of the limited amount of attention cathexis available to consciousness, each pattern constituting a distinctive mode or quality of experiencing and experience. Component structures of the ego, so-called cathectic organizations of the ego, he hypothesized, influence and govern the deployment of attention. Among these energy distributions Klein listed:

". . . (a) the energy systems constituting the component thought functions themselves, e.g., perception, memory, imaging, etc.—the different qualities of experience; (b) mobile (unbound) energies which together describe the varieties of drives; (c) bound and neutralized energies which together describe different kinds of reality adaptive motivations; (d) countercathectic energy distributions which together constitute different kinds of defensive organizations; (e) and finally, those as yet inadequately described energy distributions that constitute different kinds of adaptive cognitive styles or strategies of thought organization." (p. 17)

Thus consciousness was for Klein a function that dispenses attention, and each state of consciousness is "a distinctive *pattern* of experience, and each reflecting and vouchsafed by the existing balance among drive, defense, and controlling structure" (p. 17). Awareness assumes a "structural means of dispensing a determinate amount of attention cathexis" and states of consciousness refer to the patterns of awareness.

Motivated by the interest in consciousness shown by Rapaport, Klein, Gill, and others, specific research in this area began to appear, some of which is summarized by these same authors. In particular, the work of Gill and Brenman (1959), reported in *Hypnosis and Related States,* deserves mention as a psychoanalytic study of a specific group of phenomena related to alterations in state of consciousness. Their rich book, with its metapsychological discussions of hypnotic states and its focus on regression, while related to concepts being developed here, unfortunately cannot be discussed without lengthy detours.

Gill's (1963) monograph *Topography and Systems in Psychoanalytic Theory* deals with many of our problems. His review of Freud's topographical concepts includes a discussion of many aspects of the function of consciousness, since access to consciousness was a major criterion for the topographical systems. Gill extended this discussion to a historical survey of Freud's system *Cs.,* and the sense organ consciousness, lucidly clarifying Freud's use of these concepts.

Gill also noted that the function of consciousness may be conceived currently as a primary autonomous ego apparatus which is under the control of the ego in the waking states, but controlled more by the id (i.e., contains contents relatively more invested with drive energy and organized according to the primary process) in altered states such as sleep.

Gill described four requisites for the entry of a mental content into consciousness: first, the sense organ of consciousness itself; second, quality, an attribute derived from perceptions or sensations of pleasure or pain; third, a critical level of intensity of the particular stimulus as it vies with other stimuli to enter consciousness; and fourth, an appropriate mode of organization and appropriate cathectic conditions of the mental contents involved. There is a balance between the intensity of the drive cathexes and anticathectic forces, which determines whether a given mental content becomes conscious. Further, material organized in one mode (e.g., according to the primary process) has greater difficulty becoming conscious in a state of consciousness organized in another mode (e.g., waking consciousness, which is usually organized in accordance with the secondary process). Last, states of consciousness, according to Gill, should be viewed in terms of different kinds (degrees of neutralization) and different amounts of available attention cathexes.

Gill retained the concept of consciousness as a sense organ while discarding its use as a topographic system. He discussed the sense organ of consciousness from the five metapsychological viewpoints. Briefly, he considered the sense organ consciousness *structurally,* as a structure of the ego. The mental contents that compete for its attention cathexes are affected by executive structures that direct discharge and anticathectic structures that counteract discharge.

He discussed the *dynamic* role of conflict as a factor in the selection of those mental contents that reach consciousness. The synthetic function of the ego was related in part to the advancement in level of organization achieved through directing cathexis onto a given mental content.

Attention cathexes were considered *economically* as hypercathexes in a hierarchy of varying degrees of neutralization (see Rapaport, 1959). The roles of drive cathexes and of anticathexes were also discussed. *Genetically,* the development of attention cathexes was considered in terms of two postulated sources: Primary ego energy (see Hartmann, 1939) or neutral energy, and a secondary energy derived from structure building and the neutralization of drives. The genetic development and differentiation of states of consciousness was also considered.

Last, Gill considered consciousness *adaptively,* pointing out that the ability of attention cathexes to cathect painful stimuli leads to more adaptive regulatory principles beyond that of the pleasure principle and permits adaptive thinking and functioning.

It remained for Rapaport to bring the importance of the function of consciousness in dispensing cathexes of attention to the forefront of psychoanalytic theory. In a highly condensed, enormously rich, posthumously published paper, Rapaport (1959) enumerated a series of basic postulates regarding the role of attention cathexis in structure building and in consciousness. It was Rapaport's hope to express motivations (processes) and cognitions (processes and structures) in the same quantitative term, cathexis, and to deal as well with a number of other problems using this concept (including factors of individual differences). We can only briefly sample those of the basic postulates outlined by Rapaport regarding attention cathexis that are most pertinent to our work: (1) Excitations give rise to consciousness (e.g., perception) only if hypercathected by attention cathexis. (2) There is a limited quantity of available attention cathexis which varies with ego states and for which various excitations compete. (3) Attention cathexis is crucial in the energy of the synthetic function of the ego. (4) The supply of attention cathexis is reduced by conflict and certain drugs. (5) Drives are most likely to attract attention cathexis (unless defended against, i.e., anti-cathected). (6) In altered states, attention cathexis operates in a different way for the following possible reasons: (a) attention cathexis is the same, but its relationship to excitation changes; (b) there is a change in structural conditions; and/or (c) there is a shift in the extent to which attention cathexis exists in a neutral form. Rapaport also presented a series of postulates regarding attention cathexes as related to structures and motivations, including their role in binding energies, their displaceability, and their autonomy, but these cannot be detailed here.

Rapaport's (1958) discussion of ego autonomy also has a bearing on the concept of the relative autonomy of the function of consciousness. Drives are, he noted, the guarantors of relative autonomy from external stimulation, as reality is the guarantor of relative autonomy from drives. Regressive or altered states impair these autonomies, and with such impairment the function of attention is altered.

One last concept discussed metapsychologically by Rapaport (1953), that of activity and passivity, is relevant. Rapaport himself discussed the implications of these concepts for the conceptualization of states of consciousness. The essential meaning of these terms as used by Rapaport is as:

". . . parameters of the control of structure over drive or the relative lack of such. . . . [there terms are] parameters of the relative autonomy of the ego. The terms are applied to the function of consciousness in terms of the ability of drives to command the hypercathexis of attention (passivity), and in terms of the shift from active thought in the waking state to passive forms of experiencing in altered states." (p. 566)

Clinical Literature

Psychoanalytic clinicians who have wrestled with the problem of consciousness have done so almost entirely in terms of altered states of consciousness and their role in psychopathology. Loewald (1955) attempted to revive interest in the role of the hypnoid state in the pathogenicity of a trauma. He postulated that the state of consciousness in the child at the time of a trauma is altered, and that the alien modes of experiencing in such a state isolate memories of such traumatic experiences from later, conscious, secondary-process-dominated experiences. Niederland (1965) reported that the re-creation of altered states of consciousness during psychoanalysis fosters the recall of early traumatic experiences. According to Dickes (1965), the ego may develop an altered state of consciousness defensively to protect the individual from awareness of painful erotic and aggressive fantasies and impulses. Stein (1965) described a syndrome comprised of forgetting, pseudostupidity, and acting out, which was fostered by alterations in the state of consciousness. Rubinfine (1961), in another vein, discussed symbol formation in terms of its development during early, archaic states of consciousness. These states are dominated by the visual mode, poor separation of self and nonself, impairment of certain ego functions, and a characteristic mode of delay and control of drive impulses. Stamm (1962) and Fink (1967) have studied clinically some of the concomitants of altered ego states. Last, Arlow and Brenner (1964), in their discussion of the structural and topographic theories, touch upon changes in the mental apparatus in sleep. They emphasize that in such a state there is a regression in a variety of ego functions and in superego functioning. Further, instinctual wishes and fantasies stemming from the id play a larger role in the content of dreaming consciousness than in waking consciousness.

Although none of the writers reviewed here endeavored to define the role of specific personality features in the phenomena under consideration, awareness of individual differences was implied in much that was written. Freud approached the problem only peripherally in two places; in *The Interpretation of Dreams* (Freud, 1900) he referred to individual differences in respect to the retention of infantile wishes into adulthood; and in "The Unconscious" (Freud, 1915), he briefly discussed the role of the system *Cs.* in the structure of individual neuroses. Klein (1959a) and Rapaport (1951) acknowledged individual differences in the varieties of states of consciousness experienced by any given individual and in the underlying cognitive organizations responsible for it, but neither pursued this aspect further.

The Concept of Consciousness

This, then, is a brief survey of the psychoanalytic writings dealing with consciousness. We now attempt to present an integrated conceptualization of consciousness in all of its usages, to indicate areas of apparent confusion, and to suggest hypotheses relevant to our present research.

The term consciousness in present-day psychoanalytic theory has three meanings. First, it refers to a relatively autonomous structure (and function) of the ego, which dispenses cathexes or investments of attention. This structure is vital for awareness and conscious experience. Attention may be described along several dimensions: it can be actively directed and controlled or passively influenced and preempted; it can be focused or diffuse, discrete or vague, and full in range or limited; and it can turn upon itself (enable the person to be aware of being aware) or lack this capacity. These dimensions are considered metapsychologically in terms of vicissitudes of attention cathexes or hypercathexes, the latter possibly referring to focused attention. Further, the condition of this structure, its manner of functioning, and the availability of sensory and mental contents to its limited quantity of cathectic energies are all influenced by other specific ego functions or structures, by a variety of organizations within the ego, by a number of external and internal conditions, by the state of instinctual drives, and last, by the state of consciousness of the total organism.

Consciousness as a state of the total organism is the second psychoanalytic use of this term. This state can be described not only in terms of alterations in the function of awareness but also in terms of modifications in every aspect of the mental apparatus. The dimensions of the state of consciousness range along the continuum of full alertness or wakefulness, through clouding and sleep, to a multiplicity of other parameters (see Table A1.1) which vary independently or codependently with this first dimension. These include those related to the mode of conscious experience, the manner in which attention is dispensed, awareness of one's identity, differentiation between self and nonself, motility, and a multiplicity of changes within the mental apparatus. The metapsychology of these changes is discussed in terms of a variety of concepts including patterns of deployment of attention cathexes, differences in cognitive organizations, and the parameters proposed by Rapaport and others (Table A1.1).

Shifts in the state of consciousness may be initiated by a wide variety of means (Ludwig, 1966), essentially by any critical alteration in the self-environment totality. Thus such changes may begin with an upsurge of drives, with a shocking or monotonous reality, with sudden intrapsychic shifts in the defensive alignment, and with the ingestion of certain drugs such as LSD which may affect a number of these areas.

The third usage of the term consciousness in psychoanalytic writings is primarily a qualitative one, although this use now has wider implications than simply whether a particular mental content or mental operation is conscious or unconscious, within or outside awareness. This usage refers to the organization of such contents in terms of a hierarchy of cognitive and fantasy organizations. Of particular interest to the present research is the fact that such organizations are revealed through a variety of means (e.g., dreams, analytic working-through, lifting of repressive barriers, and so on), including alterations in the state of consciousness through drugs such as LSD.

It was in this theoretical context that our research was undertaken. By administering the drug LSD to each of our experimental subjects, we hoped to create pharmacological pressure toward an alteration in the state of consciousness in each one and to study the resultant altered state in detail, including those factors that enhance as well as minimize it. Further, we sought to focus on the ego function of consciousness, that is, of dispensing attention cathexes, and to follow its vicissitudes in these altered states. Last, in keeping with the conceptualization of conscious and unconscious cognitive organizations, we hoped to explore these organizations and the modes of functioning that emerged in the various altered states. All this was done in the context of a careful and detailed personality assessment by means of which we could correlate individual differences in the experienced altered states of consciousness (and the functioning in these states) with the various dimensions of the personality of each subject. Once data in all of these areas had been collected and analyzed, we returned to the psychoanalytic theory of consciousness to suggest refinements and clarifications (Chapter 6).

R. J. L.
H. L. B.

APPENDIX 2

Notes for Chapter 2

NOTE 1: ALTERNATIVE METHODS OF ANALYZING THE DATA

The individual differences in a specific drug effect could have been correlated with the personality measures, and a number of interesting relationships were in fact found in this way. To do this for each drug effect, however, would have yielded a maze of relationships impossible to integrate and conceptualize.

Another approach was to examine the relationships among the subjects' responses to the different experimental tasks, through correlational or other methods. There is, however, a serious limitation to this. The effects of LSD last, on the average, about 8 hours, with the strongest effects averaging 3 or 4 hours, although this varies widely for different individuals. During this time there is a progression of drug effects, by no means the same for everyone, characterized by marked qualitative and quantitative changes in the person's psychological state throughout the drug day. Since different tasks were, perforce, given at different times during the day, even the reactions of the same subject to two different tasks cannot be assumed to have occurred in the same altered state of consciousness. Any relationships between performance on different tasks (and some were found) had to work against this fact.

The relationships across tasks that were most readily found were between the various experimental procedures and either the questionnaire responses or the behavioral observations. Comparisons could have been made between performances in each experiment and the questionnaire or behavioral data obtained closest to it in time. Some of these comparisons were quite illuminating in clarifying individual differences in the laboratory tasks. They are reported in the text whenever they were found, but they proved too specific and limited to clarify the total picture.

NOTE 2: THE PRELIMINARY MMPI SCREENING OF SUBJECTS

We did accept as subjects some men who were moderately depressed or somewhat immature, who reported a moderate number of somatic or functional complaints, who were "sensitive" or within the "normal" range of paranoid tendencies. Also accepted were moderately impulsive and scattered (i.e., hypomanic) subjects and those who were somewhat eccentric, conscientious and orderly, and shy. On two scales no limits were set; homosexual subjects and those scoring in the psychopathic range were accepted. In addition to the summary scores represented by the MMPI scales, "stop items" indicating gross pathology were grounds for rejection. Examples are: "Someone has been trying to poison me"; "My soul sometimes leaves my body"; and "Someone has control over my mind." A number of additional items, while not grounds for immediate rejection, were noted on the subject's face sheet for the interviewer to inquire into. Examples of such items are: "I deserve severe punishment for my sins"; "I feel weak all over much of the time"; and "Sometimes I feel that I am about to go to pieces."

NOTE 3: THE PERSONALITY ASSESSMENT VARIABLES

For each of the 9-point scales used for the Personality Assessment items, there was a specific point used as an anchor, representing that degree of a particular characteristic which was felt to represent an average or hypothetical norm. Those items in which the mean of the study group differed significantly from the point so defined as "normal" thus identify differences from the hypothetical general population. For both the WAIS and the DPI, there are well-established normative data, and the diagnostic summaries of the pretest Rorschach protocols were written against the background of a broad general clinical experience. The description of the ways in which our 50 subjects, as a group, tend to differ from the hypothetical average young man is based on the group deviations from such normative data.

The Personality Assessment variables are:

1. Weak relationships with people, withdrawn. *Combines:* Relationships with people generally tenuous, marginal; approaches others anxiously, cautiously, defensively. Generally feels isolated and separated from others; withdrawn. Relates himself to people easily, freely, and warmly (*sign reversed*).

2. Bland and uncommunicative. *Combines:* Tends to be quiet and uncommunicative. Affect is bland or flat; lacks spontaneity and passion.

3. Narcissistic, with fluid affect. *Combines:* Is narcissistic, overly concerned with himself as object. Affects are fluid and undercontrolled; he is impulsive and labile, excitable and overenthusiastic.

4. Affect well-modulated, good-tempered. *Combines:* Generally cheerful and good-tempered. Affect expression is well-modulated, flexible, spontaneous, but not fluid.

5. Relationships manipulative and demanding. *Combines:* Manipulates people as a means to achieving personal ends; is guileful. Actively demanding in his relationships with people (e.g., "get something for nothing").

6. Is socially perceptive, responsive to interpersonal nuances.

7. Defensiveness. When faced with stress and frustration retreats to a guarded position; is self-defensive and tries to conceal feelings and thoughts.

8. Inhibition and overcontrol. Deals with impulses and feelings by inhibiting and suppressing them; overcontrols impulses and affects; needlessly delays or denies gratification.

9. Experiences diffuse anxiety readily.

10. Is tense and restless.

11. Frequently feels elated, on top of the world.

12. Separation from, or rejection by, paternal figures has been, or would be, an important source of anxiety.

13. Separation from, or rejection by, maternal figures has been, or would be, an important source of anxiety.

14. Hostile relationships, verbal aggression and resentment. *Combines:* Relationships with people are usually marred by hostility. Seeks arguments; loves to attack people verbally, to criticize, to belittle or ridicule people. Feels resentful, bitter; harbors grudges.

15. Hostility toward paternal figures and men in general. *Combines:* Rebels against paternal figures. Tends to be hostile toward men. Competes with paternal figures.

16. Hostility toward maternal figures and women in general. *Combines:* Tends to be hostile toward women. Rejects or rebels against maternal figures.

17. Aggression pent-up and expressed in fantasy. *Combines:* Is excited by eroticized thoughts of cruelty or destructive power; has fantasies of injuring or humiliating others (may be unconscious or ego-alien). His aggressions are pent-up; has a great deal of unexperienced anger.

18. Anticipates being exploited. *Combines:* Tends to anticipate that people will push him around, compel him to enter into unwanted activities. Fears possible future privation; anticipates being exploited and cheated.

19. Is passively aggressive, using indirect means of hurting or thwarting others (e.g., negativism, "forgetting" obligations, etc.).

20. Needs to rebel, to reject and defy authority, conventional values, and/or dogmatic standards.

21. Oversensitive to challenge and threat.

22. Fears losing control over his aggressive impulses.

23. Depression and self-abasement. *Combines:* Turning against the self; feels depressed as a defense against aggression, or in some other way directs hostility against self (e.g., by "objective" self-criticism), intropunitive. Is subject to feelings of shame, inferiority, and inability to live up to his standards. Easily becomes depressed, feels unworthy and self-abasing.

24. Self-punitive, disillusioned. *Combines:* Has an unconscious need for punishment; self-defeating, gets self into painful situations. Feels disillusioned, resigned.

25. Sees himself as unwanted and unloved.

26. Has an unconscious body image as physically impaired, incomplete, or damaged.

27. Somatization: Expresses anxiety and impulses somatically in the form of physical or physiological reactions.

28. Often feels angry and impatient with himself.

29. Positive attitudes toward work and responsibility. *Combines:* Rejects responsibility (*sign reversed*). Is active and resourceful in seeking work of the kind he wants. Derives personal reward and pleasure from work; values productive achievement for its own sake. Sees his role in life as a passive bystander, a nonparticipant (*sign reversed*).

30. Persistent goal striving in the face of frustration. *Combines:* Strives for his goals persistently and with endurance. Counteraction: in the face of frustration, redoubles efforts to succeed; if injured, strikes back directly against the source. Lowered ego ideal; when frustrated, withdraws cathexis from the goal (*sign reversed*).

31. Lack of self-assertion; masochism and avoidance. *Combines:* Is pessimistic about his professional future, lacks self confidence. Afraid to assert himself. Masochistically submits to other people; takes blame or punishment without a struggle; easily surrenders. Avoidance: sidesteps troublesome situations; makes concessions to avoid unpleasantness; evades and attempts to escape difficulties.

32. Independence (high score) vs. dependence (low score). *Combines:* Seeks independence in all things; hates to be beholden to anyone; prefers to work things out without help. Feels the need for protection and support; relies on and easily turns to others for help, consolation, advice, or security (*sign reversed*).

33. General passivity and passive resistance. *Combines:* Longs for peace and quiet; needs relaxation and rest; hates exertion and effort. Passive resistance: refuses to become involved in things; withdraws into self, or drags his feet rather than overtly rebelling.

34. Seeks positions of authority and identifies with authority figures. *Combines:* Tends to identify self with authority figures. Loves to influence and control others, ascendant and domineering; seeks positions of leadership.

35. Suggestible and dependent on others to take initiative.

36. Has an adequate amount of reasonable self-esteem, accepts and likes self (N.B., not narcissistic self-inflation).

37. Counterphobic and hypomanic: In the face of fearful situations and depressive feelings, takes active steps to control and cope with it; tests out fearful situations; directly wards off low moods by forced merriment.

38. Failure of defense: becomes disorganized and unadaptive under stress, feels helpless.

39. Thought and fantasy stereotyped and concrete—repression inferred. *Combines:* His thinking is stereotyped, unoriginal, and concrete (vs. imaginative and original concepts and problem-solving attempts). His fantasy life is minimal and stereotyped; clings to reality. Repression: conveniently forgets and excludes unacceptable ideas and impulses from access to action or awareness.

40. Loose thinking (high score) vs. clear thinking (low score). *Combines:*

His concepts tend to be loose, fuzzy or vague, poorly articulated, and sloppily worded. Communicates ideas clearly, effectively, and appropriately (*sign reversed*).

41. Thinking inhibited and stimulus bound. *Combines:* His thinking tends to be blocked and inhibited. Thinking is stimulus bound and requires external stimulation.

42. Given to inferential thinking and primary-process intrusion. *Combines:* His thinking and speech generally show much evidence of the primary process. Highly given to inference; tries to figure out hidden meanings, reasoning in a biased and sometimes arbitrary way.

43. Introspection and sensitive to minimal cues. *Combines:* Introspective and self-examining. Alert and sensitive to small differences and slight cues.

44. Concentrates easily on an interest or a problem and is not easily distracted.

45. Thinks in a ruminative, circumstantial, overdetailed fashion; vacillates and hesitates over decisions.

46. Has vivid imagery.

47. Analyzes a problem skillfully, actively, and accurately.

48. Has a narrow range of interests.

49. His thinking shows much evidence of naivete.

50. His thinking and language tend to be expansive, flamboyant, and colorful.

51. Heterosexual (high score) vs. homosexual (low score). *Combines:* Has a confused sexual identity (feminine identification) (*sign reversed*). Is masculine in style and manner of behavior. Has a strong interest in the opposite sex; seeks sexual gratification through love; oriented toward lasting heterosexual relationships. Homosexuality (manifest or latent): a good deal of (eroticized) interest in persons of the same sex (*sign reversed*).

52. Feelings of superiority, exclusiveness, and exhibitionism. *Combines:* Feels special, unusual, a cut above most others. Is concerned with making an impression on others; boastful, ostentatious, exhibitionistic. Feels a need to be discriminating, critical, exclusive, perhaps snobbish; intolerant of others and rejective.

53. Intellectualization and intellectuality. *Combines:* Has the identity of an intellectual. Intellectualization: seeks safety in information and knowledge; under stress gets distance from the situation and prevents emergence of anxiety by taking a "scientific" or "philosophical" attitude, dissecting the situation, and so on. Values information for its own sake; wants to be well informed.

54. Seeks creative outlets and strives for understanding. *Combines:* Needs to have an outlet for creative urges; eager to write, build, or create things or ideas. Seeks explanations; wants to understand the reasons for things; enjoys reading and study.

55. Sensitive, creative identity, and philosophical concerns. *Combines:* Has the identity of the sensitive, creative artist. Concerned with abstract and philosophical problems, for example, religion, values, and the meaning of life, and so on.

56. Identity diffusion and conflict. *Combines:* There is a serious intrinsic conflict between elements of his identity (other than sexual identity). His identifications are diffused, not well jelled; he is floundering about, playacting, in search of someone to be.

57. Ego-syntonic identity and values. *Combines:* Moral and ethical values are well internalized, ego-syntonic, and calmly accepted. The major theme of his identity fits well into his social and professional world.

58. Identity: orderly and thrifty. *Combines:* Feels a need for cleanliness and order; must keep things tidy and in place or becomes uncomfortable; hates dirt and messiness. Is thrifty, saving of money and careful of possessions; hates to throw anything away; holds onto anything of value.

59. Regression and childishness. *Combines:* Sees himself as immature and childlike; tends to identify himself with young children. Regression: regresses in the face of stress; retreats to an earlier mode of functioning.

60. Conventional and other-directed judgments, and introjection as defense. *Combines:* Introjection: defends self against a threatening person by identifying self with him, imitating his values and ways; tries to placate people by being just like them. His judgment is conventional, based mainly on "what others may think."

61. Projection and externalization. *Combines:* Externalization: disowns personal responsibility and blame by attributing them to external agents. Projection: attributes to others his own unacceptable impulses, needs, and fears; distorts reality (or takes advantage of it in some way) so it seems to be the source of his own unacceptable impulses.

62. Conceives of self as realistic, practical, and "hard-boiled."

63. Is changeable, fitting himself chameleonlike into any environment he encounters.

64. Is acutely aware of his sexual inadequacy, real or fancied (may be timid with girls, brash, ascetic, etc., in overt behavior).

65. Is constantly trying to reassure himself by proving he is "all right," acceptable to others, or competent.

66. Plays the role of "clown" when with others.

67. Seeks and enjoys sensuous and/or sensual experience.

68. Acting out: Avoids anxiety by *doing* something; prevents self from thinking by keeping on the move, involved in activities, acting out his problems.

69. Denial: Copes with disturbing external objects or events by a failure of reality testing, not perceiving their presence.

70. Substitution in fantasy: when frustrated, seeks substitute gratification in fantasy.

71. Isolation: separates affect from ideational content, which is not repressed; in poor touch with his own true feelings.

72. Reaction formation: defends self against the emergence of a repressed impulse by building up its opposite (nurturance vs. aggression; responsibility vs. dependence; saintliness vs. sex, etc.).

73. Undoing: compulsively acts so as to negate and magically annihilate a "sin" by expiation, ritualistic acts, and so on.

74. Lacks social poise and presence; becomes rattled and upset in social situations.

75. Submits to paternal figures; complies with their wishes.

76. Strives to achieve status; needs to be admired, looked up to by others.

77. Shows ordinary, unremarkable reasoning (does not imply unoriginality —simply unobtrusiveness).

78. Has dependable and practical common sense and good judgment.

79. Thinking is compulsively rigid, ordered, and planful.

80. Intuitive, reaching conclusions without knowing how or why (regardless of whether these conclusions are valid or invalid).

81. Often experiences his thoughts and impulses as ego-alien.

82. Thinks much about money and what he can get; greedy or acquisitive.

83. Has a strong sense of identity with an ethnic group or national tradition.

84. Tends to identify self with the outcast and social deviant.

85. Interest in people is feigned, overdemonstrative; facade of warmth.

86. Is curious about people, prying into others' affairs; fond of gossip and finding out the lowdown.

87. Lacks insight into his own motives and behavior.

88. Is gregarious; prefers interpersonal and group situations to working alone; seeks relatedness to others.

89. Submits to maternal figures; complies with their wishes.

90. Wants to be helpful to others; generous with time and energy; kind and sympathetic.

91. Uses words in a pompous, stilted, ostentatious way.

92. Is worried by, or suffers conflict over, homosexual thoughts, fantasies, or behavior.

93. Suffers conscious guilt over heterosexual impulses, or fears loss of control over sexual impulses.

NOTE 4: THE INADEQUACY OF RANDOM ASSIGNMENT OF SUBJECTS TO GROUPS

The first 29 subjects (19 drug and 10 placebo) were tested during the first 5 months of 1959 and testing was then suspended for the summer. A preliminary analysis made at that point revealed that, using the Total Questionnaire Score to measure the overall magnitude of the drug reaction, the score for the pretest day correlated very strongly with the drug day score within the LSD group ($r = .58$, significant at the .01 level), although the drug day scores were, as expected, much higher (on the average, more than five times the pretest scores). A problem was then apparent; the mean pretest score, intended as a baseline measure, was significantly higher (.02 level) in the drug group than it was in the placebo group. In other words, subjects who reported more drug-like reactions to the questionnaire before taking the drug experienced a stronger drug effect, and such subjects were more common in the drug than in the placebo group.

Although this imbalance could not account for the massive difference between the mean Total Questionnaire Scores of the two groups on the experimental day (see Chapter 3), it seemed wise to abandon the use of random numbers and assign the remaining subjects on the basis of their pretest scores, trying to match the groups as well as possible. By this means, when the study was completed in the latter part of 1959, we had been able to reduce the mean difference in pretest scores to one-third of its former size; this difference was no longer statistically significant. In the completed drug group, the correlation between pretest and drug day scores dropped to .37 which, although significant (.05 level), accounts for only a small portion (14%) of the variance in drug day scores. The corresponding correlation of .22 in the placebo group is not significant.

The effect of placing subjects with low pretest scores in the drug group during the later period of experimentation, in order to compensate for the earlier overinclusion of those with high pretest scores, was that we unknowingly corrected for certain major aspects of personality. We later discovered that narcissistic subjects reported more reactions on the pretest day than average, while hostile, suspicious, and anxious subjects reported fewer. As a result, the drug subjects tested before and those tested after the change in assignment procedures differed markedly in the nature of their drug reaction, although contrary to our expectation they did not differ in the overall magnitude of their effect. When subjects are grouped into the reaction type categories described in Chapter 5, we find that all but 2 of the 15 subjects in Groups I, II, and VI were from the earlier test group, while all subjects in Groups III and IV were tested later.

Two conclusions may be drawn from our experience: first, that random assignment is not adequate in studies using small samples to investigate complex reactions; and second, that such studies would be much improved by knowledgeable selection of subjects based on relevant aspects of personality.

APPENDIX 3

Notes for Chapter 3

NOTE 1: ADMINISTRATION AND SCORING OF THE QUESTIONNAIRE

The questionnaires were scored by one experimenter and reviewed by a second; scoring differences, which were not numerous, were resolved by discussion. Each "yes" answer was given 1 point, and each "partial yes" ½ point; these were summed to obtain the Total Questionnaire Score and scores for the separate subscales.

The questionnaire was usually given seven times, but omissions did occur, especially with subjects whose reaction was extreme. The actual number of subjects tested at each time period is indicated below; no subject missed more than one of the four administrations on the experimental day.

1. Pretest day, with instructions to "report whether you have had any of these feelings at all today" (obtained for all 30 LSD and 20 placebo subjects).
2. One-half hour after drug administration (all subjects).
3. Two hours after drug administration (29 LSD and 19 placebo subjects). (The actual time range was from 1½ to 2¼ hours.)
4. Five hours after drug administration (29 LSD and 20 placebo subjects). (The actual time range was from 3¾ to 6½ hours, with 76% obtained between 4½ and 5¾ hours.)
5. Eight hours after drug administration (25 LSD and 17 placebo subjects). (The actual time range was 7 to 9½ hours, with 76% obtained between 7¼ and 8¾ hours.)
6. Posttest day, given on the morning after the experimental day with instructions to answer "on the basis of how you feel today" (26 LSD and 19 placebo subjects).
7. Retrospective, given immediately after the posttest questionnaire, with instructions to report all reactions experienced at any time during the experimental day (27 LSD and 19 placebo subjects); this questionnaire is not discussed here but is fully reported elsewhere (Linton, Langs, and Paul, 1964; Paul, Langs, and Barr, 1965).

In addition to the scoring of each of the seven questionnaire protocols for each subject, a comprehensive Experimental Day score was computed. For this purpose 1 point was scored for each item to which the subject answered "yes" on any of the four experimental day protocols, and ½ point for each item to which he gave only a "partial yes" at any time. The mean scores of each group for each of the questionnaire administrations except the retrospective and for the Experimental Day summary score are given in Table A3.1.

NOTE 2: COURSE OF SPECIFIC LSD EFFECTS OVER TIME

The time curves of the total score and of 5 groups of items clustered according to their course over time are shown in Fig. A3.1.

Curve Types 1 and 2 are LSD effects that share very early onsets (½ hour). Some of these reactions diminished rapidly (Type 1); the balance continued at a high level throughout the entire 8 hours (Type 2). Type 1 reactions included feeling like a different person and the feeling one is *about to* lose control; early body image changes (feeling small, the body feeling disconnected, and losing or being about to lose control over the body); and finding it easier to move. Type 2 effects included additional feelings of alienation from oneself and body image changes but were most prominently somatic effects such as dizziness or grogginess, physical weakness, numbness or tingling, nausea, blurred vision, and feeling hot. Also early in onset, and persisting in some subjects, was a happy feeling that in a few cases reached extreme elation.

Curve Types 3 and 4 resemble each other in having a somewhat later onset; they both consist of drug effects that were minimal at the ½ hour point, close to peak level by 2 hours, and at their peak at 5 hours. They differ in that Type 3 reactions fell off after 5 hours, whereas Type 4 reactions persisted through the 8 hours. Among the Type 3 effects were: a carefree feeling, silliness and the loss of control over elation, a feeling of time passing quickly, visual distortions, and thinking disturbances (impaired judgment, difficulty in holding onto ideas and images, and loss of control over thoughts). Feelings of unreality and of standing aside and looking at oneself were of this type, as well as the feeling of having lost control, thinking about things not usually thought about (including one's childhood), and attention being held involuntarily. Body image changes, such as merging into the surroundings, were included, as were difficulty in moving and feeling cold. Anger with oneself is in this group, possibly in association with the varied forms of loss of control that typify this group of reactions.

The smaller group of the more persistent Type 4 reactions included impairments of ideation (difficulty in concentration and slower thinking), loss of meanings, an impaired sense of time, reluctance to talk, and externally directed anger. Additional somatic symptoms (unpleasant taste, dry mouth, ringing in the ears) also fit this curve.

The Type 5 group consisted of items that peaked sharply at 5 hours at the height of the LSD reaction and were comparatively rare at other times. This

Table A3.1. Comparison of Total Questionnaire Scores of LSD and Placebo Subjects

	LSD Group			Placebo Group			LSD vs. Placebo
	Mean Score	Range	t vs. Pretest	Mean Score	Range	t vs. Pretest[a]	t
Pretest	4.78	0–16	—	3.63	0–13	—	1.07
Experimental day							
½ hour	10.58	0–41.5	4.03[b]	3.40	0–12	−0.25	3.84[b]
2 hours	22.60	4–43.5	9.22[b]	3.95	0–9	0.75	8.48[b]
5 hours	27.83	3–44.5	11.33[b]	5.20	0–15.5	1.24	9.23[b]
8 hours	16.14	0–39	5.21[b]	3.82	0–14	0.79	4.96[b]
Posttest	5.02	0–28	0.02	.95	0–4.5	−3.72[c]	3.08[c]
Experimental Day summary score	38.95	15.5–56.5		11.15	0–24		10.22[b]

[a] A minus sign before a t indicates that the mean is lower than the pretest mean. The t test for correlated means was used to compare the pretest with later means.

[b] Significant at .001 level (two-tailed test).

[c] Significant at .01 level (two-tailed test).

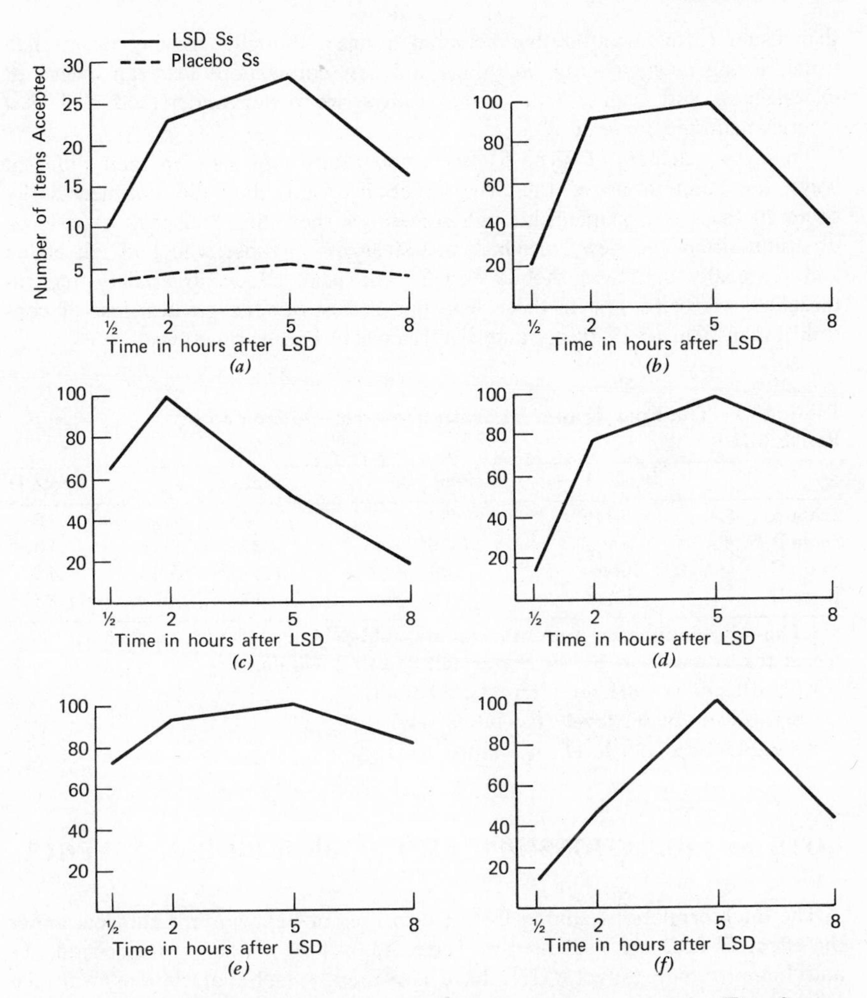

Figure A3.1. Time Curves for Total Questionnaire Scores and for Five Groups of LSD Effects. Items within each curve type are equated by assigning a value of 100 to the maximum point in time of each item. (*a*) Total questionnaire score. (*b*) Type 1 (7 items). (*c*) Type 2 (14 items). (*d*) Type 3 (25 items). (*e*) Type 4 (10 items). (*f*) Type 5 (23 items).

pattern occurred for two rather distinct aspects of the drug reaction. One set involved anxiety, depression, and retardation of time (passing slowly or stopping), along with the mind being blank, events seeming disconnected, fear (sometimes of going crazy and sometimes simply uncontrolled fear), losing hold of reality, feeling old or helpless like a child, being reluctant to talk, and being unsure of the reactions of others. The other set, in contrast, represented a loss of inhibition of thinking and the opening of new horizons: talking more than usual (often about rather personal things), thoughts moving faster than usual, seeing new meanings in things and new connections between events or experiences, and feeling that certain things are better understood and new abilities acquired under LSD.

These two clusters of Type 5 effects apparently represent, in their different ways, the culmination of the drug experience, and they did not necessarily occur in the same people, although sometimes they did. The peak experience of disinhibition and new "insights" was strongest in those who had felt elated and physically light and mobile earlier. The peak effects of anxiety and retardation were strongest in those who had earlier felt the greatest loss of control, impairment of thinking, and disturbance in bodily functions.

Table A3.2. The Four Empirical Scales: Intercorrelations and Reliabilities[a]

	Scale A	Scale B	Scale C	Scale D
Scale A	(.90)[b]	.51[c]	.36[d]	–.12
Scale B	.51[c]	(.86)[b]	.24	.10
Scale C	.36[d]	.24	(.87)[b]	.45[d]
Scale D	–.12	.10	.45[d]	(.83)[b]

[a] The correlations in parentheses are odd-even reliability coefficients, corrected for attenuation by the Spearman-Brown formula.

[b] Significant at .001 level (two-tailed test).

[c] Significant at .01 level (two-tailed test).

[d] Significant at .05 level (two-tailed test).

NOTE 3: RELATIONSHIPS AMONG BEHAVIORAL EFFECTS

The intercorrelations among the 13 measures of behavior for subjects under the effect of LSD are presented in Table A3.3. Two measures, Regression (I) and Inappropriate Affect (III), have consistently high correlations with the entire set of scores. Inappropriate Affect (III) is associated with all the specific measures of affective change: Silliness (IV), Elation (V), Anxiety (VIII), Hostility (X), and Suspiciousness (XI), and thus can be seen as an omnibus measure of the emotional changes produced by LSD. It is also correlated with Motility Deviations (VI-A) and Regressive Behavior (I).

Let us look at some of the more notable links between the other measures before considering Regression (I). Of special interest is the strong association between Anxiety (VIII) and Bodily Preoccupation (IX), which confirms the subjective reports from the questionnaire, in which they were strongly correlated and both appeared in the empirical Scale D. These two behavioral manifestations are also strongly associated with Regression (I) and Motility Changes (VI-A), while Anxiety alone correlates with Hostility (X) and Suspiciousness (XI).

Table A3.3. Intercorrelations of Behavioral Scales—LSD Subjects ($N = 30$)

		I	II	III	IV	V	V-A	VI	VI-A	VII	VIII	IX	X
I.	Regression												
II.	Visual Distortion	.76[a]											
III.	Inappropriate Affect	.76[a]	.50[b]										
IV.	Silliness	.72[a]	.61[a]	.85[a]									
V.	Depression (+) vs. Elation (−)	−.42[c]	−.54[b]	−.55[b]	−.74[a]								
V-A.	Affect, absolute deviation	.41[c]	.07	.38[c]	.25	.21							
VI.	Motility: Slow (+) vs. Fast (−)	−.05	.13	.23	−.26	.65[a]	.12						
VI-A.	Motility, absolute deviation	.59[a]	.25	.51[b]	.49[b]	−.22	.57[a]	−.15					
VII.	Withdrawal	−.28	.40[c]	.29	−.43[c]	.73[a]	.26	.55[b]	.11				
VIII.	Anxiety	.62[a]	.33[d]	.43[c]	.33[d]	−.14	.40[c]	.12	.58[a]	−.16			
IX.	Bodily Preoccupation	.57[a]	.36[c]	.29	.29	.09	.28	−.07	.46[b]	−.08	.72[a]		
X.	Hostility-Negativism	.24	−.02	.56[b]	.23	.03	.35[d]	−.05	.17	.24	.43[c]	.14	
XI.	Suspiciousness	.48[b]	.20	.48[b]	.25	−.07	.39[c]	.11	.35[d]	.11	.56[b]	.19	.55[b]

[a] Significant at .001 level (two-tailed test).
[b] Significant at .01 level (two-tailed test).
[c] Significant at .05 level (two-tailed test).
[d] Significant at .10 level (two-tailed test).

Hostility-Negativism (X) and Suspiciousness (XI) form a pair of reactions and, as we have noted, they are correlated with both Inappropriate Affect (III) and Anxiety (VIII). Only Suspiciousness, however, correlated significantly with Regression (I), suggesting that suspicion is a more psychoticlike manifestation than hostility.

Deviations of Affect (V-A) and Motility (VI-A) are related to each other and (by definition) unrelated to the bipolar measures of Depression-Elation (V) and Motility, Slow vs. Fast (VI). Both are significantly related to Regression (I), Inappropriate Affect (III), and Anxiety (VIII), while motility shift alone is also significantly related to both Silliness (IV) and Bodily Effects (IX). An altered pattern of motility, then, is associated with some of the most pervasive behavioral effects of LSD.

Shifts on the Depression-Elation scale (V) are correlated with Motility shifts (VI) and Withdrawal (VII). These cluster with other behavioral reactions to form two groups of reactions. The first is one of depression, retardation, and withdrawal; the second is a maniclike response which includes elation, pressure of speech, and hyperactivity. Elation in Scale V is associated with Silliness (IV), Inappropriate Affect (III), Visual Distortions (II), and Regression (I). This makes it clear that behavior rated as "elated" represents a maniclike loss of control rather than happiness, an interpretation supported by the questionnaire correlates of this scale (see Note 4).

To return to Regression (I), it is highly correlated with most of the other behavioral measures, especially with Visual Distortion (II), Inappropriate Affect (III), and Silliness (IV). With its components of thought confusion, loss of reality contact, regressive behavior, and uncontrolled verbalizations, it may be considered to represent the extent of the psychoticlike effects of LSD on a subject's overt behavior. The four highly intercorrelated measures (I through IV, with an average r among them of .70) may be viewed together as a measure of the most bizarre drug effects.

NOTE 4: RELATION BETWEEN SELF-REPORT AND BEHAVIOR

More specific relationships between self-report and observation were tested through the a priori scales, since they differentiate more finely among specific aspects of the drug experience (see Table A3.4). We made predictions about 49 of the 208 correlations between the a priori scales and the behavioral measures.[1] Of the predicted correlations, 43% were significant at the .01 level (two-tailed test), 59% reached the .05 level or better, and 71% at least the

[1] Nineteen predictions were considered to be direct validations (e.g., two measures of visual distortion), whereas 30 represent less direct relationships (e.g., "new meanings" might relate to behavioral measures of visual distortion, hostility, or suspiciousness). The rate of confirmation was virtually identical for direct and indirect predictions, however, so they are considered together.

Table A3.4. Correlations between Questionnaire and Behavioral Scales for Subjects unler LSD ($N = 30$)[a]

Questionnaire scales	Behavioral Scales												
	I. Regression	II. Visual Distortion	III. Inappropriate Affect	IV. Silliness	V. Depression (+) Elation (—)	V-A. Affect, absolute deviation	VI. Motility, Slow (+), Fast (—)	VI-A. Motility, absolute deviation	VII. Withdrawal	VIII. Anxiety	IX. Bodily preoccupation	X. Hostility-Negativism	XI. Suspiciousness
Scale A	.44[d]	.50[c]	.41[d]	.47[c]	—.34[e]	.34[e]	—.08	.27	—.19	.21	.29	.22	.29
Scale B	.80[b]	.78[b]	.52[c]	.66[b]	—.53[c]	.23	—.15	.35[e]	—.33[e]	.50[c]	.46[c]	.11	.26
Scale C	.20	.12	.01	—.03	.14	.14	.27	.32[e]	.29	.39[d]	.45[d]	.10	.30
Scale D	—.01	—.05	—.02	—.25	.16	—.07	—.02	.01	.17	.41[d]	.46[c]	.29	.19
I. Elation	—	—	—	*.10*	*—.04*	—	—	—	—	—	—	—	—
II. New Meanings	.33[e]	*.35[e]*	—	.35[e]	—	.39[d]	—	—	—	—	—	*.33[e]*	*32[e]*
III. Improved Functioning Felt	—	—	—	—	—	.38[d]	—	—	—	—	—	—	—
IV. Less Inhibition: Open	.49[c]	.48[c]	.36[d]	*.39[e]*	*—.30*	.31[e]	*—.11*	.32[e]	—	.35[e]	.46[c]	—	—
V. Disturbed Time Sense	*.35[e]*	.39[d]	—	.31[e]	—	—	—	—	—	—	—	—	—
VI. Thinking Difficulty	*.50[c]*	.50[c]	.48[c]	*.59[b]*	—.43[d]	—	—	—	—	—	—	—	—
VII. Control Loss Felt	*.50[c]*	*.54[c]*	—	*.40[d]*	—.33[e]	*.16*	—	*.19*	—	*.38[d]*	*.47[c]*	—	—
VIII. Visual Distortions	*.69[b]*	*.78[b]*	.52[c]	.67[b]	—.55[c]	—	—	.42[d]	—	.45[d]	.43[d]	—	—
IX. Loss of Contact	*.62[b]*	*.64[b]*	*.49[c]*	.55[c]	—.37[d]	.31[e]	—	.44[d]	*—.24*	*.38[d]*	.33[e]	—	—
X. Ego Change, Alienation	*.69[b]*	.50[c]	.43[d]	.49[c]	—.34[e]	—	—	.47[c]	—	*.50[c]*	*.63[b]*	—	37[d]
XI. Loss of Meaning	*.52[c]*	.62[b]	.44[d]	.41[d]	—.51[c]	—	—.39[d]	—	—.34[e]	*.37[d]*	—	.33[e]	.48[c]
XII. Suspiciousness	*.50[c]*	.48[c]	*.50[c]*	.56[c]	—.42[d]	—	—	.34[e]	*—.30*	—	—	*.19*	*.29*
XIII. Inhibited, Slowed	—	—	—	—	*.23*	—	*.28*	—	*.46[c]*	.31[e]	—	—	—
XIV. Body Image Change	—	—	—	—	—	—	—	*.36[d]*	—	.31[e]	*.49[c]*	—	—
XV. Somatic Symptoms	—	—	—	—	—	—	—	*.07*	—	.32[e]	*.53[c]*	—	—
XVI. Unpleasant Affect	—	—	—	—	*.00*	—	—	—	—	*.41[d]*	—	*.63[b]*	*.42[d]*

[a] All correlations between empirical and behavioral scales are given. For the 16 a priori scales, correlations are given only if they reach the .10 level, were predicted, or both. Predicted correlations are italicized.
[b] .001 level (two-tailed test). [c] .01 level (two-tailed test). [d] .05 level (two-tailed test). [e] .10 level (two-tailed test).

.10 level. Of the 159 correlations for which predictions were not made, only 10% reached the .01 level (20% reached the .05 level, and 29% the .10 level). The majority of the predicted relationships were thus confirmed, although there were important exceptions, and a much smaller, although significantly greater-than-chance, proportion of unpredicted relationships was discovered. For some aspects of behavior, the majority of predictions were confirmed; in others, prediction failed almost completely. The fact that the level of confirmation of the predictions varied according to the behavioral scales, rather than the questionnaire scales, indicates that, of the two ways of learning about the LSD effects, the experimenters' observations are the less valid. The predictions involving the first four behavioral scales (Regression, Visual Distortion, Inappropriate Affect, and Silliness) were confirmed most strongly,[2] followed by those involving Anxiety and Bodily Effects[3] and, at a somewhat lower level, the predictions for Hostility and Suspiciousness were also confirmed.[4] Thirty-three of the 36 predictions made for these eight aspects of behavior were confirmed. Prediction failed almost completely, however, in the areas of Affective Shifts, Motility, and Withdrawal.

Furthermore, the additional unpredicted relationships found for the eight behavioral scales where predictions were confirmed are easily understood, expanding rather than contradicting the predictions. The one real contradiction in this group was in the failure of the questionnaire measure of suspiciousness (Q-XII) to correlate with the behavioral measures of Hostility or Suspiciousness. This was, as we discovered on the posttest day, one area in which a straightforward report of subjective feelings did not occur. Paranoid features were largely inferred from other questionnaire data. A subject who, for example, feared the experimenter's evil intent might, for that very reason, not be willing to admit it openly. Others were unaware of their mistrust or suspiciousness. Subjects who appeared suspicious to the observer tended to report that things seemed meaningless, that events took on a new light, or that they were experiencing other unpleasant emotions, but they did not necessarily admit directly that they were suspicious. In contrast, those subjects who did report that they were suspicious were, in their overt behavior, regressed, silly, and inappropriate, and showed evidence of visual distortions. Within the questionnaire, reports of suspiciousness were generally related to the psychoticlike Scale B and specifically to experience of loss of contact (Q-IX) and visual distortions (Q-VIII).

The predictions relating to behavioral changes in affect, motility, and withdrawal failed almost completely, although 18 unpredicted relationships were found. Elation (negative pole of B-V) was associated with questionnaire scales VI through XII, which consist essentially of Scale B items (those related to the most psychoticlike LSD effects) but was unrelated to the questionnaire measures of elation (Q-I) or unpleasant affect (Q-XVI). We conclude there-

[2] Median $r = .50$.
[3] Median $r = .41$.
[4] Median $r = .33$.

fore that the behavioral measure of elation-depression (B-V) does not represent a dimension ranging from happiness to unhappiness but rather reflects, in its negative direction, a maniclike loss of inhibition, including press of speech. There was no behavioral measure of happiness as such.

The absolute amount of affect deviation (B-V-A) is the only behavioral measure with significant correlations with new meanings (Q-II) and the subjective experience of improved functioning (Q-III).[5] The sense that one has reached a new understanding of oneself or others that is embodied in these scales is, then, accompanied by observable affect, but the nature of the affect presumably depends on the nature of the insight. In another area, the amount of motility deviation (B-VI-A) correlated moderately with reports of body image change (Q-XIV) and somewhat more strongly with ego change (Q-X), loss of contact (Q-IX), and visual distortion (Q-VIII). The amount of alteration in motility thus seems to be related to the deepest changes in the self (body image and ego change), in the environment (visual distortion), and in the relationship between the two (loss of contact). It is not related to changes reported by the subjects in ideation, affect, or purely somatic symptoms.

The behavioral measure of withdrawal (B-VII) was not an effective measure, as seen in the data on behavioral effects in which it failed to show a drug effect. Its only significant correlation is with Q-XIII, which represents feelings of being slowed down and inhibited; what appeared to the observers as withdrawal apparently was more a lack of responsiveness (a reluctance to talk and a rather generalized feeling of exhaustion and slowing down).

The accuracy of prediction is limited to some extent by the fact that the areas covered by the behavioral and questionnaire scales often do not correspond very closely. For more direct comparison a special questionnaire scale was constructed for each of the original 18 behavioral scales, consisting of the specific items corresponding most closely to the behavior in question, and the two sources of data were then compared. These relationships were even stronger than the ones shown in Table A3.4, including a significant, although still only moderate, correlation between the two measures of suspiciousness (.47 as against .29). Elation or happiness was detected by the questionnaire but not by the behavioral measures, in which the elation-depression scale actually represented a maniclike loss of control rather than happiness.

[5] These two scales are highly correlated ($r = .62$).

APPENDIX 4

Details of Experimental Procedures and Statistical Techniques

NOTE 1: THE EGO ADEQUACY AND PARANOID-PRONE SCORES

The Ego Adequacy Score for each subject was obtained by summing (with appropriate plus or minus signs) his scores on the 19 personality assessment items that, in the consensus of a group of clinically trained judges, were considered indicative of adequate or inadequate ego functioning.[1] As a check on the internal consistency of the scale, the 10 highest scoring subjects of the total group of 50 were compared with the 9 lowest scoring subjects on all 93 personality assessment items. Of the original 19 items, 11 differentiated the two groups at the .001 level and 1 additional item reached the .01 level. These 12 items thus convey the core meaning of the scale; they comprise the first group listed in Table A4.1. An additional 14 items differentiated between high and low scorers at the .01 level; they comprise the second group listed in Table A4.1. Although they were not used in the actual scoring of Ego Adequacy, they should be kept in mind when we consider the kinds of people characterized by high and low scores. The last group of items in the table includes five that did not differentiate between high and low scorers and two items that reached only the .05 level. Although used in the scoring, they were apparently tangential to the core group of items.

The Paranoid-Prone Score is derived from a separate study in which we administered the questionnaire developed for this study to two groups of hospitalized patients, paranoid schizophrenics and nonparanoid schizophrenics (Langs and Barr, 1968). The paranoid patients had a typical pattern of questionnaire responses that was also found in nine of our subjects while under the effects of LSD. The personality assessment variables on which those subjects differ significantly from the other drug subjects may be considered as a set of "paranoid-prone" personality characteristics, that is, the predrug characteristics

[1] This scale was developed by Helene Kafka for a dissertation study in which she used the same group of subjects (Kafka, 1963); she labeled it "Ego Autonomy Scale."

Table A4.1. Scoring for Ego Adequacy

I. Items used in Ego Adequacy scoring, related to total score
  A. Scored for adequate ego (four items)
    4. Affects well modulated, good tempered
    29. Positive attitudes toward work and responsibility
    30. Goal striving in the face of frustration
    57. Ego-syntonic identity and values
  B. Scored for inadequate ego (eight items)
    1. Weak relationships with people, withdrawn
    2. Bland and uncommunicative
    9. Experiences diffuse anxiety readily
    35. Suggestible and dependent on others to take initiative
    38. Failure of defense: Becomes disorganized and unadaptive under stress; feels helpless
    41. Thinking inhibited and stimulus bound
    56. Identity diffusion and conflict
    59. Regression and childishness
II. Items not used in scoring, but differentiating extreme subjects at better than the .01 level
  A. Associated with adequate ego (five items)
    11. Frequently feels elated, on top of the world
    36. Has an adequate amount of reasonable self-esteem; accepts and likes self
    37. Counterphobic and hypomanic: In the face of fearful situations and depressive feelings, takes active steps to control and cope with it; tests out fearful situations
    53. Intellectualization and intellectuality
    78. Has dependable and practical common sense and good judgment
  B. Associated with inadequate ego (nine items)
    13. Separation from, or rejection by, maternal figures has been, or would be, an important source of anxiety
    17. Aggression pent-up and expressed in fantasy
    24. Self-punitive, disillusioned
    25. Sees himself as unwanted and unloved
    31. Lack of self-assertion; masochism and avoidance
    33. General passivity and passive resistance
    40. Loose thinking (high score) vs. clear thinking (low score)
    48. Has a narrow range of interests
    69. Denial: Copes with disturbing objects or events by a failure of reality testing, not perceiving their presence
III. Items used in scoring, but not sufficiently related to total score
  B. Scored for adequate ego (two items)
    44. Concentrates easily on an interest or a problem and is not easily distracted
    54. Seeks creative outlets and strives for understanding
  B. Scored for inadequate ego (five items)
    3. Narcissistic, with fluid affect
    8. Inhibition and overcontrol
    22. Fears losing control over his aggressive impulses
    39. Thought and fantasy stereotyped—repression inferred
    63. Is changeable, fitting himself chameleonlike into any environment he encounters

of those in whom LSD is likely to produce an altered state with paranoid features.

The items that comprise that scoring, with two additional items found, by an analysis of extreme scorers, to be strongly associated with them, are presented in Table A4.2.

Table A4.2. Scoring for Paranoid Proneness

I. Items used in paranoid-proneness scoring, related to total score (twelve items)

10. Is tense and restless
14. Hostile relationships, verbal aggression, and resentment
15. Hostility toward paternal figures and men in general
16. Hostility toward maternal figures and women in general
20. Needs to rebel, to reject and defy authority, conventional values, and/or dogmatic standards
23. Depression and self-abasement
24. Self-punitive, disillusioned
25. See himself as unwanted and unloved
26. Has an unconscious body image as physically impaired, incomplete, or damaged
50. Thinking and language tend to be expansive, flamboyant, and colorful
56. Identity diffusion and conflict
57. (Lacking in) ego-syntonic identity and values

II. Items not used in scoring, but related to paranoid-prone score at .01 level (two items)

5. Relationships manipulative and demanding
18. Anticipates being exploited

III. Items used in scoring, but not strongly related (two items)

17. Aggression pent-up and expressed in fantasy
45. Thinks in a ruminative, circumstantial, overdetailed fashion; vacillates and hesitates over decisions

NOTE 2: COGNITIVE TESTS

Two alternate forms of the cognitive test battery were used; for each test in the battery, one form was always used on the experimental day and the other on the control day. Control data were usually obtained on the pretest day, in a few cases, on the posttest day.

Although the control day performance of the drug and placebo groups differed significantly on only one of the eight subtests (long passage comprehension, .05 level), their means differed noticeably, although not significantly, on several others. As a safeguard, it was therefore decided to use analysis of covariance, thus adjusting the experimental day group means on the basis of control day scores, and evaluating the significance of the differences between the adjusted group means. The cognitive tests were not scheduled for all subjects, and some missed a portion of the battery. The number of drug cases

Table A4.3. Comparison of LSD and Placebo Groups on Cognitive Tests[a]

Test	Adjusted Means		*p* Value of Difference
	LSD	Placebo	
Digit Span	13.27	14.08	n.s.
Short Passage Comprehension	6.79	7.48	n.s.
Long Passage Comprehension	5.98	7.24	n.s.
Word Naming	27.01	40.48	.01
Serial Seven (errors)	3.09	1.22	.02
Serial Seven (time[b])	100	47	.01
Simple Rhyming	14.82	18.50	n.s.
Robinson Rhymes (errors)	3.64	1.91	.02
Robinson Numbers (errors)	4.04	2.15	.02
Robinson Numbers (requests for repetition)	7.21	5.47	(.06)

[a] The drug group *N* varies from 20 to 22 for different subtests; the placebo group *N* varies from 13 to 14. The data were analyzed by analysis of covariance in order to partial out the effect of each subject's pretest performance. The adjusted means therefore represent experimental day performance with the effect of the pretest score partialled out. The *F* test was used and the *p* values are based on two-tailed tests of significance.

[b] The logarithm of time was used in analyzing the data; it is reconverted to time in seconds.

therefore varies from 20 to 22; 14 placebo subjects were tested, dropping to 13 for one test. Table A4.3 presents the results of the analysis of covariance.

Table A4.4 presents relationships among the impaired cognitive tests and other measures; here, the relationships between the impairment scores, on the one hand, and anxiety and ego adequacy, on the other, are affected by the significant association between ego inadequacy and anxiety. Note that, at the bottom of the two right-hand columns in Table A4.4, the correlation between each of these and each impairment score is presented with the effect of the other measure partialled out.

NOTE 3: COLOR-WORD TEST

The colors-alone page consists of 10 lines of 10 units, each a row of asterisks, equivalent in size to the words, with red, green, blue, and yellow arranged in random order. Total reading time is recorded in seconds.

The color-word interference page, with the four color names printed in incongruous colors, also contains 10 lines of 10 words each. It is preceded by a sample line, to check the subject's understanding of the instructions to ignore the words and name the colors. After the sample line the experimenter records the reading time for every two rows (i.e., each block of 20 words), as well as for the entire page. Errors, which are rare, are also noted. The following scores were used.

Table A4.4. Relationships among Cognitive Test Performance, Verbal IQ, Ego Adequacy, and Anxiety under LSD (22 LSD Subjects)[a]

	Pretest[b]					Impairment, LSD[b]	
	WN, SS, RN	RRhy	Verbal IQ	Ego Adequacy	Anxiety, LSD	WN, SS, RN	RRhy
Pretest: cognitive tests							
Word Naming, Serial Sevens, Robinson Numbers	—	.31	.79[c]	.52[e]	.12	.00	—.26
Robinson Rhymes	.31	—	.28	.09	.29	.30	.00
Verbal IQ (WAIS)	.79[c]	.28	—	.33	.17	.18	—.15
Ego Adequacy	.52[e]	.09	.33	—	—.42[e]	—.49[e]	—.62[d]
Anxiety under LSD	.12	.29	.17	—.42[e]	—	.85[c]	.38
LSD: cognitive impairment							
Word Naming, Serial Sevens, Robinson Numbers	.00	.30	.18	—.49[e]	.85[c]	—	.50[e]
Robinson Rhymes	—.26	.00	—.15	—.62[d]	.38	.50[e]	—
Correlation with Ego Adequacy, Anxiety partialled out						—.28	—.55[d]
Correlation with Anxiety, Ego Adequacy partialled out						.81[c]	.17

[a] A high pretest score indicates better performance; a high impairment score indicates greater impairment. Note that the correlation between pretest and impairment is .00 by definition, since the impairment score is obtained by partialling pretest performance out of drug day scores.

[b] WN, Word Naming; SS, Serial Sevens; RN, Robinson Numbers; RRhy, Robinson Rhymes.

[c] Significant at .001 level (two-tailed test).

[d] Significant at .01 level.

[e] Significant at .05 level.

1. *Colors-alone time.* The time, in seconds, required to read the entire first page.

2. *Interference score.* The raw time taken to read the Color-Word Series is determined not only by the degree of interference from the words but by the subject's color-naming ability as well. Because color naming is an important component of Color-Word reading time, times on the two pages are highly correlated. In this study the pretest correlations were .69 for drug subjects and .82 for placebo subjects; in three previous studies pooled, it was .69. Color-Word reading times were therefore adjusted by partialling out the effect of colors-alone reading time, thus providing a pure measure of interference; this was done separately for pretest and experimental day scores. The adjusted score is expressed in terms of time, in seconds, taken to read the Color-Word page.

3. *Variability.* Variability in the five subtimes of the Color-Word Series is separated mathematically into two components (see Klein and Smith, 1953, for formula). The first component, called *R,* is the slope of the best-fitting straight line when the five times are graphed. It is usually positive, indicating a tendency to slow down as the series progresses. *R* was not affected by LSD, and so will not be presented here. The second component, called *V,* is the residual variance around this trend line; a high *V* score thus reflects an erratic performance.

Complete data for both pretest and experimental days were obtained from 24 drug subjects and 19 placebo subjects. The five Color-Word subtimes were not obtained under LSD for 1 drug subject, so his variability could not be evaluated; in the LSD group, therefore, $N = 25$ for colors-alone time and interference, and 24 for the variability score.

The two groups were not well-matched on the pretest day, the placebo group being significantly higher in interference and nonsignificantly higher in colors-alone time and variability. Comparison with data from 87 male subjects in three previous studies shows that it is the placebo group that is deviant, particularly in interference proneness (.001 level), while the LSD group did not differ significantly from the previous samples in pretest performance. The placebo group improved markedly on the experimental day, much beyond the usual test-retest improvement, suggesting that their initially poor performance may have been attributable at least in part to the anxiety that this group showed on the pretest day. In order to correct for the poor matching of the two groups, the experimental day scores of all subjects were adjusted through covariance techniques to partial out the effect of pretest performance. The experimental day comparisons, based on these adjusted scores, are presented in Table A4.5.

Table A4.6 presents correlations between each of the Color-Word test measures of drug effect and (1) the Cognitive Test impairment scores and (2) the empirical questionnaire scales. Scales A and C were unrelated to the Color-Word test measures and so are omitted from the table. Product-moment correlations were used for colors-alone time and interference; in the case of the variability increase, the distribution of scores was quite discontinuous, that is,

Table A4.5. Color-Word Test: Adjusted Mean Experimental Day Scores of LSD and Placebo Groups; Correlations between Pretest and Experimental Day Scores[a]

	Reading Time		Variability: Color-Word Page	Variability	
	Colors Alone	Interference[b]		Number of *Ss* High	Number of *Ss* Moderate-Low
Adjusted means					
LSD *Ss*	70.11	102.90	5.78	13	11
Placebo *Ss*	61.04	103.17	4.32	4	15
t: LSD vs. Placebo	3.85[c]	0.07	1.56	—	
Chi-square	—	—	—	4.83[e]	
Actual shifts within each group: experimental minus pretest					
LSD *Ss*	7.10	− 4.90	2.32		
LSD *t* value	2.12[e]	1.25	4.08[c]		
Placebo *Ss*	−6.00	−14.64	−.09		
Placebo *t* value	1.83[f]	3.54[d]	0.10		
***r*: pretest × experimental**					
LSD *Ss*	.73[c]	.26	.47[e]		
Placebo *Ss*	.87[c]	.48[e]	.03		

[a] For the LSD group, *N* is 25 for reading times and 24 for variability. For the placebo group, *N* is 19 throughout.

[b] The interference reading time is the time for the Color-Word Series, with its correlation with colors alone partialled out. Adjusted means were obtained by partialling out the relationship with pretest scores from experimental day scores. Variability data were analyzed after logarithmic conversion.

[c] .001 level (two-tailed test).

[d] .01 level (two-tailed test).

[e] .05 level (two-tailed test).

[f] .10 level (two-tailed test).

variability either increased very much or hardly at all, so that a biserial correlation was considered the appropriate statistic.

It should be kept in mind that a subject whose Color-Word time is highly variable must speed up in some segments to make up for those in which his attention flags, in order to achieve the same total reading time as a subject who reads consistently at a moderate pace. Consider, for example, two subjects, each with an average total time of 102 seconds. The five subtimes for

Table A4.6. Correlations between LSD Effects on the Color-Word Test and Other Measures[a]

	Product-Moment r:		
	Colors alone	Interference score	Biserial r: High vs. Low Variability
Cognitive test impairment			
Word-naming, Serial Sevens, Robinson Numbers	.37	.21	.61[b]
Robinson Rhymes	.28	.34	.18
Questionnaire scales			
Scale B	.31	.45[c]	.04
Scale D	.03	.07	.59[b]

[a] For correlations with cognitive tests, $N = 19$ for reading times and 18 for variability. Questionnaire scores are from the protocol closest in time to the color-word testing. Two subjects were not given the questionnaire close enough to be valid, so that $N = 23$ for reading times and 22 for variability. Color-Word scores are adjusted experimental day scores, with the effect of pretest scores partialled out.

[b] .01 level (two-tailed test).

[c] .05 level (two-tailed test).

one were 19, 21, 19, 22, and 21 seconds, which is moderately slow but steady. For the other they were 15, 23, 17, 28, and 19 seconds; twice, after rather poor segments, he showed a striking improvement, something that must have required a good deal of effort. Thus the highly variable subject is one who continues to struggle actively to maintain control in the face of great difficulty; hence the association with Scale D and the fear of losing control. If the struggle is given up or never attempted in the first place, the reading times become progressively slower or are slow throughout. An example of progressive slowing is the sequence 13, 16, 23, 18, and 24 seconds, from a subject who had a very enjoyable psychedelic experience but little true impairment. An example of extreme passivity is the sequence 35, 31, 32, 37, and 34 seconds, from a subject with a very psychoticlike loss of ego controls, as reflected in greatly increased interference and strong Scale B effects. Neither of these men became anxious under LSD.

NOTE 4: THEME LIST EXPERIMENT

Complete Theme List data were obtained from all 20 placebo subjects and from 25 drug subjects; some usable data were obtained from four of the remaining 5 drug subjects, so that in the LSD group N varies from 25 to 29 for different portions of the data analysis.

Subjects were tested once in the morning and once in the afternoon on both pretest and experimental days. The four lists were presented in a preestablished and balanced scrambled order, with the limitation that a drive theme list and its control were always given on the same day. An equal number of subjects had each theme list in each position. In reading the theme lists, each theme was read twice in succession, quite slowly, with a slight break between each information unit. The subject was instructed to listen carefully in order to learn the themes. Immediately after the presentation his attention was diverted for about 5 minutes while he filled out a Feeling Tone Checklist. He was then asked to recall the list of themes, being as precise and as word-perfect as possible. His reproduction was recorded verbatim, after which he was asked "Anything more?" On the morning of the experimental day, before the new theme list was administered, and again on the posttest day, the subject was asked for a precise recall of the previous day's lists.

The two drive-related lists are reproduced in the main body of the text. The control for the aggressive list was:

The Monkey

Theme 1: The costumed general was filled with pride that Spring morning.
Theme 2: Children were chanting gay nursery rhymes.
Theme 3: They circled round him with dancing smiles.
Theme 4: A glittering coin rolled among feet.
Theme 5: She heard the frenzied scramble.
Theme 6: A hairy paw scooped it up.
Theme 7: There was noisy crying.

The control for the sexual theme list was:

Strange Lyrics

Theme 1: He listened raptly to the brunette singing on the air.
Theme 2: Lisping she told of sorrow.
Theme 3: Violins swayed with silken tones.
Theme 4: She crooned of love forgotten.
Theme 5: He hummed through clenched similing lips.
Theme 6: In the final stanza she pronounced a man's name.
Theme 7: "Heavens, is that me or him!"

Each reproduction was scored, without knowledge of whether it was given by a drug or placebo subject, for accuracy, intrusions, and distortions. *Accuracy* was scored on a 3-point scale: 2 points for a word-perfect information unit, and 1 point for a synonym or closely related meaning. *Intrusions* are information units that have no corresponding referent in the stimulus, and *distortions* are units whose meaning has been substantially changed. Two examiners scored all protocols and eliminated discrepancies afterward by discussion. Three steps were taken to promote consistent scoring. (1) All decisions were noted; these decisions formed the basis for a manual that could be consulted when scoring; (2) scoring was done by theme list and not by subject; and (3) each scorer rescored the entire set a second time several weeks after he had completed his first scoring. Although the intrusion and distortion scores differed significantly among the four theme lists under LSD, they did not vary systematically with the presence or absence of drive content nor did they show a significant overall drug effect, and so will not be reported here.

Accuracy scores were analyzed in two ways: by comparing the two groups on drive-related and neutral lists on each day, and by performing separate analyses of variance for each group. These are shown in Table A4.7. Although the placebo subjects were more accurate than drug subjects on the pretest day, the difference was not significant for either type of list. On the experimental day, however, they differed quite significantly, more so on the neutral lists (.001 level) than on the drive lists (.01 level). The analyses of variance show that this occurred because, in the placebo group, there were no significant differences attributable to either conditions or the interaction of conditions with lists; the borderline effect of drive vs. neutral lists is discussed in the main body of the text.

The analysis of variance for the LSD group shows that both the drug condition and the drive content of the lists, as separate main effects, affected accuracy at the .001 level, while the interaction between them reached the .05 level. If we compare the accuracy of recall of the separate lists on the drug day, each drive list was superior to its control at the .05 level and the difference reaches the .01 level when they are combined. Examination of the respective mean accuracy scores in the upper half of Table A4.7 shows that under the drug the difference between each drive list and its control was substantial and comparable for the two pairs of lists. When we examine the pretest to drug day loss in retention ability separately for each kind of list, we find that the loss in the two neutral lists combined was highly significant (.001 level), and significant for each sequence analyzed separately (.01 level). As for the drive lists, the 12 subjects who heard the aggressive theme list on the pretest day and the sexual list under LSD showed virtually no loss, whereas the 14 subjects who heard the sexual list on the pretest day and the aggressive list under the drug showed considerable loss (.01 level), so that the loss in retention ability on drive lists for the entire group reached the .05 level. The results for placebo subjects, however, suggest that this primarily reflects the superior memorability of the sexual list under nondrug conditions.

Table A4.8 presents the correlations among IQ, Ego Adequacy, and the four Theme List accuracy scores. Drive and neutral lists were combined for both the measure of pretest learning and the measure of drug day recall of the pretest lists (see footnote[14] in Chapter 4).

Full-scale IQ is used because pretest accuracy correlated uniformly with verbal and performance subtests. For the 24-hour recall measure, the percent of material learned on the pretest day was used rather than the amount; this effectively partialled out the effect on the recall measure of how much was originally learned, leaving the two scores essentially uncorrelated ($r = .15$). We might note that the moderate, although nonsignificant, correlation of .35 between Ego Adequacy and the drug day learning of the drive lists results entirely from

Table A4.7. Mean Accuracy of Retention of the Four Theme Lists on Pretest and Experimental Days and Summary of Results of Analyses of Variance[a]

	LSD Subjects[b]		Placebo Subjects[b]		Significance of LSD vs. Placebo Difference	
	Pretest	Experimental Day	Pretest	Experimental Day	Pretest	Experimental Day
Aggressive	26.4 (14)	24.5 (14)	28.6 (10)	29.7 (10)	n.s.	n.s.
Aggressive control	26.3 (14)	17.5 (15)	29.4 (10)	31.3 (10)	n.s.	.001
Sexual	32.1 (15)	24.5 (12)	34.5 (10)	33.7 (10)	n.s.	.01
Sexual control	26.5 (15)	15.8 (13)	26.5 (10)	30.4 (10)	n.s.	.001
All drive	29.3 (29)	24.5 (26)	31.5 (20)	31.7 (20)	n.s.	.01
All control	26.4 (29)	16.8(28)	27.9 (20)	30.8 (20)	n.s.	.001

Analyses of Variance (Significance of Sources of Variance)

	p Value	*p* Value
Main effects		
Subject differences	.001	.001
Conditions (pretest vs. experimental)	.001	n.s.
Lists (drive vs. neutral)	.001	.07
Interactions		
Conditions × Lists	.05	n.s.
Conditions × Subjects	n.s.	n.s.
Lists × Subjects	n.s.	n.s.

[a] Separate analyses of variance were carried out for the drug and placebo groups. The drug group analysis is based on the 25 subjects for whom all four measures (drive, neutral; pretest, experimental) were available. The placebo analysis is quacy for LSD Subjects[a]

[b] Numbers in parentheses indicate number of cases.

Table A4.8. Intercorrelations among Theme List Measures, IQ, and Ego Adequacy for LSD Subjects[a]

			Theme List			
				Drug Day		
	IQ	Ego Adequacy	Pretest: Drive + Neutral[b]	Percent Recall[b]	Neutral	Drive
Full IQ	—	.18	.55[c]	.07	.13	.18
Ego Adequacy	.18	—	.48[c]	.52[c]	.45[d]	.35
Theme list						
Pretest: drive + neutral	.55[c]	.48[c]	(.81)	.15	.14	.55[c]
Drug day: percent of pretest recalled	.07	.52[c]	.15	(.81)	.57[c]	.27
Neutral list	.13	.45[d]	.14	.57[c]	—	.20
Drive list	.18	.35	.55[c]	.27	.20	—

[a] For pretest $N = 29$; for recall and drug day neutral lists, $N = 28$; and for the drug day drive list, $N = 26$.

[b] For pretest learning and drug day recall of pretest material, combining the two lists provides a measure of reliability. The *r* values in parentheses are the reliability coefficients obtained through the Spearman-Brown prophecy formula.

[c] Significant at .01 level (two-tailed test).

[d] Significant at .05 level (two-tailed test).

the correlation between Ego Adequacy and pretest accuracy; when this is partialled out, the correlation of .35 drops to .11.

Table A4.9 presents the correlations between the two Theme List scores that showed a drug effect and drug effect measures from the questionnaire, behavioral observations, cognitive test battery, and Color-Word test. The empirical questionnaire scales and behavioral scales that were not significantly related to either Theme List measure are omitted from the table.

NOTE 5: RESPONSIVENESS TO THE EXPRESSIVE CONNOTATIONS OF WORDS

Twelve drug subjects and 15 placebo subjects participated in this experiment. To evaluate the overall degree of discrepancy between sets of ratings, the absolute difference between the two sets on each adjective pair was calculated. For example, for "angular-round," when the face was rated as "slightly angular," it was scored +1, and when a word was rated as "very rounded," it was scored −3, yielding a discrepancy of 4; the possible range was from 0 to 6. These differences were averaged over all adjective pairs to yield the mean discrepancies presented in Table A4.10. Each set of discrepancies was corrected for individual rating patterns, since differences in such response sets would bias the

Table A4.9. Correlations between Theme List Performance under LSD and Other Measures of Drug Effect[a]

	Percent Recalled of Pretest List	Neutral List Immediate Recall
Cognitive test impairment		
Word Naming, Serial Sevens, Robinson Numbers	−.66[c]	−.39[e]
Robinson Rhymes	−.63[c]	−.52[d]
Color-Word test impairment		
Interference	−.04	−.47[d]
Variability	.00	.15
Nearest questionnaire		
Scale A	−.07	−.42[d]
Scale B	−.34	−.63[b]
Behavior, same time		
I. Regressive Behavior	−.48[c]	−.25
II. Visual Distortion	−.03	−.48[c]
VIII. Anxiety	−.07	−.02
XI. Suspiciousness	−.10	−.30
Behavior, average for day		
I. Regressive Behavior	−.41[d]	−.47[d]
II. Visual Distortion	−.15	−.54[c]
VIII. Anxiety	−.49[c]	−.21
XI. Suspiciousness	−.40[d]	−.30

[a] Correlations with behavior and questionnaire are based on 28 cases; with the Color-Word test measures on 23 and 22; with cognitive tests on 20.

[b] .001 level (two-tailed).

[c] .01 level (two-tailed).

[d] .05 level (two-tailed).

[e] .10 level (two-tailed).

results. Although there was no consistent difference between drug and placebo groups in their use of the scales (i.e., the tendency to use the extreme scale points or to be restricted to the middle of the range), there were wide individual variations. For each comparison between two sets of ratings for each subject, the average expected discrepancy that would have occurred by chance was computed, based on his own scale-point distribution for the two sets of ratings. The difference between the chance expectancy thus computed and the actual discrepancy then became the measure of the degree of similarity between the two sets of ratings.[2] If they are not significantly different from each other,

[2] The discrepancy to be expected by chance was computed in the following manner. If, for example, we are comparing W-1 and W-2 as rated by a particular subject, the frequency distribution of his 69 ratings of W-1 over the 7 scale points was ascertained, and the same for his ratings of W-2. These distributions then formed the row and

the two concepts rated are no more similar than any pair of unrelated concepts; that is, they are clearly differentiated. If the observed discrepancies are significantly smaller than chance, the two concepts do, to some extent, resemble each other.

Table A4.10. Mean Discrepancies between Pairs of Ratings: Observed vs. Chance Expectancy[a]

	Lists I and II (69 Items)			List I (25 Items)	List II (44 Items)
	W-1 vs. W-2 (Uloomoo vs. Takete)	Face vs. W-1[b]	Face vs. W-2	Face vs. W-1[b]	Face vs. W-1[b]
LSD subjects					
Observed mean	2.07	1.45	2.27	1.55	1.40
Chance mean	2.27	2.31	2.32	2.27	2.33
Observed minus chance	−.20	−.86	−.05	−.72	−.93
p value (two-tailed) of difference	n.s.	.001	n.s.	.01	.001
Placebo subjects					
Observed mean	2.59	2.16	2.02	1.98	2.26
Chance mean	2.34	2.33	2.33	2.29	2.35
Observed minus chance	.25	−.17	−.31	−.31	−.09
p value (two-tailed) of difference	n.s.	n.s.	n.s.	n.s.	n.s.
LSD vs. placebo					
p value of difference	n.s.	.01	n.s.	n.s.	.01

[a] For the LSD group $N = 11$, since one subject did not rate W-2; for the placebo group $N = 15$.

[b] Since the face is always assigned a "name," W, the face ratings are ratings of the face plus the name; W-1 is the same name when presented alone.

column marginal totals of a 7×7 table; the chance expectancies for each cell of this table were then calculated from the marginals (as in a chi-square analysis). The mean of the discrepancies in that table was then calculated (e.g., each −1, +2 entry as a discrepancy of 3; a −3, −2 entry as 1, and so on); this mean is that subject's chance discrepancy for the W-1–W-2 comparison. Table A4.10 gives, for each set of comparisons, the mean of these chance discrepancies and the mean of the actual discrepancies that were observed. The p value of the difference between the two is based on the t test for correlated means, using the difference between actual and observed discrepancies found for each subject.

The normative scoring of the word ratings, presented in Section B of Table A.4.11, was obtained by taking the nine items in List I that most consistently differentiated between Uloomoo and Takete in both Hochberg's study and our placebo group. Each item was given a score ranging from +3 (extreme Uloomoo-like rating) to −3 (extreme Takete-like rating); the nine scores were then averaged after adjustment for individual rating tendencies. Each word was presented as W-1 (the word given to the face) for half of the subjects in each group and as W-2 (the word not presented with a face) for the other half.

The scores in Table A4.12 were obtained in a fashion similar to the normative scores in Table A4.11. The word-differentiating items applied to the face were the same ones used in the normative scoring, with the exclusion of three items that also characterized the face, and they were scored in the same way. For the face-typical items, the original pool of 26 items consisted of all those on which the combined drug and placebo groups averaged at least 1.5 points (of a possible 3) away from the midpoint of the scale in a consistent direction. After elimination of the 18 items that also differentiated between the words, the remaining 8 items were scored from +3 to −3 with +3 representing an extreme rating in the direction typical of the face; the 8 scores were then averaged. It may be noted that, over the original set of 26 items, the mean face ratings of the drug and placebo groups were virtually identical (2.00 vs. 2.09). This means that the attributes of the face that were most consistently seen by placebo subjects were also seen by subjects under LSD.

NOTE 6: COLOR VS. FORM IN PERCEPTUAL ORGANIZATION

The apparatus was copied as exactly as possible from that used by Thurstone (1944). On each day of testing, each subject's threshold for perceiving apparent movement was determined by two ascending trials, and the alternation rate of the two stimuli then adjusted to his optimal rate for perceiving movement.

Each trial lasted for 1 minute, after which the experimenter recorded the total time for perceived rightward and leftward movement and the number of spontaneous alternations. The direction of movement was reversed by changing shutters; in one direction form-determination produced rotation to the left, in the other direction to the right. Since it was thought possible that individual subjects might have left or right rotational preferences, each subject had one trial in each direction, the order counterbalanced among subjects. As it turned out, there were no consistent response patterns associated with form-right vs. form-left trials, so they are considered together. Each subject was tested on the pretest day and again under LSD or the placebo.

There were 22 drug subjects and 19 placebo subjects for whom both pretest and experimental day data were available. Alternation was not recorded for 1 placebo subject, reducing the placebo N to 18 for the analyses of alternation rate.

In the analysis of the data presented in Table A4.13, experimental day scores

Table A4.11. Ratings of Words on List I

A. Significance of Differences between Uloomoo and Takete on Each Item

Hochberg's Data	Item (Uloomoo Given First)	p Value of Mean Difference (Two-Tailed)	
		LSD Ss	Placebo Ss
Strong items	Low-high[a]	.05	.01
	Rounded-angular[a]	.10	.01
	Soft-loud[a]	.10	.01
	Dull-sharp[a]	.10	.01
	Passive-active[a]	.10	.01
	Relaxed-tense[a]	—	.05
	Smooth-rough[a]	.10	—
Moderate items	Peaceful-ferocious	.05	—
	Hazy-clear[a]	—	.01
	Heavy-light[a]	—	.05
	Weak-strong	—	.10
	Sick-healthy	—	.10
	Stale-fresh	—	.10
	Old-young	—	—
	Wet-dry	—	—
	Deep-shallow	—	—
	Awkward-graceful[b]	—	—
Weak items	Boring-interesting	—	.05
	Cold-hot[b]	—	.10
	Ugly-beautiful[b]	—	.10
	Large-small	—	—
	Empty-full[b]	—	—
	Sad-happy	—	—
	Abstract-concrete	—	—
	Bad-good[b]	—	—

B. Normative Scoring: Mean Scores for Each Word in Each Position for Nine Best Items[c]

	LSD Ss		Placebo Ss	
	Mean	p Value	Mean	p Value
Word 1				
Uloomoo (p vs. zero)	.46	n.s.	.64	.10
Takete (p vs. zero)	– .59	n.s.	–1.46	.001
Uloomoo-Takete (p of difference)	1.05	n.s.	2.10	.001
Word 2				
Uloomoo (p vs. zero)	1.02	.02	1.33	.02
Takete (p vs. zero)	–1.15	.05	–1.28	.01
Uloomoo-Takete (p of difference)	2.17	.01	2.61	.001

[a] The nine items used in the normative scoring; these are the pairs most consistently differentiating the two words in Hochberg's study and confirmed in the present placebo sample.

[b] The differences for these five items are opposite in direction to those found by Hochberg.

[c] Possible range from +3 (Uloomoo) to –3 (Takete).

Table A4.12. Mean Ratings of the Face on Word-Differentiating Items and Mean Ratings of the Words on Face-Typical Items[a,b]

	LSD Ss	N	Placebo Ss	N	p Value of LSD-Placebo Difference
Ratings of face on six word-differentiating items					
Uloomoo face, mean	.15	6	−.07	8	n.s.
Takete face, mean	−.44	6	−.27	7	n.s.
Uloomoo face-Takete face, mean difference	.59		.20		n.s.
p value of difference	.05		n.s.		
Ratings of words on eight items typical of face					
Word 1					
Takete, mean	1.96	6	1.02	7	.10
Uloomoo, mean	1.58	6	.69	8	.05
All subjects	1.77	12	.84	15	.01
Word 2					
Takete, mean	.23	6	.92	8	n.s.
Uloomoo, mean	.62	5	.54	7	n.s.
All subjects	.41	11	.74	15	n.s.
Word 1-Word 2, mean difference	1.28	11	.10	15	.05
p value of difference	.01		n.s.		

[a] Word-differentiating items are oriented so that a positive score characterizes Uloomoo and a negative score Takete. For face-typical items, a positive score is assigned to the adjective typical of the face. For both, the possible range is +3 to −3.

[b] All p values are two-tailed.

were adjusted through covariance techniques to partial out the effect of pretest level. The pretest alternation rates of the two groups were badly matched. Although the pretest t value of 1.82 between groups is only at the .10 level (two-tailed test), it is lowered by the extreme variance of placebo scores which minimizes the difference. In fact, 7 of the 18 placebo subjects for whom alternation rate was measured had three or fewer alternations (i.e., two shifts) on the first pretest trial (3 of these did not alternate at all, remaining on form for the entire time). None of the drug subjects had so few alternations, and the difference between the groups in this regard is beyond the .01 level (Fisher's Exact Test, two-tailed p). Thus the moderately significant difference between the groups on the experimental day arises because scores were adjusted for

Table A4.13. Comparison of % Color, Alternation Rate, and Their Correlations: LSD vs. Placebo Subjects and Pretest vs. Experimental Days[a,b]

	Pretest	Experimental Day	t: Experimental vs. Pretest	r: Pretest × Experimental
Mean % Color				
LSD ($N = 22$)	27.27	35.63	5.50[c]	.39
Placebo ($N = 19$)	25.92	30.16	2.64[e]	.73[c]
t: LSD vs. Placebo	0.43	2.47[e]		1.52
Logarithm of number of Alternations				
LSD ($N = 22$)	1.53	1.46	1.32	.78[c]
Placebo ($N = 18$)	1.29	1.60	6.36[c]	.79[c]
t: LSD vs. Placebo	1.82	2.07[e]		0.08
r: % Color × log Alternation				
LSD ($N = 22$)	.71[c]	.06	2.92[d]	
Placebo ($N = 18$)	.75[c]	.80[c]	0.36	
t: LSD vs. Placebo	0.24	3.34[d]		

[a] Since pretest and experimental day scores are highly correlated, the experimental day scores were adjusted through covariance techniques to partial out the influence of the pretest level.

[b] All t tests between correlations were performed on the z transformation of r, which is normally distributed.

[c] Significant at .001 level (two-tailed test).

[d] Significant at .01 level (two-tailed test).

[e] Significant at .05 level (two-tailed test).

pretest level; the experimental day unadjusted score means of the two groups were in fact identical (1.52).

In evaluating individual differences among drug subjects in the effect of LSD on their Color-Form performance, a special score was devised, as a purer measure of the drug effect than raw % Color. This was obtained by partialling out the effect of alternation rate. To do this, using a regression formula based on the experimental day scores for drug subjects would have no effect because the two measures are uncorrelated. A regression formula for predicting % Color from log alternation was derived from the placebo sample on the experimental day. From this, a "predicted % Color" was obtained based on each drug subject's experimental day alternation rate. The difference between the % Color thus predicted and the actual % Color was taken to represent the effect of the drug states on Color-Form preference, eliminating that portion of the score that can be attributed to the subject's characteristic, nondrug style of perceptual organization, as reflected in the alternation rate. This score is called C', and

Table A4.14. Questionnaire Correlates of the *C′* Score for 21 LSD Subjects

Questionnaire Score	*r*	*p* Value (Two-Tailed)
Total Questionnaire Score	.31	n.s.
Empirical scales		
Scale A	.51	.05
Scale B	.48	.05
Scale C	.21	n.s.
Scale D	–.41	(.10)
A priori scales		
VIII. Visual distortion	.73	.01
IX. Loss of contact	.50	.05
IV. Feeling less inhibited, opened up	.49	.05
V. Disturbed time sense	.49	.05
XIV. Body image change	.47	.05
X. Ego change, alienation	.36	n.s.
XV. Somatic symptoms	–.36	n.s.
Partial correlations		
XIV. (Body image) with XV (somatic symptoms) partialled out	.71	.01
XV. (Somatic symptoms) with XIV (body image) partialled out)	–.66	.01

it is the score used in Table A4.14. The number of cases represented in this table is reduced from 22 to 21 because for one subject there was no questionnaire obtained at a time close enough to the Color-Form testing to be considered valid.

NOTE 7: EARLIEST MEMORIES

Complete data were obtained from all 20 placebo subjects and from 28 of the 30 drug subjects. Replies were recorded verbatim, with additional probing only when the response was not clear; an inquiry followed. All first memories were given code numbers, with the two memories from each subject paired, but the sequence (pretest-experimental or experimental-pretest) and the drug or placebo condition randomized. They were then scored separately on a blind basis by two experimenters using the method developed by Langs et al. (1960); disagreements were resolved by discussion. The scoring covers a broad range of categories and has two major divisions. The first refers to directly mentioned items, such as persons present, setting, indications of movement, and direct

subject dated it from an earlier period; and those with a new memory that was not more regressed in any sense.

NOTE 8: THE RORSCHACH TEST

Although all 50 subjects were given the pretest assessment Rorschach test, on the experimental day it was given to only 19 drug subjects and 10 placebo subjects. The primary-process scoring is done with a special manual (Holt, 1959), which requires training. Under the supervision of the manual's author, each protocol was scored by two raters to insure reliability. The primary-process scoring was done "blind" for all pretest and experimental records, intermixed and assigned arbitrary code numbers.

Scores

This presentation of the effects of the LSD states on the Rorschach test is based almost entirely on the scores from Holt's primary-process manual, with the limited addition of four conventional scoring categories: number of responses (*R*), human movement (*M*), amount of color usage (*Sum C*), and specific color scores. Another conventional score examined was the weighted form level, scored according to the system of Mayman (1960), which is included in Holt's manual as well.[3]

Statistical Method

The analysis of drug effects was made primarily in terms of changes between pretest and experimental day scores. In this way the significance of mean shifts could be evaluated, both within the drug group and through the comparison of shifts for the drug and placebo groups. In addition, the correlations between pretest and experimental scores for all measures were obtained separately for each group, and changes in score variances of the major measures were evaluated. Many scores that showed no mean change under LSD did show a significant increase in variance; this means that subjects *were* affected, but some in one direction and others in the opposite direction. These effects were also evaluated. The overall drug effects are presented first, followed by a description of the Rorschach changes associated with each of the four empirical questionnaire scales.

The Rorschach scores generated a massive and complex set of statistical findings; their presentation in tables would be confusing rather than clarifying.

[3] Three components of this score were also examined: $F+\%$ (superior forms), $F-\%$ (misperceptions, not matching the blot), and the percentage of poor forms other than $F-$ (vague forms or weak matches). Most responses were of adequate but ordinary form level, and thus were placed in none of these categories (63%, under both normal and drug conditions).

Accordingly, the findings are presented descriptively, with significance levels or actual correlation coefficients presented only in special cases. All of the findings cited as significant are at the .05 level of significance (two-tailed test) or better; findings described as "borderline" are between the .05 and .10 levels and are cited only when they enrich the interpretation of more significant findings. Nonsignificant effects are not cited except in special cases in which the failure to find an expected effect is of interest.

NOTE 9: DRAWINGS OF THE HUMAN FIGURE

Although all subjects made pretest drawings, experimental day drawings were obtained from only 20 drug and 16 placebo subjects. They were chosen on a prearranged schedule because it was not possible to test all subjects in all the experiments planned. Drawings were obtained from all of the scheduled subjects. It was not always possible to test subjects during the height of the drug's effects, and a few were tested either early or late in the day, when the effect was comparatively weak.

All scoring was done "blind," with each subject's drawings identified only by a code number. The four drawings made by each subject were kept together as a set, with the pretest and experimental day pairs identified as "A" or "B" in randomized order. All variables were scored by two raters, and an average or consensus was reached; initial reliabilities were quite high throughout. The code was broken only after all scoring had been done in order to compare the Human Figure Drawing scores with other aspects of the drug reaction and the personality measures.

Before scoring, a staff member guessed which drawings were made by drug and which by placebo subjects and, within each set, which were done on the pretest and which on the experimental day. A number of the scoring signs developed by Karen Machover for Witkin's study (Witkin et al., 1954) were then selected and scored. These signs, as well as additional ones that were devised for this study, were mostly dichotomous categories (absence or presence).

The drawings were also scored for four scaled variables. One was the sophistication-of-body-concept scale developed by Hanna Marlens as a single global measure of the level of psychological differentiation.[4] Based on the form level, degree of identity and sex differentiation, and amount of detailing of the figures, it is a 5-point scale ranging from very primitive or infantile to highly sophisticated and differentiated. Two additional 5-point scales were developed. One measured the degree of activity-passivity of the figure as expressed in its posture or the activity depicted, and the other was the degree of sexualization. The fourth scaled measure was the height of the figure in inches.

[4] We wish to thank Dr. H. A. Witkin for providing us with the scoring criteria, including a set of sample drawings; they are presented in some detail in Witkin, et al., 1962.

Drug effects were evaluated for the scaled variables by the *t* test, using the *t* test for correlated means to evaluate pretest to experimental day shifts within each group. Comparisons between the two groups on the experimental day were based on adjusted scores in which the effect of pretest variance had been partialled out. Changes in the signs were evaluated by McNemar's sign test. Although some predictions were made, many of the comparisons were without predictions. The predictions were, essentially, that the drug would produce a shift toward primitivization, missing parts, and peculiar elements. Two-tailed tests of significance were used throughout, so that the distinction between predicted and unpredicted relationships may be ignored in this presentation.[5]

In relating Human Figure Drawing changes under LSD to other aspects of the drug reaction, the questionnaires and behavioral measures obtained closest in time to the Human Figure Drawing testing were used, since different subjects were tested at different stages of their drug reaction. For the four scaled measures, each subject's pretest score was partialled out of his drug day score, yielding an adjusted measure that is a purer measure of the drug's effect on each variable. As for the specific indicators, subjects who received them only for their drug day drawings were compared with all others, unless otherwise specified (when an indicator had been present in a subject's pretest drawings, its appearance on the experimental day could not be considered a drug effect).

[5] As with the Rorschach test, the number of statistical tests made is too great to present in tabular form without a loss of clarity. Findings are therefore presented descriptively, with only those at the .05 level or better cited.

APPENDIX 5

Statistical Basis for the Reaction Pattern Groups

For each group the Personality Assessment items on which its members differed from the rest of the sample at the .05, .10, and .20 levels were determined.[1] For purposes of comparison four "chance" groups were also examined. They consisted of the four subjects who did not fall into any cluster and three groups formed by combining pairs of groups (I and V, III and IV, and IV and V) whose drug reactions were moderately similar to each other.

The upper half of Table A5.1 shows that the reaction pattern groups are internally consistent on significantly more of the Personality Assessment items than would be expected by chance. This is true of the .05, .10, and .20 level criteria, and regardless of whether the reaction pattern groups are compared with the actual "chance" groups or with the theoretical chance expectancy.

The 93 Personality Assessment items are, however, not independent of each other; representing, as they do, various aspects of personality, many of them are substantially intercorrelated. To eliminate the possibility that the number of items reaching significance might be inflated by overlapping items, a factor analysis of the personality items was made, yielding 14 relatively independent factors. The lower half of Table A5.1 shows that at the .05, .10 and .20 levels there is within-group consistency for significantly more factors than would be expected by chance. While the smaller number of items involved reduces the significance levels of the findings, the groups are consistent on a larger *proportion* of the factors than of the individual items. If it is fair to assume that the factors represent more basic dimensions of personality than the items, since the latter deal in part with very limited aspects of functioning, further support is lent to the proposition that each kind of drug reaction occurs in subjects with a particular set of personality characteristics.[2]

[1] The .05 level is achieved for the group of seven subjects if the mean differs from the sample mean by .65 sigma, groups of four if by .92 sigma, groups of three if by 1.08 sigma, and groups of two if by 1.35 sigma. The corresponding sigma scores for the .10 level are .55, .78, .92, and 1.14, respectively, and for the .20 level, .44, .61, .72, and .90, respectively.

[2] By the chi-square test, each group has significantly more of the 93 Personality Assessment items at either the .05 or .10 levels than chance. For the 14 personality factors, this is true for only three groups.

Table A5.1 Mean Number of Personality Measures on Which Groups Deviate Significantly from Rest of Sample[a]

	Chance Expectancy: Mean Number at Each Level	Results, Four "Chance" Groups: Mean Number at Each Level	Seven Reaction Type Groups		
			Mean Number at Each Level	t vs. Chance Expectancy	t vs. Four "Chance" Groups
93 Personality Assessment scores					
At .05 level	4.65 = 5%	3.00 = 3%	7.00 = 8%	2.88[c]	3.27[b]
At .10 level	9.30 = 10%	7.25 = 8%	13.86 = 15%	4.41[b]	3.47[b]
At .20 level	18.60 = 20%	17.50 = 19%	27.00 = 29%	3.90[b]	2.86[b]
14 Personality factors					
At .05 level	.70 = 5%	.25 = 2%	2.14 = 15%	1.96[c]	2.44[c]
At .10 level	1.40 = 10%	1.25 = 9%	3.43 = 24%	2.03[c]	1.97[c]
At .20 level	2.80 = 20%	2.25 = 16%	5.71 = 41%	4.07[b]	3.11[b]

[a] The significance levels used as criteria for item deviation are all two-tailed, since no directions were predicted.
[b] Significant at .01 level (one-tailed test).
[c] Significant at .05 level (one-tailed test).

As might be expected, consistencies in personality are more apparent when the two smallest groups, each consisting of only two subjects, are eliminated. The criteria for significance of an item deviation become more stringent as group size decreases.

References

Abramson, H. A. Lysergic acid diethylamide (LSD-25): The questionnaire technique with notes on its use. *Journal of Psychology*, **49**:57–65, 1960.

Abramson, H. A., Jarvik, M. E., Kaufman, M. R., Kornetsky, C., Levine, A., and Wagner, M. Lysergic acid diethylamide (LSD-25): I. Physiological and perceptual responses. *Journal of Psychology*, **39**:3–60, 1955a.

Abramson, H. A., Kornetsky, C., Jarvik, M. E., Kaufman, M. R., and Ferguson, M. W. Lysergic acid diethylamide (LSD-25): XI. Content analysis of clinical reactions. *Journal of Psychology*, **40**:53–60, 1955b.

Abramson, H. A., Waxenberg, S. E., Levine, A., Kaufman, M. R., and Kornetsky, C. Lysergic acid diethylamide (LSD-25): XIII. Effect on Bender-Gestalt test performance. *Journal of Psychology*, **40**:341–349, 1955c.

Angyal, A. *Foundations for a Science of Personality*. New York: Commonwealth Fund, 1941.

Arlow, J. A., and Brenner, C. *Psychoanalytic Concepts and the Structural Theory*. New York: International Universities Press, 1964.

Arnheim, R. The Gestalt theory of expression. *Psychological Review*, **56**:156–171, 1949.

Aronson, H., and Klee, G. D. The effect of lysergic acid diethylamide (LSD-25) on impulse control. *Journal of Nervous and Mental Disease*, **131**:536–539, 1960.

Aronson, H., Silverstein, A. B., and Klee, G. D. Influence of lysergic acid diethylamide (LSD-25) on subjective time. *AMA Archives of General Psychiatry*, **1**:469–472, 1959.

Auerbach, E. *Mimesis: The Representation of Reality in Western Literature*. Princeton, N.J.: Princeton University Press, 1953.

Barber, T. X. *LSD, Marihuana, Yoga and Hypnosis*. Chicago: Aldine, 1970.

Bercel, N. A., Travis, L. E., Olinger, L. B., and Dreikurs, E. Model psychoses induced by LSD-25 in normals. I. Psychophysiological investigations, with special reference to the mechanism of the paranoid reaction. *AMA Archives of Neurology and Psychiatry*, **75**:588–611, 1956a.

Bercel, N. A., Travis, L. E., Olinger, L. B., and Dreikurs, E. Model psychoses induced by LSD-25 in normals. II. Rorschach test findings. *AMA Archives of Neurology and Psychiatry*, **75**:612–618, 1956b.

Blacker, K. H., Jones, R. T., Stone, G. C., and Pfefferbaum, D. Chronic users of LSD: The "acidheads." *American Journal of Psychiatry*, **125**:341–351, 1968.

Bleuler, E. (1911). The basic symptoms of schizophrenia. In Rapaport, D., ed. *Organization and Pathology of Thought*. New York: Columbia University Press, 1951.

Bleuler, E. *Dementia Praecox or the Group of Schizophrenias*. Translated by Joseph Zinkin. New York: International Universities Press, 1950.

Breuer, J., and Freud, S. (1895). Studies on hysteria. *Standard Edition*, Vol. II. London: Hogarth, 1955.

Cheek, Frances E., Newell, S., and Joffee, M. Deceptions in the illicit drug market. *Science*, **167**:1276, 1970.

Cohen, J. A factor-analytically based rationale for the WAIS. *Journal of Consulting Psychology*, **21**:451–457, 1957.

Dickes, R. The defensive function of an altered state of consciousness: A hypnoid state. *Journal of the American Psychoanalytic Association*, **13**:356–403, 1965.

Dishotsky, N. I., Loughman, W. D., Mogar, R. E., and Lipscomb, W. R. LSD and genetic damage. *Science*, **172**:431–440, 1971.

Ditman, K. S., Tietz, W., Prince, Blanche S., Forgy, E., and Moss, Thelma. Harmful aspects of the LSD experience. *Journal of Nervous and Mental Disease*, **145**:464–474, 1967.

Eagle, Carol J. An Investigation of Individual Consistencies in the Manifestations of Primary Process. New York University, unpublished doctoral dissertation, 1964.

Fink, Geraldine. Analysis of the Isakower phenomenon. *Journal of the American Psychoanalytic Association*, **15**:281–293, 1967.

Fink, M., and Itil, T. M. Neurophysiology of phantastica: EEG and behavioral relations in man. Efron, D. H. et al., eds. *Psychopharmacology: A Review of Progress 1957–1967*. Washington, D.C.: U.S. Government Printing Office, 1968.

Fiss, H., Klein, G. S., and Bokert, E. Waking fantasies following interruption of two types of sleep. *Archives of General Psychiatry*, **14**:543–551, 1966.

Fiss, H., Klein, G. S., Shollar, E., and Levine, B. E. Changes in dream content as a function of prolonged REM sleep interruption. *Sleep Study Abstracts*, September, 1968, p. 217.

Freud, S. (1891). Hypnosis. *Standard Edition*, Vol. I. London: Hogarth, 1966, pp. 103–114.

Freud, S. (1895). Project for a scientific psychology. *Standard Edition*, Vol. 1. London: Hogarth, 1966, pp. 281–397.

Freud, S. (1899). Screen memories. *Standard Edition*, Vol. III. London: Hogarth, 1962, pp. 301–322.

Freud, S. (1900). The interpretation of dreams. *Standard Edition*, Vols. IV and V. London: Hogarth, 1953.

Freud, S. (1905). Fragment of an analysis of a case of hysteria. *Standard Edition*, Vol. VII. London: Hogarth, 1953, pp. 1–122.

Freud, S. (1912). A note on the unconscious in psycho-analysis. *Standard Edition*, Vol. XII. London: Hogarth, 1958, pp. 255–266.

Freud, S. (1915). The unconscious. *Standard Edition*, Vol. XIV. London: Hogarth, 1957, pp. 159–215.

Freud, S. (1917). A metapsychological supplement to the theory of dreams. *Standard Edition*, Vol. XIV. London: Hogarth, 1957, pp. 217–235.

Freud, S. (1923). The ego and the id. *Standard Edition*, Vol. XIX. London: Hogarth, 1961, pp. 3–66.

Freud, S. (1925a). A note upon the 'mystic writing-pad.' *Standard Edition*, Vol. XIX. London: Hogarth, 1961, pp. 227–232.

Freud, S. (1925b). Negation. *Standard Edition*, Vol. XIX. London: Hogarth, 1961, pp. 233–239.

Freud, S. (1926). Inhibitions, symptoms and anxiety. *Standard Edition*, Vol. XX. London: Hogarth, 1959, pp. 75–174.

Freud, S. (1933). New introductory lectures on psycho-analysis. *Standard Edition*, Vol. XXII. London: Hogarth, 1964, pp. 3–182.

Freud, S. (1939). Moses and monotheism. *Standard Edition*, Vol. XXIII. London: Hogarth, 1964, pp. 3–137.

Freud, S. (1940a). An outline of psycho-analysis. *Standard Edition*, Vol. XXIII. London: Hogarth, 1964, pp. 141–207.

Freud, S. (1940b). Some elementary lessons in psycho-analysis. *Standard Edition*, Vol. XXIII. London: Hogarth, 1964, pp. 279–286.

Gardner, R. W., Holzman, P. S., Klein, G. S., Linton, Harriet B., and Spence, D. P. Cognitive control: A study of individual consistencies in cognitive behavior. *Psychological Issues*, **1,** Monograph 4, 1–186, 1959.

Gill, M. M. Topography and systems in psychoanalytic theory. *Psychological Issues*, **3,** Monograph 10, 1–179, 1963.

Gill, M. M., ed. *The Collected Papers of David Rapaport*. New York: Basic Books, 1967.

Gill, M. M., and Brenman, Margaret. *Hypnosis and Related States*. New York: International Universities Press, 1959.

Gill, M. M., and Klein, G. S. The structuring of drive and reality: David Rapaport's contributions to psychoanalysis and psychology. In Gill, M. M., ed. *The Collected Papers of David Rapaport*. New York: Basic Books, 1967, pp. 8–34.

Glover, E. The "screening" function of traumatic memories. *International Journal of Psycho-Analysis*, **10:**90–93, 1929.

Goldberger, L. Reactions to perceptual isolation and Rorschach manifestations of the primary process. *Journal of Projective Techniques*, **25:**287–303, 1961.

Goldberger, L. Cognitive test performance under LSD-25, placebo and isolation. *Journal of Nervous and Mental Disease*, **142:**4–9, 1966.

Goldberger, L., and Holt, R. R. Experimental interference with reality contact (perceptual isolation): Method and group results. *Journal of Nervous and Mental Disease*, **127:**99–112, 1958.

Goldstein, K. *The Organism*. New York: American Book, 1939.

Greenacre, Phyllis. *Trauma, Growth and Personality*. New York: International Universities Press, 1969.

Grygier, T. G. *The Dynamic Personality Inventory*. Slough, England: National Foundation for Educational Research in England and Wales, 1956.

Grygier, T. G. Statistical and psychoanalytical criteria in the development of the dynamic personality inventory. *Rorschach Newsletter*, **3:**5–7, 1958.

Haertzen, C. A. Subjective drug effects: A factorial representation of subjective drug effects on the Addiction Research Center Inventory. *Journal of Nervous and Mental Disease*, **140:**280–289, 1965a.

Haertzen, C. A. Addiction Research Center Inventory (ARCI): Development of a general drug estimation scale. *Journal of Nervous and Mental Disease*, **141:**300–307, 1965b.

Haertzen, C. A., Hill, H. E., and Belleville, R. E. Development of the Addiction Research Center Inventory (ARCI): Selection of items that are sensitive to the effects of various drugs. *Psychopharmacologia*, **4:**155–166, 1963.

Hardison, J., and Purcell, K. The effects of psychological stress as a function of need and cognitive control. *Journal of Personality*, **27:**250–258, 1959.

Hartmann, H. (1939). *Ego Psychology and the Problem of Adaptation*. New York: International Universities Press, 1958.

Hill, H. E., Haertzen, C. A., Wolbach, A. B., Jr., and Miner, E. J. The Addiction Research Center Inventory: Standardization of scales which evaluate subjective effects of morphine, amphetamine, pentobarbital, alcohol, LSD-25, pyrahexyl and chlorpromazine. *Psychopharmacologia*, **4:**167–183, 1963a.

Hill, H. E., Haertzen, C. A., Wolbach, A. B., Jr., and Miner, E. J. The Addiction Research Center Inventory: Appendix: I. Items comprising empirical scales for seven drugs; II. Items which do not differentiate placebo from any drug condition. *Psychopharmacologia*, **4:**184–205, 1963b.

Hochberg, J., and Brooks, Virginia. Takete and Uloomu: An item analysis of physiognomic connotation. New York: Columbia University, 1957 (mimeo).

Holt, R. R. Gauging primary and secondary processes in Rorschach responses. *Journal of Projective Techniques*, **20:**14–25, 1956.

Holt, R. R. (with the collaboration and assistance of Joan Havel, L. Goldberger, A. Philip, and Reeva Safrin). Manual for the scoring of primary process manifestations in Rorschach responses, 7th Ed. New York: Research Center for Mental Health, New York University, 1959 (ditto).

Holt, R. R. A critical examination of Freud's concept of bound vs. free cathexis. *Journal of the American Psychoanalytic Association*, **10:**475–525, 1962.

Holt, R. R. Ego autonomy re-evaluated. *International Journal of Psycho-Analysis*, **46:**151–167, 1965. Reprinted with critical evaluations by S. C. Miller, A. Namnum, B. B. Rubinstein, J. Sandler and W. G. Joffe, R. Schafer, H. Weiner, and the author's rejoinder. *International Journal of Psychiatry*, **3:**481–536, 1967.

Holt, R. R. Measuring libidinal and aggressive motives and their controls by means of the Rorschach test. In Levine, D., ed. *Nebraska Symposium on Motivation, 1966.* Lincoln: University of Nebraska Press, 1966, pp. 1–47.

Holt, R. R. The development of the primary process: A structural view. In Holt, R. R., ed. Motives and thought: Psychoanalytic essays in honor of David Rapaport. *Psychological Issues,* **5,** Monograph 18/19. New York: International Universities Press, 1967a, pp. 345–383.

Holt, R. R. On the insufficiency of drive as a motivational concept, in the light of evidence from experimental psychology. Unpublished paper presented at the meetings of the American Psychoanalytic Association, December 15, 1967b.

Holt, R. R. Artistic creativity and Rorschach measures of adaptive regression. In Klopfer, B., Meyer, M. M., and Brawer, F. B., eds. *Developments in the Rorschach Technique,* Vol. III: *Aspects of Personality Structure.* New York: Harcourt, 1970, pp. 263–320.

Holt, R. R. On the nature and generality of mental imagery. In Sheehan, P. W., ed. *The Function and Nature of Imagery.* New York: Academic, 1972.

Holt, R. R., and Goldberger, L. Personological correlates of reactions to perceptual isolation. *USAF WADC Technical Report* No. 59-735, 1959, 46 pp.

Holt, R. R., and Goldberger, L. Research on the effects of isolation on cognitive functioning. *USAF WADC Technical Report* No. 60-260, 1960, 22 pp.

Holt, R. R., and Havel, Joan. A method for assessing primary and secondary process in the Rorschach. In Rickers-Ovsiankina, Maria A., ed. *Rorschach Psychology.* New York: Wiley, 1960, pp. 263–315.

Holt, R. R., Havel, Joan, Goldberger, L., Philip, A., and Safrin, Reeva. Manual for the scoring of primary process manifestations in Rorschach responses, 10th Ed. New York: Research Center for Mental Health, New York University, 1969 (mimeo).

Houston, Jean. A different kind of mysticism. *Jubilee,* June, 1967.

Huxley, A. *The Doors of Perception.* New York: Harper, 1954.

Hyde, R. W. Psychological and social determinants of drug action. Conference on Psychodynamics, Psychoanalysis, and Sociologic Aspects of the Neuroleptic Drugs in Psychiatry, Montreal, 1959. In Sarwer-Foner, G. J., ed. *The Dynamics of Psychiatric Drug Therapy.* Springfield, Ill.: Thomas, 1960.

Itil, T. Electroencephalography and pharmacopsychiatry. *Modern Problems of Pharmacopsychiatry,* **1:** 163–194, 1968.

Kafka, Helene. The Use of Color in Projective Tests and Dreams in Relation to the Theory of Ego Autonomy. New York University, unpublished doctoral dissertation, 1963.

Kasamatsu, A., and Hirai, T. (1966). An electroencephalographic study on the Zen meditation (Zazen). In Tart, C. T., ed. *Altered States of Consciousness.* New York: Wiley, 1969, Chapter 33.

Klee, G. D. LSD-25 and ego functions. *Archives of General Psychiatry,* **8:**461–474, 1963.

Klee, G. D., and Weintraub, W. (1959). Paranoid reactions following lysergic acid diethylamide (LSD-25). In Bradley, P. B., Deniker, P., and Radouco-Thomas, C., eds. *Neuro-Psychopharmacology: Proceedings of the 1st International Congress of Neuro-Psychopharmacology*, Rome, September, 1958.

Klein, G. S. Need and regulation. In Jones, M. R., ed. *Nebraska Symposium on Motivation.* Lincoln: University of Nebraska Press, 1954, pp. 224–274. Also: In Klein, G. S. *Perception, Motives and Personality.* New York: Knopf, 1970, pp. 162–200.

Klein, G. S. Consciousness in psychoanalytic theory: Some implications for current research in perception. *Journal of the American Psychoanalytic Association*, **7**:5–34, 1959a. Also: In Klein, G. S. *Perception, Motives and Personality.* New York: Knopf, 1970, pp. 235–263.

Klein, G. S. On subliminal activation. *Journal of Nervous and Mental Disease*, **128**:293–301, 1959b. Also: In Klein, G. S., *Perception, Motives and Personality.* New York: Knopf, 1970, pp. 264–277.

Klein, G. S. Peremptory ideation: Structure and force in motivated ideas. In Holt, R. R., ed. Motives and thought: Psychoanalytic essays in honor of David Rapaport. *Psychological Issues,* **5,** Monograph 18/19. New York: International Universities Press, 1967, pp. 80–128.

Klein, G. S. The vital pleasures. In Goldberger, L. et al., eds. *Psychoanalysis and Contemporary Science*, Vol. 1. New York: Free Press, 1972.

Klein, G. S., and Holt, R. R. Problems and issues in current studies of subliminal activation. In Peatman, J. G., and Hartley, E. L., eds. *Festschrift for Gardner Murphy*, New York: Harper, 1960, pp. 75–93.

Klein, G. S., and Smith, G. J. W. Cognitive controls in serial behavior patterns. *Journal of Personality*, **22:**188–213, 1953.

Klein, G. S., Spence, D. P., Holt, R. R., and Gourevitch, Susannah. Cognition without awareness: Subliminal influences upon conscious thought. *Journal of Abnormal and Social Psychology*, **57:**255–266, 1958.

Koffka, K. *Principles of Gestalt Psychology.* New York: Harcourt, 1935.

Kott, M. G. Learning and retention of words of sexual and nonsexual meaning. *Journal of Abnormal and Social Psychology*, **50:**378–382, 1955.

Krippner, S. Drug deceptions. *Science*, **168:**654–655, 1970.

Kris, E. *Psychoanalytic Explorations in Art.* New York: International Universities Press, 1952.

Kris, E. The recovery of childhood memories in psychoanalysis. *Psychoanalytic Study of the Child*, **11:**54–88, 1956.

Langs, R. J. Earliest memories and personality: A predictive study. *Archives of General Psychiatry*, **12:**379–390, 1965a.

Langs, R. J. First memories and characterologic diagnosis. *Journal of Nervous and Mental Disease*, **141:**318–320, 1965b.

Langs, R. J. Stability of earliest memories under LSD-25 and placebo. *Journal of Nervous and Mental Disease*, **144:**171–184. 1967.

Langs, R. J. Altered states of consciousness: An experimental case study. *Psychoanalytic Quarterly,* **40:**40–58, 1971.

Langs, R. J., and Barr, Harriet L. Lysergic acid diethylamide (LSD-25) and schizophrenic reactions: A comparative study. *Journal of Nervous and Mental Disease*, **147**:163–172, 1968.

Langs, R. J., Rothenberg, M. B., Fishman, J. R., and Reiser, M. F. A method for clinical and theoretical study of the earliest memory. *Archives of General Psychiatry*, **3**:523–534, 1960.

Levine, A., Abramson, H. A., Kaufman, M. R., Markham, S., and Kornetsky, C. Lysergic acid diethylamide (LSD-25): XIV. Effect on personality as observed in psychological tests. *Journal of Psychology*, **40**:351–366, 1955a.

Levine, A., Abramson, H. A., Kaufman, M. R., and Markham, S. Lysergic acid diethylamide (LSD-25): XVI. The effect on intellectual functioning as measured by the Wechsler-Bellevue Intelligence Scale. *Journal of Psychology*, **40**:385–395, 1955b.

Levy, J., and Grigg, K. Early memories. *Archives of General Psychiatry*, **7**:57–69, 1962.

Linton, Harriet B., and Langs, R. J. Subjective reactions to lysergic acid diethylamide (LSD-25). *Archives of General Psychiatry*, **6**:352–368, 1962a.

Linton, Harriet B., and Langs, R. J. Placebo reactions in a study of lysergic acid diethylamide (LSD-25). *Archives of General Psychiatry*, **6**:369–383, 1962b.

Linton, Harriet B., and Langs, R. J. Empirical dimensions of LSD-25 reaction. *Archives of General Psychiatry*, **10**:469–485, 1964.

Linton, Harriet B., Langs, R. J., and Paul I. H. Retrospective alterations of the LSD-25 experience. *Journal of Nervous and Mental Disease*, **138**:409–423, 1964.

Loewald, H. W. Hypnoid state, repression, abreaction and recollection. *Journal of the American Psychoanalytic Association*, **3**:201–210, 1955.

Loomis, Helen K., and Moskowitz, S. Cognitive style and stimulus ambiguity. *Journal of Personality*, **26**:349–364, 1958.

Ludwig, A. M. Altered states of consciousness. *Archives of General Psychiatry*, **15**:225–234, 1966.

McGlothlin, W., Cohen, S., and McGlothlin, M. S. Long lasting effects of LSD on normals. *Archives of General Psychiatry*, **17**:521–532, 1967.

Mayman, M. *Form-Level Scoring Manual.* Topeka: Menninger Foundation, 1960 (mimeo).

Meili-Dworetzki, Gertrude. The development of perception in the Rorschach. In Klopfer, B., ed., *Developments in the Rorschach Technique*, Vol. 2. Yonkers-on-Hudson, N.Y.: World Book, 1956, pp. 104–176.

Mischel, W. *Personality and Assessment*. New York: Wiley, 1968.

Mogar, R. E. Current status and future trends in psychedelic research. *Journal of Humanistic Psychology*, **4**:147–166, 1965. Also: In Tart, C. T., ed. *Altered States of Consciousness: A Book of Readings*. New York: Wiley, 1969, Chapter 26.

Mogar, R. E., and Savage, C. Personality change associated with psychedelic (LSD) therapy: A preliminary report. *Psychotherapy: Theory, Research and Practice,* **1**:154–162, 1964.

Niederland, W. G. The role of the ego in the recovery of early memories. *Psychoanalytic Quarterly*, **34:**564–571, 1965.

Paul, I. H. Some preliminary studies of memory styles: Importers versus skeletonizers. Paper read at the annual convention of the American Psychological Association, Washington, D.C., 1958.

Paul, I. H. Studies in remembering: The reproduction of connected and extended verbal material. *Psychological Issues*, **1,** Monograph 2. New York: International Universities Press, 1959.

Paul, I. H. The effects of a drug-induced alteration in state of consciousness on retention of drive-related verbal material. *Journal of Nervous and Mental Disease*, **138:**367–374, 1964.

Paul, I. H., Langs, R. J., and Barr, Harriet L. Individual differences in the recall of a drug experience. *Journal of Nervous and Mental Disease*, **140:** 132–145, 1965.

Philip, A. F. The effect of lysergic acid diethylamide (LSD-25) on primary process thought manifestations. New York University, unpublished doctoral dissertation, 1960.

Pine, F., and Holt, R. R. Creativity and primary process: A study of adaptive regression. *Journal of Abnormal and Social Psychology*, **61:**370–379, 1960.

Pollard, J. C., Uhr, L., and Stern, Elizabeth. *Drugs and Phantasy. The Effects of LSD, Psilocybin, and Sernyl on College Students.* Boston: Little, Brown, 1965.

Rapaport, D. (1942). *Emotions and Memory.* 2nd Ed., New York: International Universities Press, 1959.

Rapaport, D. (1951). States of consciousness: A psychopathological and psychodynamic view. In Gill, M. M., ed. *The Collected Papers of David Rapaport.* New York: Basic Books, 1967, pp. 385–404.

Rapaport, D. (1953). Some metapsychological considerations concerning activity and passivity. In Gill, M. M., ed. *The Collected Papers of David Rapaport.* New York: Basic Books, 1967, pp. 530–568.

Rapaport, D. (1957). Cognitive structures. In Gill, M. M., ed. *The Collected Papers of David Rapaport.* New York: Basic Books, 1967, pp. 631–664.

Rapaport, D. (1958). The theory of ego autonomy: A generalization. In Gill, M. M., ed. *The Collected Papers of David Rapaport.* New York: Basic Books, 1967, pp. 722–744.

Rapaport, D. (1959). The theory of attention cathexis: An economic and structural attempt at the explanation of cognitive processes. In Gill, M. M., ed. *The Collected Papers of David Rapaport.* New York: Basic Books, 1967, pp. 778–794.

Rapaport, D. (1960). On the psychoanalytic theory of motivation. In Gill, M. M., ed. *The Collected Papers of David Rapaport.* New York: Basic Books, 1967, pp. 853–915.

Rapaport, D., Gill, M. M., and Schafer, R. (1945). *Diagnostic Psychological Testing*, Vol. I. Chicago: Yearbook Publishers, 1945. Revised edition, Holt, R. R., ed. New York: International Universities Press, 1968.

Reider, N. Reconstruction and screen function. *Journal of the American Psychoanalytic Association*, **1**:389–405, 1953.

Riggs, Margaret M. Recall and organization of aggressive words under varied conditions of emphasis. *Perceptual and Motor Skills*, **6**:273–284, 1956.

Rinkel, M., DeShon, H. J., Hyde, R. W., and Solomon, H. C. Experimental schizophrenia-like symptoms. *American Journal of Psychiatry*, **108**:572–578, 1952.

Rinkel, M., DiMascio, A., Robey, A., and Atwell, C. (1961). Personality patterns and reaction to psilocybin. In Rothlin, E., ed. *Neuro-Psychopharmacology*, Vol. 2, Proceedings of the 2nd International Meeting of the Collegium Internationale Neuro-Psychopharmacologicum, Basel, 1960.

Robinson, Mary F. What price lobotomy? *Journal of Abnormal and Social Psychology*, **41**:421–436, 1946.

Rubinfine, D. L. Perception, reality testing and symbolism, *Psychoanalytic Study of the Child,* **16**:73–89, 1961.

Salvatore, S., and Hyde, R. W. Progression of effects of lysergic acid diethylamide. *AMA Archives of Neurology and Psychiatry*, **76**:50–59, 1956.

Saul, L. J., Snyder, T. R., Jr., and Sheppard, Edith. On earliest memories. *Psychoanalytic Quarterly*, **25**:228–237, 1956.

Savage, C. Lysergic acid diethylamide (LSD-25): A clinical-psychological study. *American Journal of Psychiatry*, **108**:896–900, 1952.

Scheerer, M., and Lyons, J. Line drawings and matching responses to words. *Journal of Personality*, **25**:251–273, 1957.

Schmidt, B. Reflektorische Reaktionen auf Form und Farbe und ihre typologische Bedeutung. *Zhurnal Psychologie*, **137**:245–310, 1936.

Schur, M. Comments on the metapsychology of somatization. *Psychoanalytic Study of the Child*, **10**:119–164, 1955.

Shorr, Marcia. Trust, orality and openness to sensory experience: A study of some personality correlates of creativity. New York University, unpublished doctoral dissertation, 1971.

Silverstein, A. B., and Klee, G. D. The effect of lysergic acid diethylamide on digit span. *Journal of Clinical and Experimental Psychopathology*, **21**:11–14, 1960a.

Silverstein, A. B., and Klee, G. D. The effect of lysergic acid diethylamide on dual pursuit performance. *Journal of Clinical and Experimental Psychopathology*, **21**:300–303, 1960b.

Smith, G. J. W., Spence, D. P., and Klein, G. S. Subliminal effects of verbal stimuli. *Journal of Abnormal and Social Psychology*, **59**:167–176, 1959.

Smith, J. G. Influence of failure, expressed hostility and stimulus characteristics on verbal learning and recognition. *Journal of Personality*, **22**:475–493, 1954.

Stamm, J. Altered ego states allied to depersonalization. *Journal of the American Psychoanalytic Association*, **10**:762–783, 1962.

Stein, M. H. States of consciousness in the analytic situation: Including a note on the traumatic dream. In Schur, M., ed. *Drives, Affects, Behavior*, Vol. II. New York: International Universities Press, 1965, pp. 60–86.

Stroop, J. R. Studies of interference in serial verbal reactions. *Journal of Experimental Psychology*, **18:**643–662, 1935.

Tart, C. T., ed. *Altered States of Consciousness: A Book of Readings.* New York: Wiley, 1969a.

Tart, C. T. Guide to the literature on psychedelic drugs. In Tart, C. T., ed. *Altered States of Consciousness: A Book of Readings.* New York: Wiley, 1969b, Chapter 32.

Thurstone, L. L. A factorial study of perception. *Psychometric Monographs*, Vol. 4. Chicago: University of Chicago Press, 1944.

Weintraub, W., Silverstein, A. B., and Klee, G. D. The effect of LSD on the associative processes. *Journal of Nervous and Mental Disease*, **128:**409–414, 1959.

Weintraub, W., Silverstein, A. B., and Klee, G. D. The "correction" of deviant responses on a word association test. *Archives of General Psychiatry*, **3:** 17–20, 1960.

Werner, H. *Comparative Psychology of Mental Development.* New York: International Universities Press, 1966.

Witkin, H. A., Dyk, Ruth B., Faterson, Hanna F., Goodenough, D. R., and Karp, S. A. *Psychological Differentiation.* New York: Wiley, 1962.

Witkin, H. A., Lewis, Helen B., Hertzman, M., Machover, Karen, Meissner, Pearl B., and Wapner, S. *Personality Through Perception.* New York: Harper, 1954.

Wolitzky, D. L. Cognitive control and cognitive dissonance. *Journal of Personality and Social Psychology*, **5:**486–490, 1967.

Name Index

Subject Index

Bert therefore has a poorly integrated personality, with noteworthy borderline schizophrenic features. Basically, he is a narcissistic character with schizoid features, along with some hysterical and weak obsessive-compulsive tendencies and some mild paranoid tendencies.

Bert's LSD state was in most respects typical of Group II, with extensive loss of control and contact, thinking difficulties, visual hallucinations, and experiences of altered meanings. His behavior was more regressed than that of any of the others in Group II and was described as "grossly psychotic." Body image changes were extreme; he became very anxious, rather than manic, with a marked loss of motility. He felt that his arms were useless and his legs paralyzed, cut off, or numb from the waist down (which made him think of a childhood figure with whom he identified himself), as if he were old or, at the same time, like a baby. He also felt "like a little ball floating in space, while you're talking to me as a man possessing arms and legs and a body."

At times he felt smaller: ". . . as you mentioned it [i.e., asking if he felt like a child], I thought of being all curled up, womblike." The childlike feeling was pervasive: "The reason I want to give up cigarettes—now, I'm a child—the connection with guilt, legs, school teachers—I never saw a teacher smoke." This relates to the way he viewed one of the female experimenters while she was asking him questions: ". . . enormous, towering like a queen, enormous breasts getting bigger and bigger, undulations of legs and skirt. Very seductive, also forbidden, like a prison warden, or teacher." This of course concretizes the conception of women that was apparent in his pretest projective tests. He also felt that the desk at which she was sitting became bigger and in fact that "everyone was much bigger than I."

He saw well-worked-out scenes from the past, including long-repressed recollections (a funeral procession, for one), in the folds of the curtains and said, "I seemed to be drawn into them." The loss of boundaries was evident in many ways. He was the subject already quoted who felt as if his body were beyond his control, plugged into electric currents, ". . . floating, no responsibilities, I'm a child—I'm so light." As this suggests, the drug experience was by no means totally unpleasant for him, but in his case an early elated mood was succeeded by a flat depression during the latter part of the day.

The effect of the drug on his performance in the experimental tasks was, as we would expect, very great, particularly in the projective tests. His loss of reality contact was reflected in a very marked shift to perceptual organization on the basis of color in the Color-Form test, and extremely poor learning of the neutral theme lists under LSD. It is noteworthy, however, that although his behavior was noted as anxious he, like the other subjects in Group II, did not exhibit the cognitive disruptions that stem from anxiety.

Under the drug his recall of the pretest theme lists was excellent, and his Color-Word reading was very stable, without the increased variability usually shown by more anxious subjects (he was not given the cognitive test battery).

His Rorschach test performance which, as we have seen, reflected severe pathology on the pretest day, became grossly psychotic under the drug. His previous vagueness and obsessional vacillation vanished; there was a great loss of distance, with an eruption of oral, anal, and sexual material. The fit between the blots and his percepts became grossly inappropriate, and both his use of color and the links between the parts of his images were often arbitrary. His verbalizations became at times bizarre, and self-references were prominent. Projection became apparent, and his use of the primitive defense of denial was extreme.

The change in his figure drawings was equally extreme (see Figure 5.2). Both the male and female figures became larger, less organized, and fragmented. The regressive emergence of blatant homosexuality was expressed through an extreme emphasis on the buttocks, and his loss of reality testing, evident in the missing parts of both figures, was most marked in the male figure which, after an abandoned attempt in the center of the page, ran off the page and was drawn too large for the entire figure to fit had it been centered. While the pretest male and female figure drawings were identical with each other except for hair and clothing, the male figure drawn under LSD was, despite its musculature, depleted and unsupported, and dominated by the potent and seductive-looking female figure. (The fact that the female was drawn first on both days is an expression of his homosexuality.)

Under LSD he recalled a more regressive Earliest Memory, which had been repressed until that time. We may note that when the Earliest Memories given on the two days are compared, the one reported on the pretest is seen to be a screen memory for the one that emerged under LSD (see Langs, 1971, where they are presented in detail).

To summarize his pretest personality and his drug reaction: Bert typifies this group of borderline subjects with impaired defenses and poor ego functioning in the waking state who experienced under LSD a pervasively regressed altered state, with markedly impaired cognitive functioning, loss of ego boundaries, and altered reality contact and testing.

GROUP III

Since Group III consists of only two subjects, its status is more dubious than that of the other groups, and the presentation of data is therefore limited to those features in which these two men are both extremely deviant from other subjects and are very similar to each other.

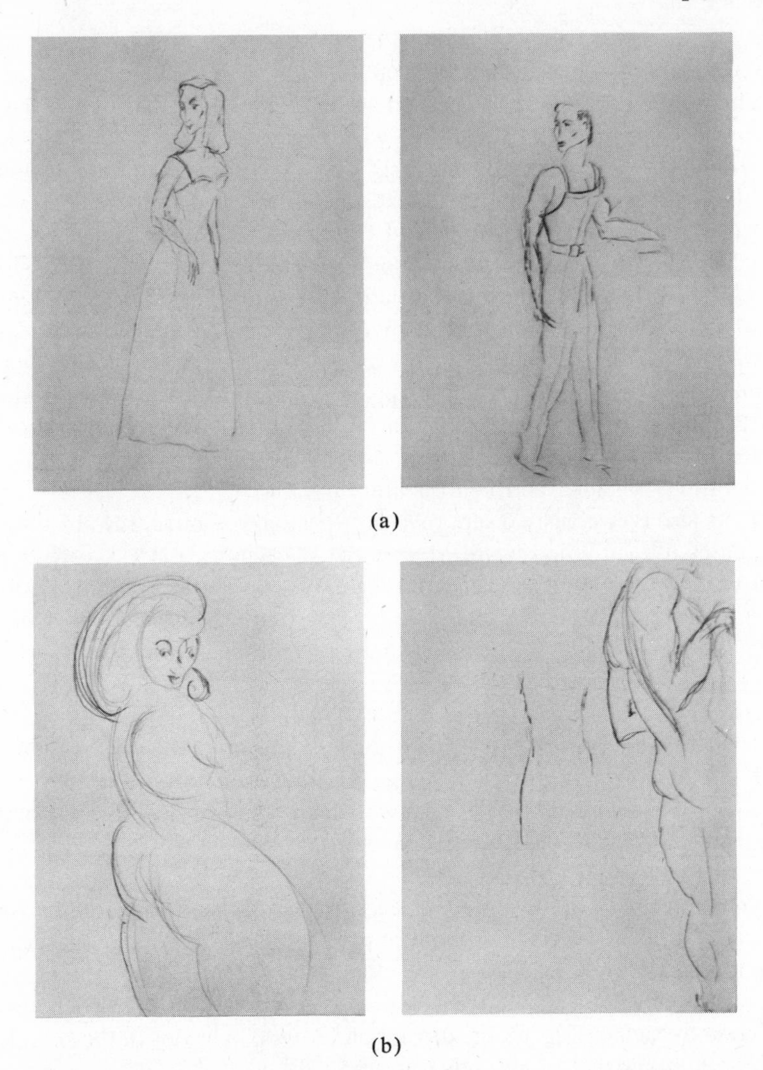

(a)

(b)

Figure 5.2. Bert's Human Figure Drawings. (a) Pretest Day; (b) LSD Day. The left-hand figure of each pair was drawn first.

These two subjects are characterized by a good deal of inner turmoil, much of it within awareness, against which they exercise strong controls that normally operate fairly well. They are notably prone to depression and disillusionment and often experience anxiety. They suppress their anger rigidly, expressing it only in the form of passive aggression. Some hostility to women is evident, but they have a marked tendency to submit to paternal figures. They feel sexually inadequate and suppress sensuality. Thus their emotions and impulses are generally inhibited but do break through at times in sudden outbursts during which they are experienced as ego-alien. Phobic manifestations also appear at times.

These men have, however, certain strong assets. They have considerable intelligence (IQs of 134 and 144) which they use effectively. They have wide intellectual and creative interests, are good at solving problems, interested in knowledge for its own sake, and sensitive to minimal cues. As expected, intellectualization is one of their most often used and most effective defenses, often used in conjunction with isolation. Obsessive-compulsive trends are prominent; they are orderly and thrifty, and their thinking is often rigid, overly planful and ruminative. We saw evidence of undoing, as well as denial, in their personality assessment. They also seemed lacking in imagery. Reaction formation is apparent, and they are conventional and conscientious, with a strong need to be helpful to others. They are deliberate, prefer routines, and dislike adventure. In their conscious values moderation, balance, and control are emphasized.

They also consciously disapprove of a passive-receptive, inward-turning, contemplative attitude toward life. At the same time, a streak of passivity and yearning for comfort comes through. We got the impression of strong underlying passive tendencies which are defended against by reaction formations. In regard to their LSD state, it is of special interest that their Rorschachs indicate that they tend to regress to a passive position under stress.

Their relationships are marred by anxiety and are not smooth; they also tend to somatize. By and large, however, they function rather effectively, although not comfortably, by means of their rigid controls and by relying on their skills, competence, and knowledge, in a seemingly independent manner.

The effect of LSD on these subjects was cataclysmic. Their total questionnaire score was very high, indicating a most pervasive and overwhelming altered state experience. Three other groups (I, II, and IV) reported about as many subjective effects as this group (although the patterns were different in each case), but the disruption of overt behavior in these subjects exceeded by far that of any other group.

The most remarkable thing about their reaction, however, was its course over time. While their peak effect, 2–5 hours after drug ingestion, was greater than that of any other group, their reaction was minimal during the first hour (the lowest of any group) and declined sharply by 8 hours to one-third of peak level. The other three high-effect groups, in contrast, reached about one-half their peak effect within the first hour, and remained at about two-thirds of this peak level at 8 hours. Groups I and II also reported more LSD-like effects than average on pretest and posttest days, while the Group III subjects reported virtually none. For this group, then,